Contents

From the Editor • 1

PRESIDENTIAL FORUM: In Dreams Begin Responsibilities

Introduction
Patricia Meyer Spacks • 3

Responsibilities? Dream On!
David T. Gies • 5

Flaubert's Nightmare
Myra Jehlen • 10

Literary Reading in Interdisciplinary Study
Margery Sabin • 14

The Responsibility to Dream
Bryan Wolf • 19

SIGNIFICANCE OF PRIMARY RECORDS

Statement on the Significance of Primary Records • 27

Introduction
G. Thomas Tanselle • 29

What Is the Future of the Print Record?
J. Hillis Miller • 33

Traces of a Lost Woman
Susan Staves • 36

The Diaries of Queen Lili'uokalani
Miriam Fuchs • 38

Manuscripts on Microfilm: The Disturbing Case of Proust
Anthony R. Pugh • 41

Twentieth-Century Undergraduates and an Eighteenth-Century Edition
of Diderot's *Encyclopédie*
Manon Anne Ress • 43

On the Importance of Judging Books by Their Covers
Gregg Camfield • 44

Rekindling the Reading Experience of the Victorian Age
Catherine Golden • 45

Postscript about the Public Libraries
Ruth Perry • 48

Young and Highly Educated in the 1990s: Job Prospects in the Professional Labor Market
Lori G. Kletzer • 51

Speculating about the Labor Market for Academic Humanists: "Once More unto the Breach"
Jack H. Schuster • 56

Graduate Programs and Job Training
Seth R. Katz • 62

Burning In / Burning Out
H. L. Hertz • 68

English in a Postcolonial Situation: The Example of India
R. K. Gupta • 73

Teaching Old English in the Next Millennium: Why? And How?
M. J. Toswell • 79

The Profession and the National Education Scene: A Collaborative Model
Edward J. Ahearn and Arnold Weinstein • 85

Global Thinking, Local Teaching: Departments, Curricula, and Culture
Russell A. Berman • 89

Dealing with Difference: Being an Administrator in the 1990s
Patricia Meyer Spacks • 94

Forum • 100

Recommendations on Extramural Evaluations • 114

From the Editor

With this issue, *Profession* enters a new phase in its history, and I therefore begin with some background. In 1972 the MLA Executive Council approved the establishment of an annual publication that would focus on matters of importance to the profession, but the money to support such a project was not available until 1977. That year, Executive Director William Schaefer offered the first issue of *Profession* as an experiment he would continue only if MLA members found the journal useful. Initially, *Profession* was intended to carry reprints of articles published in the *ADE Bulletin* or the *ADFL Bulletin* that the editors of these journals selected, but by 1981 the new publication was well enough established that the editors began to include, along with bulletin reprints, MLA committee reports and previously unpublished articles of general interest. In 1986, as the journal approached the end of its first decade, the Executive Council named the executive director its editor and further encouraged the use of new material by authorizing an invitation to MLA members to submit articles directly to *Profession*. At first, essays arrived in small numbers and were easy enough to handle; by the early 1990s, however, the number of submissions had grown substantially, and decisions about what to publish became increasingly difficult to make.

Last year the Executive Council reviewed the journal's evolution and confirmed its purpose: to publish articles that, in Schaefer's words, "say important things about our profession" (*Profession 77*, inside front cover) and to carry MLA policy statements, committee reports, talks from the annual presidential forum, and reprints from the bulletins. The council also concluded that members' growing interest in writing for the journal warranted a membership committee to read and evaluate submissions; they therefore established the Advisory Committee for *Profession*. With this change, *Profession* became a refereed journal. Serving on the first *Profession* Advisory Committee are Marga Cottino-Jones (Univ. of California, Los Angeles), Joan Ferrante (Columbia Univ.), John W. Kronik (Cornell Univ.), and Jerry W. Ward, Jr. (Tougaloo Coll.). As in the past, the editors of the ADE and ADFL bulletins, David Laurence and Elizabeth Welles, also review articles and propose bulletin essays for reprinting, and the editor makes final publication decisions. I'm happy to say that the new arrangement has fallen into place rather easily.

Reports from Advisory Committee members have greatly simplified the review process and should be helpful to authors as well.

I am in the habit of studying the essays we receive for *Profession* for evidence of what MLA members have on their minds, and, insofar as submissions permit, I try to include a variety of professional perspectives in each issue. This year's essays reminded me that our community has been living in interesting times for quite a while and now faces unusual professional and intellectual challenges. I take as a good sign that, after years of lively theoretical debates, MLA members are considering the practical implications of these discussions for the curriculum, scholarship, the discipline itself, and departments.

The first set of essays in *Profession 95* was presented at the 1994 convention in the presidential forum that Patricia Meyer Spacks organized about the theme of dreams and responsibilities. Looking at the difficulties facing the field, David T. Gies calls for optimism and action. Responsibility, for him, means less specialization in graduate education in order to encourage flexibility in the careers available to students; he also urges renewed commitment to improving undergraduate programs for schoolteachers. Myra Jehlen similarly focuses on responsibility, asking what the obligation of a reader is when art and evil seem to agree. Margery Sabin turns to the meaning of literary study and argues that "the learned and teachable skills of literary reading . . . are central to what our profession of language and literature has to offer students across disciplines and in interdisciplinary study." Bryan Wolf explores the dreams that education in our society can make possible, and he thereby also emphasizes the responsibilities of educators.

As it happens, the theme of dreams and responsibilities runs throughout this issue of *Profession*. A second group of essays grows out of the work of an MLA committee that has been considering how to ensure the survival of primary materials during a period of growing interest in electronic communication and publication. Articles by G. Thomas Tanselle, J. Hillis Miller, Susan Staves, Miriam Fuchs, Anthony R. Pugh, Manon Anne Ress, Gregg Camfield, and Catherine Golden present the issues committee members discussed before developing their "Statement on the Significance of Primary

Records." Although the publication of a policy statement usually signals the conclusion of a project, this committee's work will continue, and Tanselle asks MLA members' help in encouraging libraries to retain collections that will be important to future generations of scholars. In addition, Ruth Perry asks us to share her concern about the future of public libraries.

A third group of essays also touches on professional dreams and responsibilities, in this case as they relate to the job market. Two articles look forward; one looks back. Lori G. Kletzer, an economist, tries to put academic employment prospects in the larger context of the professional labor market, while Jack H. Schuster, who has been studying the academic market, examines the factors that are likely to continue to influence employment in higher education. After three years in a tenure-track position, Seth R. Katz writes about what he wishes he had known when he began his search for an academic position. His insights are likely to assist both graduate advisers and job seekers.

The other essays in *Profession 95* touch on a variety of professional issues, but they too relate to the dreams and responsibilities of modern language teachers and scholars. H. L. Hertz writes about the effects of years of teaching on teachers, R. K. Gupta discusses the complex attitudes people in one culture can have about learning the language and literature of another culture, and M. J. Toswell considers whether the study of Old English will survive as departments face the task of "compressing another century into [the] curriculum." Edward J. Ahearn and Arnold Weinstein argue for more collaborative efforts between higher education and the schools and describe how well a rigorous comparative literature program can serve both secondary school and college students. Russell A. Berman explores ways that recent theoretical developments in the field might affect departmental and curricular arrangements, noting that "everything is due for review: the connections between language and literature, between literature and culture, between Europe and the globe, and between the literature of single nations and comparative literature." Patricia Meyer Spacks also considers how recent developments in the field have affected departments. She looks at the relations between generations of scholars who are committed to different approaches to work in the field, and she maintains that departments would benefit from completing the following difficult assignments. She proposes that each "department reflect collectively on its differences and their meanings until it discovers its points of congruence," that each department assess the job it is doing of "representing its discipline and teaching its students," and that it discuss whether faculty autonomy should not sometimes be discouraged if autonomy prevents a department from achieving its institutional responsibilities.

The members of *Profession's* new advisory committee and my colleagues on staff join me in inviting you to comment on and explore further in *Profession 96* the topics presented in the essays that follow. In addition, we seek discussions of subjects that are of interest both within and outside the academy: for example, the NEH-sponsored National Conversation about American pluralism, ideal school and college curricula in English and foreign languages for various groups of students, the voluntary standards for English and foreign languages that have been conceptualized in accordance with Goals 2000, the internationalization of the college curriculum, and the status of bilingual education. Above all, we welcome essays on the topics you believe "say important things about our profession."

Phyllis Franklin

Introduction

Patricia Meyer Spacks

The topic I provided for the participants in this forum had no specifications attached. When I asked people to ponder the matter of dreams and responsibilities, I had nothing particular in mind, beyond my sense that our professional responsibilities have multiplied alarmingly in recent years and that those responsibilities often bear little obvious relation to the dreams that motivated many to enter the profession in the first place. The four essays generated by my original directive to write under a vague general rubric, however, give substance to vagueness and sharply delineate the complexity of the expanding responsibilities that the teaching of modern languages and literatures has entailed. The essays also mark the complexity of the relation between those responsibilities and the dreams in which they somehow originated.

Those of us lucky enough to teach literature invite our students to experience vicariously the dreams of other men and women: thus to grow. Our responsibility as teachers begins with our fidelity to the dreams that initiated our study. I'm using "dreams," of course, in a metaphoric sense, to designate all the nonrational or suprarational constructs that originate and support imaginative creation and imaginative study. The metaphor is exact. Think of what we know and believe about the literal dreams that attend our sleep. Dreams often don't make immediate obvious sense, but they may yield to investigation various kinds of profound meaning and suggestion. They are by their nature ambiguous and frequently complicated, sometimes beneath apparently simple surfaces. They can tell us—people have thought this for a long time, well before Freud—important truths about ourselves.

Everything I have said about literal dreams can be accurately applied to the metaphoric dreams that provoke and inhabit literature. They too demand investigation and make elucidation difficult by their ambiguity and complications. They too teach us about ourselves. Literature teachers profess a discipline of dreams—and, ideally, demonstrate the rigor of such a discipline.

The radical differences of approach exemplified by the four papers indicate the multiplicity of dreams and of responsibilities and the complications involved in fleshing out the kind of general statement I presented as a forum topic—as well as the diversity within the profession. Yet these disparate reflections on dreams and responsibilities also have something in common. They ponder what social imperatives govern (or should govern) pedagogical and critical activity.

David Gies speaks of the immediate professional responsibility of teachers to make their graduate students employable, reminding his readers that academics, like carpenters and accountants, must operate within the perplexing economic and social context of our historical moment. We cannot pretend, he insists, that our responsibilities end in the classroom. Every teacher of postbaccalaureate students has to worry about how the next generation of teachers will sustain itself. We need to think about practical ways to limit excess production of academic job candidates as well as about how to nurture and direct, or redirect, those sufficiently determined, talented, and optimistic to persist in pursuing graduate education. In other words, academics must act as well as dream. Only thus will we fulfill our responsibilities.

Myra Jehlen calls attention to problematic aspects of the notion of responsibility in relation to the actions of both writing and reading. "The ability to imagine

The author is Edgar F. Shannon Professor of English at the University of Virginia and a past President of the Modern Language Association.

a world entails a duty to that world," Jehlen writes, outlining a conventional concept of literary responsibility. But then she raises the question of what happens in the mind when literary dreams turn into nightmares. Her example is Flaubert's novel *Salammbô*, which steadily demands the reader's response to horrifying material represented with formal elegance. Ethical and aesthetic reactions come into violent conflict. Not only does Flaubert convert moral evil into linguistic beauty, he also uses evil as a means to enhance beauty. And he leaves the reader no way to resolve the resulting discomfort. All one can finally do, Jehlen maintains, is to recognize and acknowledge as fully as possible how the tension is created, how it works. Such awareness fulfills one kind of literary responsibility, but it compels recognition that literature as an expressive mode does not necessarily make either the world or its readers better. We cannot lightly assume that as responsible readers we exercise any specifically moral discriminations.

For Margery Sabin, too, reading provides a relevant arena of responsibility, but the possibility of moral activity seems more immediate. "The whole action of language within a text," Sabin asserts, should engage the attention of those professionally committed to the study of literature. Many recent writers, she points out, have challenged the value of such study in the name of political or social agendas, but Raymond Williams, acknowledged precursor of much socially inflected criticism, provides a model for a critique that fully acknowledges the value of what it attacks. Unlike his recent followers, Williams, according to Sabin, respected the achievement of language within a text and assumed the permanence of the literary. The current decline in attentiveness to linguistic activity has resulted in a carelessness that obscures both political purpose and literary effect, a point Sabin supports by reference to late-twentieth-century misreadings of a sentence by a nineteenth-century historian. Teachers of literature, Sabin argues, need productive ways to think about what literature is. Their responsibility to reading demands full consciousness, the consciousness threatened by facile assumptions of every kind.

If Sabin considers the politics of criticism, Bryan Wolf directs our attention to the politics of culture,

using visual texts as a means to locate the crucial splits and closures characteristic of late-twentieth-century culture, some of which, as Wolf demonstrates, originated in the nineteenth century. He begins with a complex image by a Chicana artist, a reflection on childhood, the body, and education, and ends with an allusion to the Wizard of Oz. In between, his points of reference include Descartes and Freud, Charles Willson Peale and John Singleton Copley, Frederick Douglass and P. T. Barnum. The responsibility he implicitly recommends is that of making connections, seeing links that education may have occluded, and using education as a mode of perception. Placing the institution of education in the context of other cultural institutions, Wolf reminds his readers that thinking about their professions and professionalism constitutes part of their ethical obligation.

Although each of these essays raises troubling issues about our current professional, critical, or cultural situation and each suggests the difficulty of acting responsibly in relation to the social imperatives inherent in our profession, the variety of comment here offered remains heartening. Each articulation of the subject of dream and responsibility reveals a different aspect of the burdens and opportunities that academics share. All the papers reiterate, at least by implication, the fundamental notion that dreams provide the source or impetus for responsibilities and that the concepts of dream and responsibility involve each other. They suggest a considerable range of possibility for academic self-awareness. The four essays remind their readers of various kinds of urgency: about caring for our graduate students, about paying attention to language, about reimagining the moral obligations inherent in reading, about bringing together apparently disparate areas of concern. Equally important: they exemplify different approaches to the issues they interrogate. As a group they demonstrate how the fundamental responsibility to language implicit in the professional tasks of MLA members, assuming diverse forms, in all those forms possesses enabling power for those who accept it. And they suggest the multiplicity of dreams at work as academics think about the perplexities of their profession.

Responsibilities? Dream On!

David T. Gies

Too many years of life in academia—this is my twenty-sixth year as a member of the MLA—have made me pleasantly schizophrenic. As I contemplate our profession—and its future—my mood swings between great optimism and scary despair. The optimism surges from the ever-enriching and ever-changing nature of the undergraduate and graduate students who appear in our classes each September. Quite unlike Allan Bloom (*The Closing of the American Mind*), I see the new generation of students as a bright, enthusiastic, creative, and challenging lot who not only are eager to move into the profession and to wrest control of so-called power from those of us they so foolishly think wield it but also are eminently capable of doing so. (Unlike Bloom, who thought that rock music has made this generation dumb, I believe it has only made them deaf.) When my mood shifts, however, I find myself nodding in agreement with my Chicken Little colleagues who bewail this new bunch's lack of seriousness, lack of training, lack of energy, and lack of interest. But even I must admit that to their list of lack-ofs can now be added one that is probably justified and that is most likely the driving force behind this forum: lack of jobs. As Phyllis Franklin informed us rather understatedly in her memo of 28 July 1994, "The job market and the fate of full-time faculty positions in English and foreign language departments received much attention" at the Executive Council meeting.

In fact, some of you might think this forum should be titled not "In Dreams Begin Responsibilities" but rather "In Nightmares Begin Panic." The job market looks bleak. The MLA reports that in the past five years we have experienced a double whammy: we have seen a significant increase in applicants to and enrollments in English and foreign language graduate programs (41% in my field, Spanish), but this increase has been combined with a marked decline in the number of jobs advertised in the English and foreign language editions of the *Job Information List*. *Profession 94* had a special section on the job market, replete with ominous-sounding titles such as Erik D. Curren's "No Openings at This Time: Job Market Collapse and Graduate Education."

Given this reality, what can we do? Many possible options have been envisioned and some have even been voiced at those beloved forums for tension, egomania, conflict, and sometimes open warfare, that is, at departmental faculty meetings. We could cut back sharply on our PhD programs, a move contemplated by university financial officers facing severe budget cuts and suggested as a possibility by the MLA itself (Spacks, Letter). We could lie more about our students to get them placed (this strategy would obviously not produce more jobs, but a cynic might argue that it would at least produce better statistics for the hired students' departments). We could demand "longer and better financial support from graduate programs," as Curren suggests in his article (60). We could refuse to hire foreign born or foreign-trained professors—erect a kind of Atlantic Wall against an invasion of foreign talent, thus presumably keeping the few jobs for our own students—as Robert Holub rather surprisingly suggests in his article "Professional Responsibility: On Graduate Education and Hiring Practices." We could ignore the problem, hope it goes away, and simply shrug. Or we could take a different step, a more productive one and one I advocate here: instead of following this curve, we could direct it by taking the initiative to retrain our students away from overspecialization in fields and to present them with more flexible career options.

The author is Commonwealth Professor of Spanish at the University of Virginia. A version of this paper was presented at the 1994 MLA convention in San Diego.

One of the great dissonances of today's modern language profession is that students, well trained to teach upper-level courses in literature and literary theory in major research-oriented institutions, frequently find themselves asked to teach composition, grammar, conversation, and entry-level language classes either in part-time jobs or in small, out-of-the-way, nonresearch-oriented institutions. Or both. This fact has created a significant tension in English and foreign language departments—between those who insist on teaching a narrow range of lit-crit, in-vogue, and with-it courses and those who want to roll over and play dead, that is, those who insist on teaching only the broadest, most basic carpenter courses that provide students with what they call the tools of the trade. Neither of these groups, it seems to me, takes full responsibility for its beliefs and actions. Each argues cogently, passionately, and, at times, convincingly for its view. The first group claims that it is essential to train students in the most exciting, cutting-edge theories, to create new knowledge and new ways of looking at language and literature, to force students to stretch their minds and creative impulses to the limit. This argument is right, of course. The second group claims that the bulk of our students go on not to become academic superstars but rather to become mere bright lights in the intellectual firmament across the country, that our students need to read "canonical" literature (as now redefined by that other Bloom, Harold) and to arm themselves with as much how-to as we can possibly give them. This argument too, alas, is right. Yet between what might be called the totalitarianism of trendiness and the totalitarianism of dumbing down exists—it seems to me—a middle, and wiser, course.

> **Many of my colleagues still refuse to become contaminated by reality.**

Most graduate programs in American colleges and universities are clone factories. That is, we train our students as we were trained and to do what we do. Sure, we continually update our approaches or even invent new -isms to keep them puzzled and ourselves amused, but the fact is we strive to produce what we are: literary critics prepared to teach in the top ten or twenty or thirty graduate programs in the country. Yet when we look at where our students are getting jobs and when we consider what they are being called on to teach, we discover a discrepancy that is only now becoming a real problem for us. In the past, we could safely do what we do and ignore the consequences. In Spanish literature, except for that frightening period in the late 1970s when we were asked to dissuade students from going into college teaching, there have been jobs galore, jobs for everyone. Academia was a growth industry, and, even in the years when it was not, we could not lower ourselves to be concerned with the realities of the marketplace. We called the MLA convention, dismissively, the meat market when we were involved in job searches; today it is called, simply, frustratingly, the buyer's market (see Caminero-Santangelo). Many of my colleagues still refuse to become contaminated by reality; that is, they hold to their now-worn "high standards" with an attitude of "the marketplace be damned." We are, after all, professors of literature and language, above the crass concerns of corporate America, and we will never allow ourselves to be corrupted by the demands of the bottom-line people or reactionary politicians that colleges and universities be more attuned to some external reality, more sensitive to the future employment needs of Dick and Jane (well, today, of Justin and Melissa, Caleb and Kristin).

I think that this ivory-tower attitude is precisely what is wrong with higher education today. Many of us take no responsibility for the disparity between what we are teaching our students and what they will be called on to teach. If we are to take responsibility, the question becomes, What do we teach our students for today's and tomorrow's reality? The suggestions I offer here are nothing new, of course, nor are they particularly radical, but perhaps this is the appropriate forum and the appropriate time to contemplate them as we discuss the future of the profession. In the spirit of the title of the presidential forum, I would urge us to dream. Herein, three dreams.

First, I would urge us to dream to be flexible. That is, I would encourage us to broaden our scope of interest to include things beyond the traditional focus of graduate-level literature studies. With this aim in mind, my institution has developed an innovative—and very well funded, I might add—program to bring content courses to the secondary school classroom, which is strengthening the teaching of language, literature, and culture across the Commonwealth of Virginia. But beyond this move to educate already working teachers, I think that we must convince some of our best graduate students to consider secondary school teaching as a career option. I remember listening with great alarm and growing anger to members of the profession who counseled students pursuing a Master of Arts in Teaching— no doubt having what they thought to be the students' best interests in mind—with the following words of advice: "You are too smart for this. Have you considered not going into high school teaching and getting a PhD instead?" I would rant, plead, and attempt to educate my colleagues about what I felt to be a fundamentally important principle: that our strongest students should be encouraged to go into secondary school teaching, not our weakest. My colleagues would nod, agree, and seem contrite—until the next advising session with a "too smart" master's student, when the default mechanism built into them from years of considering PhD the only respectable university degree would have them once again proffering the same old advice.

Patricia Meyer Spacks, the 1994 president of the MLA, has recognized the seriousness of the situation and called for us to focus attention on secondary education. In the Winter 1994 *MLA Newsletter* she writes, "The assumed separation of interests between primary and secondary education and postsecondary education begins to blur; those engaged in higher education now clearly must think about what precedes the college years." She adds, "We cannot finally insulate ourselves from at least indirect responsibility for what happens in earlier years of education" ("Enlargements" 3). I would go a step further and say that we must take *direct* responsibility for that education, and we can begin to do so by training our graduate students for secondary school teaching. This does not mean, as some might wail, a lowering of standards, a dumbing down of what we do. On the contrary, anyone who has worked closely with secondary school teachers knows the dedication, intelligence, conviction, and sense of excitement they bring to their jobs. Spacks expressed it clearly in the Fall 1994 *Newsletter*: We must "advocate secondary school teaching as an appropriate profession for MAs and PhDs" ("Voices" 3). Yes, indeed. It is an honorable alternative.

Sadly, American colleges and universities have abdicated their responsibilities to American high schools. At least colleges of arts and sciences have, either ignoring the needs of high schools or, worse, turning over the teaching and credentialing process to schools of education, where touchy-feely, "sharing," and "how to organize your grade book" courses frequently win out over content and intellectual discipline. It is worse than a problem; it is a national disgrace.

Yet why would any bright student want to go into secondary school teaching, with its low prestige and tense working conditions? Teachers have no easy access to phones. They are hassled continually by undermotivated if not gun- and knife-toting students parked there by parents who have forgotten what education should be. Theirs is one of the few professions in which, as a teacher once said to me, "We have to go to work ready to do our work, work when we are there, then come home to grade, prepare lessons, and get ready to go to work again." I repeat, Why would anyone want to enter this profession? Aside from the usual answers—calling, commitment, love of teaching, love of students (powerful reasons in themselves)—one might be, surprisingly, money (always a topic that makes graduate students sit up and pay attention). In Virginia, many high school teachers in the north (the outskirts of DC) and in the Tidewater area make more money than tenured associate professors at the university do. Entry-level high school teaching jobs pay competitive salaries: for someone with only a BA the salary begins at $28,000; a new teacher with a master's can command $31,000; and a teacher with a PhD begins at $34,200. Beginning college salaries generally range from $28,000 to $37,000. What is more, a seasoned secondary school teacher with a PhD can earn up to $70,000 by retirement. Not exactly chicken feed: I know many full professors who have retired comfortably on less. For one to keep a job and rise on the salary ladder, an MA degree is no longer a luxury in Virginia, it is a necessity, so there is a built-in market for what we offer, if we can just begin to offer it coherently and sensibly. I say this because when are the majority of our graduate courses offered—many of which are courses a high school teacher might want to take? Right; exactly when a high school teacher cannot take them.

But are our best professors likely to get involved in programs for that forgotten constituency, "school teachers"? If the example of the Center for the Liberal Arts at the University of Virginia or of any number of National Endowment for the Humanities–funded institutes and seminars for high school teachers is any indication, the answer is a resounding yes. In the ten years since its inception, the Center for the Liberal Arts has provided lectures, seminars, workshops, and institutes by more than 217 professors from the University of Virginia alone, who have found the challenge of thinking along new lines, of reconceptualizing the how and the what of their teaching, extremely rewarding. This enthusiasm and this discovery are certainly exportable to other institutions, if those institutions are willing to be flexible.

In addition, the MLA is currently developing an exciting new initiative on teacher education, aimed at the preparation of secondary school teachers in English and foreign languages. The grant money is in hand: all schools need to do now is bid for it and move toward fulfilling the goal of the grant, which is "to determine how well existing curricula prepare students to respond to changing circumstances in the schools and to teach the content required by state frameworks" (Franklin, Letter). This is a move that should be applauded and encouraged and one in which we can and should be closely involved. Which brings me to my next dream.

Second, I would urge us to dream to be relevant. It is well and good that we offer specialized literature and theory courses for our students, but not all graduate students—nor all career goals—demand courses with titles like Postmodernism, Multiculturalism, and the Lesbian Body in Two Short Stories by a Seventeenth-Century French Monk You Have Never Heard Of. I exaggerate, of course, but academic self-indulgence may be a luxury we can no longer afford. Relevance and trendiness are not the same thing. We might consider expanding our curricula to include broad literature, culture, and perhaps even advanced language courses for students who wish to go into secondary school teaching or into publishing, international business, government service, or the like. Aren't we bright enough to develop courses that would be as rigorous as our psycho-Bakhtin-multi-historicism-Derrida courses but with a different—dare I say it, more *relevant* for some—content? For me relevance means coming down off our pedestals and offering nuts-and-bolts career counseling for graduate students. Many of us already do this, of course (some very reluctantly), but counseling and similar steps can make our students more marketable and provide them with more alternatives. We can help them with the revision of papers, encourage them (and find money for them) to attend conferences (not only literature conferences, to be sure) and deliver conference papers; we can move them through mock interviews, help them write cover letters and prepare their résumés, listen to mock conference presentations (perhaps even videotaping these for later viewing and critiquing), help them with grant writing, prepare them better as *teachers* of language and literature, and so on.

> **Academic self-indulgence may be a luxury we can no longer afford. Relevance and trendiness are not the same thing.**

We must help students hone their teaching skills, since they will be called on to be Jacks and Jills of all trades. Universities must shift resources, even scarce and precious resources, into teacher training. This does not mean caving in to the frequently imperialistic demands of those in education who would have our students learn how to prepare better bulletin boards and help their wards "get in touch with their feelings" whether or not those wards know the subject matter being taught to them. It simply means that as we teach our courses, we can also teach our students techniques they can use in the courses they will teach. That is, we might embed in our courses tested models of pedagogy along with tested (and untested) models of theory. We might contemplate hiring people whose expertise is in content-based education to help our graduate students (and, I suspect, us too) deliver with more effectiveness and drive the material to be taught. It also means, of course, working closely and in harmony with those in the schools of education—and there are many—who value content over process and intellect over emotion. The University of Virginia's dynamic Teaching Resource Center has been an invaluable new ally in our quest for better teaching. Measures like opening such a center might help resolve the conflict between overspecialized and general courses and, ultimately, provide more flexibility and better job options for our students.

Third, I would urge us to dream of optimism. Even though the current job market looks tight (*grim, dark, bleak* are other words that appear with alarming frequency) and the philistines of the Conservative Right seem to be slashing and burning our educational budgets with a glee not seen in decades, the future does not look hopeless. In Spanish, for example, we have burgeoning enrollments, and national demographics indicate that we will be in an upward spiral for years to come. The October 1993 *Job Information List* announced 181 jobs in Spanish, and some of us are in the enviable position of placing all our graduate students in full-time jobs every year. Granted, I was once accused by a frustrated colleague of possessing the irritating quality of what he called evangelical optimism, to which I had to plead guilty, but I do not think that my optimistic nature is entirely unfounded. Bettina Huber's most recent statistics prove beyond question that the number of positions advertised in the *Job Information List* has declined sharply from the high of 1988–89, but the 1993–94 figures are not too much lower than those of 1976–77, and they deal primarily with teaching positions in four-year colleges and universities. What about other options? What about secondary school teaching? We are clever and resourceful people, and if we are willing to move with optimism into the future, I see no reason why we cannot control and shape that future.

What will that future look like? Carlos Fuentes recently said that we were living in the shortest century in history, one that went—by his reckoning—from 1914 to 1994. According to him, then, we are already at the juncture of a new century, a new millennium in fact, and we must ask ourselves whether the new century will be a short one or a long one. What will the MLA of the twenty-first century be like? Will there even be an MLA? Recent cracks in the wall made by the hammering of members of the newly formed Association of Literary Scholars and Critics, who have become disillusioned with what they perceive to be—incorrectly, I believe—the over-politically-correctization of the MLA convention, can be viewed as a threat to our future. The emergence of a new organization can also provide new voices in the ongoing dialogue about the profession. The MLA is more heterogeneous than it has ever been, than it was ten, twenty, or thirty years ago, and we must, it seems to me, dare to dream in different languages, different shapes, different colors, and different themes.

I conclude these brief remarks by quoting that model of American cultural and literary studies, Neil Sedaka, who sang so perceptively many years ago "Breaking Up Is Hard to Do." It will be difficult for us to break up our lock on the clone factory, but it must be done and done now. I return to the terms in my title and in the title of this forum. We do have responsibilities, and we can dream about them if we wish. Or we can act, and act now, to bring those dreams into reality.

Works Cited

Bloom, Allan. *The Closing of the American Mind: How Higher Education Has Failed Democracy and Impoverished the Souls of Today's Students*. New York: Simon, 1987.

Bloom, Harold. *The Western Canon*. New York: Harcourt, 1994.

Caminero-Santangelo, Marta. "The Ethics of Hiring." *Profession 94*. New York: MLA, 1994. 62–63.

Curren, Erik D. "No Openings at This Time: Job Market Collapse and Graduate Education." *Profession 94*. New York: MLA, 1994. 57–61.

Franklin, Phyllis. Letter to the author. 4 Nov. 1994.

———. Report on the May 1994 Executive Council meeting to members of the MLA Delegate Assembly. 28 July 1994.

Fuentes, Carlos. Address. Bridgewater College. 18 Apr. 1994.

Holub, Robert C. "Professional Responsibility: On Graduate Education and Hiring Practices." *Profession 94*. New York: MLA, 1994. 79–86.

Huber, Bettina J. "Recent Trends in the Modern Language Job Market." *Profession 94*. New York: MLA, 1994. 87–105.

Spacks, Patricia Meyer. "Enlargements of Interest." *MLA Newsletter* 26.4 (1994): 3.

———. Letter to chairs of PhD-granting departments in the modern languages. 1 Aug. 1994.

———. "Voices of the Membership." *MLA Newsletter* 26.3 (1994): 3.

Flaubert's Nightmare

Myra Jehlen

The very nice notion that Patricia Spacks offered as a theme for this forum raises the alarming possibility latent in all nice notions, the possibility of a commensurately unpleasant inversion, of something in the nature of lilies festering. Such negativity doesn't invalidate the pleasure of the positive, but it does complicate things. The dreams of literature bring responsibilities the way moral capacity grows out of self-consciousness. The ability to imagine a world entails a duty to that world; the same ethical implication flows from just being able to read, for reading ought to engage the imagination not only aesthetically but ethically as well. Or so Spacks seems to be suggesting, and I agree; but not everyone, either writing or reading, does. Let us consider an example of the contrary view, incarnate in a text that seems to have issued more from a nightmare than from a dream and seems to advance at each step in defiance of all duties save one, and that one hardly moral.

The text is Flaubert's novel *Salammbô*, which recounts the history of a war between Carthage and the mercenaries the Carthaginians had hired to fight in the first Punic War. When the promised wages were not forthcoming after the victory, the mercenaries turned on their employers. I want to look at a passage early in the story, where the suspicious soldiers have been nonetheless persuaded to leave the gates of the city and regroup at a safer distance to await their pay. A babel of tongues and a chaos of tribes and nations, the barbarian mercenary army marches through the farming country surrounding Carthage and out into the desert. After three days of march comes this incident:

They were marching through a kind of large gulley, flanked by two chains of reddish dunes, when a sickening stench struck their nostrils, and on top of a carob-tree they seemed to see something extraordinary: a lion's head rose above the leaves. They ran to it. It was a lion, its limbs fastened to a cross like a criminal. Its huge muzzle drooped onto its chest, and its two forepaws, half concealed under its luxuriant mane, were widely separated like the wings of a bird. Its ribs stuck out, one by one, beneath the taut skin; its hind legs, nailed one on top of the other, rose a little; and black blood, flowing through the hair, had collected in stalactites at the bottom of its tail, which hung straight down along the cross. The soldiers stood round amusing themselves; they called it consul and Roman citizen and threw stones at its eyes to drive away the flies. (38)

This is not pleasant reading, but *Salammbô* is famous for worse. In selecting the passage, I hesitated over a wealth of repugnant examples: a description of the Carthaginian Hanno whose monstrously corpulent body is covered by a suppurating leprosy (44–45, 99–101); the sight of slaves turning millstones, "the bridle round their armpits [having] formed purulent scabs as one sees on a donkey's withers" (132); a depiction of men being whipped, in which "the striker used both arms; as the thongs swished they made the bark fly from the plane-trees. Blood showered up into the foliage, and red shapeless masses howled as they writhed at the foot of the trees" (134); the account of child sacrifice to the god Baal-Moloch, with the iron arms of the god's statue working by cranks to carry the children up toward the roaring oven of its maw. Losing count, the priests feed the children in faster and faster, and

[a]s the priests hurried, so the people's frenzy increased. . . . It looked as though the walls crammed with people were crumbling under the screams of horror and mystic pleasure. Then the faithful came into the avenues, dragging along their clinging children; they beat them to make them let go and handed them over to the men in red. The musicians sometimes stopped in exhaustion: then the cries of the mothers could be heard and the sizzling of fat falling on the embers. (241)

The author is Board of Governors Professor of English at Rutgers University, New Brunswick. A version of this paper was presented at the 1994 MLA convention in San Diego.

You get the idea. But what idea? Let me take up the first passage, the one about the crucified lion, and try to decipher from it what Flaubert's idea was in detailing a scene that elicits such horror and disgust. Within the story, the torture of animals conveys a clear message. When the soldiers move on from tormenting the first crucified beast, they come upon a whole line of them, which illustrates a wide variety of horrors. The narrator explains that the Carthaginian peasants avenged themselves thus on wild animals hoping to set a discouraging example. The barbarian mercenaries draw their own conclusion: "'What sort of people are these,' they thought, 'who amuse themselves by crucifying lions!'" (38). As the barbarians and the reader will discover, the Carthaginians are the sort of people who burn their children alive and tear their enemies limb from limb, and the passage is there to bode such ill.

The same kind of explanation applies to the other passages I've indicated and to the many I could have cited: Flaubert wants to portray a civilization given over to extravagant violence as well as to the utmost sensual enjoyments, however bizarre. His Carthage is a fleshpot, a den of iniquity, an inferno of perversity, a satanic cauldron. There is critical consensus that it stands in for the mid-nineteenth-century bourgeois society Flaubert is famous for having loathed. The consensus recognizes, however, that the repulsiveness of Carthage far exceeds the requirement of denouncing Rouen or even Paris. As history, the savagery portrayed in *Salammbô* is wildly sensationalized. At this point, the critical tradition on Flaubert raises the issue of the author's sadistic imagination. Contemporary responses to this novel have invoked Flaubert's fascination with the infamous Marquis de Sade, generally deprecating that fascination and the kinds of excess noted above. It does seem that in the episode of the crucified lion, Flaubert is writing not just to describe a horrifying world and to inspire the reader's horror at it but also to cause the reader to experience horror as such, to experience horror, as it were, intransitively. In short (in very short and with all acknowledgment that the case is immensely complicated), I agree with the critics who find *Salammbô* sadistic in itself.

This sadism has been much analyzed, but for obvious reasons I won't recapitulate the analysis and instead will move directly to the question of the relation of sadism to Flaubert's literary project. And here I propose that in the lion passage, as in the descriptions of the torture of children, Flaubert achieves something that less repulsive accounts might not achieve, namely, a separation of exquisite form from hideous content and

the subsequent triumph of form over content. The separation occurs when readers are repelled by the content and attracted by the form; it occurs when a content, by its repulsiveness, forces the reader to become conscious of the difference between it and an attractive form. Significantly, content is the active proponent of this process, which can be seen to unfold within the word itself. The word *content*, is a noun, pronounced cón-tent; pronounced contént, it is also an adjective. Both come from the Latin *continere*, to contain. The noun denotes a quantity contained, the adjective a psychological state of pleasant calm. But when juxtaposed with the noun, the adjective, describing the calm of fulfillment, reveals that the noun means not just any quantity but one that suffices, a plenitude; reciprocally, the noun explicates the adjective, showing that the calm of fulfillment requires plenitude.

Now it can be said that the *con*tent of the lion passage arouses radical *dis*content in the reader,

> *Not only is the aesthetic distinct from the ethical; the one contradicts the other.*

who is repelled by its plenitude of horror. The reader's repugnance may well be tinged with fascination, but the essential thing is that Flaubert has created a tension between the repellent unpleasantness of the scene described and the aesthetic attraction of the description as art. My point is that this tension works to enhance the aesthetic experience by making it stand apart, distinctly valuable and moreover ultimately redemptive of the repugnance engendered by the disgusting content.

When the beauty of the literary expression triumphs over the ugliness of the lion's torment, however, it also triumphs over the reader's ethical impulse to condemn this torment. The reader is of two minds, on the one hand censuring the torture of animals but on the other admiring Flaubert's account. Since this is art, not life, the admiration reasonably wins. But the reader's moral sympathy, in losing out to artistic appreciation, yields a further point; the reader is now brought to actually value the lion's suffering, since it permits such beautiful writing. At this point, not only is the aesthetic distinct from the ethical; the one contradicts the other. In opposition to the theme of this forum, the reader of the crucifixion passage abjures her or his moral responsibility in order to enjoy Flaubert's dream. As for Flaubert, he did it first.

What he did was write not just apart from ethical considerations but at their expense; in fact, against them. *Salammbô* represents brilliantly, inspiringly an art that nourishes itself from the contemplation of suffering. Sade's explanation for the superiority of causing pain over causing pleasure was that pain, engendering a more violent and visible reaction, was more exciting for the perpetrator. Flaubert derives a similar advantage in his novel when the reader feels the aesthetic experience the more acutely for its being devoid of, indeed antithetical to, moral pleasure. We don't have to enjoy the sight of a beast bleeding and squirming on a cross as a scene in itself to enjoy Flaubert's description. Evil as such is not the issue, nor does he advocate it. But if evil enhances beauty, that is another matter; and this, I would argue, Flaubert does advocate.

More precisely, he practices in *Salammbô* an enhancement of beauty through evil. The most elaborate images evoke the most revolting characters and events. It is frequently noted that in the novel that bears her name as its title, the Carthaginian princess Salammbô appears remarkably rarely. The romance that ostensibly centers the plot, the passion of the barbarian Matho for Salammbô, is lost to view through long chapters until we almost forget it. But we never lose the beat of the real heart of the novel: the war and the horrors it breeds. The first chapter sets out these terms clearly. The story opens with a great feast that the Carthaginian general Hamilcar, father of Salammbô, offers to the mercenaries, hoping to propitiate them. At this feast, replete with gorgings and regurgitations, Salammbô does eventually appear, gorgeous in silks, feathers, and precious stones, to descend from her palace to the field of disgusting revels below. Flaubert's description is certainly lush:

> Her hair, powdered with mauve sand, was piled up like a tower in the style of the Canaanite virgins and made her look taller. Ropes of pearls fastened to her temples fell to the corners of her mouth, rose red like a half-open pomegranate. On her breast clustered luminous stones iridescent as a lamprey's scales. Her arms, adorned with diamonds, were left bare outside a sleeveless tunic, spangled with red flowers on a dead black background. Between her ankles she wore a golden chain to control her pace, and her great, dark purple mantle, cut from some unknown material, trailed a broad wake behind her with every step she took. (25)

Compare this with the first appearance of the corrupt and perverted Hanno, who represents the Carthaginians in their efforts to cheat the mercenaries:

> He wore black felt boots, sprinkled with silver moons. Strips of cloth, as on a mummy, were wound round his legs, and the flesh bulged out between the crossed material. His stomach overflowed on to the scarlet jacket that covered his thighs; the folds of his neck fell down to his chest like an ox's dewlaps; his tunic, painted with flowers, was split at the armpits; he wore a scarf, a belt, and a full black cloak with double laced sleeves. The richness of his dress, his great necklace of blue stones, his gold clasps, and heavy earrings only served to make his deformity more hideous. He looked like some gross idol roughly hewn out of a block of stone; for a pale leprosy, spread all over his body, gave him the appearance of an inert object. However his nose, hooked like a vulture's beak, dilated violently to breathe in the air, and his small eyes, with sticky lashes, shone with a hard metallic glint. In his hand he held a spatula of aloes for scratching his skin. (44–45)

Both Salammbô and Hanno are depicted more eventfully later; these are formal introductions, somewhat reminiscent of the genre of medieval portraiture. But even through the formality, the difference is patent. Salammbô is rote, though very fine rote. Hanno's reverse depiction, beginning with his feet, is a black mass of a portrait, animate with the author's hatred, as Salammbô never is with the passion she promises but only rarely embodies. *Salammbô* belongs to a subcategory of orientalism, in which not the rich beauty of the East is celebrated but its festering disease.

If, then, art may exist not only independent of morality but dependent on the violation of morality, what does this entail for the critic who aspires to be a moral human being as well? Some have used abstraction as a way out of the dilemma; they talk not about the events unfolding on the surface of the text but about the truth of suffering and the courage of the writer who depicts that suffering. Jean-Paul Sartre's portraits of two of the evil men of letters, Jean Genêt and Flaubert, goes this route, retracing their reprehensible paths to arrive finally at a transcendence composed of truth and courage. One difficulty with this solution is that it requires that we not take Genêt and Flaubert at their word. Moreover, translating their accounts of evil into brave allegories of truth implies that they could have represented that truth differently, using other, less objectionable, allegorical images; and this implication risks trivializing the very problem the defense takes up, by suggesting that the problem need not have arisen.

This is not the place to rehearse the literature on the relations of the aesthetic to evil. Besides, the question of responsibility is not quite that of morality as such, for responsibility is a particular instance of morality, having particular characteristics. Responsibility denotes a relation to morality and is not a moral principle in itself. Like loyalty, responsibility can be applied to a bad cause. I take Spacks's dictum as having to do less with the lessons to be embodied in or derived from works of the imagination than with one's relation as author or reader to those lessons. But what would it mean for Flaubert to behave responsibly toward the nightmares he projects in *Salammbô*? And what does it mean to be a responsible reader of those nightmares?

I suppose that in the first instance responsibility involves pointing out that the nightmares are indeed nightmares: in other words, it involves making a moral judgment. But facing squarely the immorality of Flaubert's pleasure in pain—of his sadism—what does a reader do to be responsible toward it? I have no answer and have been wondering whether there is anything beyond recognition to be done. But if there is nothing more to be done in relation to such art, there is perhaps some value in acknowledging the weakness of that conclusion, taking *weakness* not in its negative sense but as describing a positive force with its own peculiar effectiveness. The effectiveness of the weak conclusion (that all one can do is recognize the possible agreement of evil and art) might lie in what this conclusion implies for the place of art in society. Perhaps art as such does not properly inhabit the prophetic place that some today wish it to inhabit. Perhaps society should cease to await from literature lessons about life or a sense of life's order or meaning. With the example of Flaubert, one would be better advised to see literature as related to life not directly but through a dialectic without any necessary resolution. Reading Flaubert is an experience not just of contradiction but at times also of incoherence, as one realizes that the contradiction is permanent, that its terms can only grow farther apart. In *some* dreams begin terrorism, and critical responsibility to them, I propose, begins in recognizing them for what they are.

Work Cited

Flaubert, Gustave. *Salammbô*. Trans. with introd. A. J. Krailsheimer. London: Penguin, 1977.

Literary Reading in Interdisciplinary Study

Margery Sabin

As far as dreams go, all I can say is—you have to be a real dreamer to write an essay in 1994 and presume to say anything persuasive on behalf of what used to be called literary reading. Even our most adaptive senior representatives are sounding daunted. Denis Donoghue, in his recent book *The Old Moderns*, observes, without really expecting to overcome, a situation where "many of our students don't understand . . . what it means to read literature 'as literature,'" while what passes for theory in contemporary discourse makes it ever harder to establish "the fictive and the aesthetic as calling for a distinctive form of attention" (85). George Levine, in his essay "Reclaiming the Aesthetic," confesses anxiety and a sense of high risk in defending literary experience (11). And Frank Kermode worries aloud about the repudiation of literature in the aftermath of the "critical revolution" he helped foster in England. Literature as a distinct category "is what we're being asked to give up," he says in a recent interview. "And that seems a lot to give up without making any kind of enquiry" (Tredell 35).

Unfortunately, the critical revolution has at once so undermined and overcomplicated the terms of our professional discourse that we have no shared language of inquiry. The May 1994 *PMLA*, for example, skirts inquiry by emptying the terms *literature* and *literary study* of any distinct meaning. To legitimize what is broadly called *cultural studies*, the editorial column asks, in a conciliatory tone, "[I]sn't *literature* today, for some readers at least, capacious enough to include any text that can be studied from a historical or sociological perspective?" (Stanton 359). I believe that this rhetorical question has serious professional as well as intellectual implications and itself cannot be accepted without inquiry. For if *literature* is no longer to designate a set of objects distinct from those in, say, anthropology, or

even anything as loose as a perspective distinguishable from history or sociology, what is left as the professional contribution that justifies our continuing existence? I agree with George Levine that it is the responsibility of literary study to confront this question anew (8)—not in a spirit of nostalgia, but as a practical and progressive inquiry into an enterprise that cannot thrive, or perhaps even survive, if it cannot articulate what it is.

I want to sketch briefly one among many possible lines of argument here by inquiring what kinds of attention to language may be said to constitute a distinct literary discipline, leaving aside the separate vexed question of what texts should principally command literary attention. I proceed by first reviewing, in a very abbreviated way, the crucial turn in the recent history of English studies marked by Raymond Williams's much publicized split in the 1960s from the "practical criticism" identified with F. R. Leavis and Cambridge English, a split that inaugurated the English version of cultural studies. Then I identify a second turning point that I somewhat loosely locate in the late 1980s, after Williams's death, not so much because of his individual absence as because his death coincided with the rise of an academic generation that was no longer obsessed by earlier literary battles and that often did not even engage with them at all. I illustrate this contemporary situation with a small example from current postcolonial studies in America of how the drive to indict the politics of the past is draining current reading practice

The author is Lorraine Chiu Wang Professor of English at Wellesley College. A version of this paper was presented at the 1994 MLA convention in San Diego.

of the attention to language still energetically alive in Williams's own work.

To begin: Raymond Williams liked to assert that he had renounced literary criticism, had even renounced literature altogether, and that he looked forward to a socialist, democratic future when our very consciousness of such elitist categories would be fundamentally revised. However, under the pressure of questioning— for example in *Politics and Letters*, a brilliant volume of interviews put together in 1979—Williams tended to retreat from this revolutionary frontier into more local combat with Leavisite practical criticism centered in Cambridge, England.

There are many interpretations of what this famous academic split was and was not really about. I do not see it as mainly about the connectedness of literature to other academic disciplines. Williams himself often acknowledged Leavis as his embattled precursor in the effort to understand literature in relation to social, cultural, and even economic phenomena (*Politics* 65; *Writing* 187–88, 214). In the experimental plan for a seventeenth-century tripos laid out in a little book of 1943 called *Education and the University*, Leavis had argued that literary training "demands, of its very nature, to be associated with work in other fields," such as sociology, anthropology, history, and political thought (8, 61). His list of two dozen possible topics for "extended pieces of writing" anticipated the kind of investigations still being proposed as interdisciplinary novelties today: "the social-economic correlations of literary history," "the changing relations between sophisticated and popular culture," "economic individualism," "the reaction against Whig History" (53). It is not the concept of interdisciplinary understanding that divides Williams from Leavis. Nor is it the vision of literary study as engaged in a positive form of cultural resistance, in a strenuous effort of advocacy and protest conducted through trained attention to the historical development of language. Here, too, Leavis was more a precursor to Williams than an opponent.

Yet Williams did decisively repudiate Leavis. His quarrel, as I understand it, had principally to do with the kind of cultural resistance literature was to promote. For Leavis, the literature of the past offered a means of resistance to what he called the "drift of modern life" into technology, abstraction, and cliché (22). He hoped that direct, active, detailed engagement with particular performances of written language from the past could strengthen connection to a humane tradition of what he called "human intelligence, choice, and will" (30). This Leavisite humanism is far from complacent, however, for it is driven by the anxiety that the cultural continuity he values exists only insofar as literary study creates and sustains it.

Williams came to deplore the alienation from the present in Leavis and his followers, which he saw as snobbish and depressing. Williams based his radically different conception of cultural resistance on a radically different judgment of the present in relation to the past. He argued that the literature of the past admired by Leavis for still valuable examples of "human intelligence, choice, and will" needed to be more skeptically viewed within a history of inherited privilege and exploitation, a history that the dominant literary tradition tended to mystify because of its own participation in it. Especially since the nineteenth century, Williams asserted, educated language, which is to say the language of what was traditionally called literature, passed itself off as "ordinary" and "universal," thereby masking its own conditions of privilege (*Writing* 102). Williams wanted to strengthen contemporary resistance to this elite tradition. At the same time, he raised for higher regard an alternative English tradition of radical dissent, communal energy, and connection to spoken forms of language. He looked to this alternative tradition to challenge "official" versions of the past and to reinforce another kind of cultural continuity, a democratic, socialist continuity between past and contemporary working class and popular culture.

When I formulate the Williams and Leavis split in these terms, I mean to underscore a familial quality to their conflict. Williams renounced (more exactly, he *de*nounced) his literary inheritance while remaining inside the house, as it were. In part, the quarrel began as a battle of the books: Williams championing the Milton of the political pamphlets against the metaphysical poets; Hardy's *Jude the Obscure* against the novels of Henry James; early George Eliot against late George Eliot; customary, collective, assertive speech forms against the complex, individualized imagery and syntax of the reflected-upon written sentence. The entire challenge of Williams against Leavis evolved in relation to particulars of English language in the designs of specific texts and conventions of composition.

I don't have time to trace Williams's further movement toward a more radical cultural politics in the late 1970s. What stands out to me as almost poignant, in reviewing his career for this paper, was his continuing conviction that the dominant literary tradition and training would survive his attack on them. "If we put such prose down," he remarked of the elite tradition in his introduction to the *Pelican Book of English Prose* in

1969, "it is still with the certainty that in its special achievement it continues to be there" (*Writing* 83). How should we understand this certainty? Is it a sign of pessimism about the real likelihood of the cultural change he desires? Or does it show willed optimism in the face of Leavisite anxiety about the "drift of modern life"? Even through the 1980s, Williams continued to punctuate his repudiations of the literary tradition by interjections like "of course," "naturally," it is "bound to be the case." "Certainly," he says, we still need to know what he calls "this important, indispensable central culture" (*What* 155). Why did Williams think that this indispensable central culture was bound to remain known and knowable without his assistance? Did his own oppositional position at a high moment of English studies in Cambridge University lead him to overrate the stability of what he could then feel free to attack without fear that it might really collapse? Perhaps Williams attributed perpetual strength to the central literary culture of the past because it continued to be so strong in his own mind and work, which remained, right to the end, not so much revolutionary as dramatic—"dialogic," in current Bakhtinian terminology. Williams's family quarrel with Leavis was of that interminable sort that continues within, as a dramatic internalized conflict.

How little tone and context have come to matter to critics.

I have one quick example of Williams's dramatic cast of thought even at the end of his career. It comes from a 1984 essay published in *What I Came to Say* as "Writing, Speech, and 'the Classical.'" Williams begins with his trademark insistence on the "disproportionate advantages" that writing has conferred on those who possess it, so that "theirs . . . is the record, and, if we are not careful, the verdict of history" (47). But then he turns to demonstrate an almost opposite appreciation of the written record for the dramatic contests it contains. He cites an episode in the *Agricola* of Tacitus, where a soon-to-be-defeated Briton swordsman makes a stirring speech of protest against Roman power. "Raptores orbis" is the phrase Williams especially likes. He singles it out for its "concentrated power" and its "unforgettable underlying image of hands seizing the round globe itself" (49).

What most engages Williams here, however, is not only the swordsman's phrase of protest but also the dramatic interplay of opposing voices in the narrative by Tacitus. It is the "whole action" of these different voices that Williams examines, as the swordsman's heroic denunciation of Roman imperialism is followed by the very different voice of the "practical, moderate, loyal servant of Empire who goes on to defeat him" (52). Williams demonstrates through Tacitus how the written record, even a narrative eulogy in Latin, yields more than a simple verdict in favor of the historical victor. Williams will not belittle the dramatic vitality of the Roman text by containing it within an ideological structure, even though he notes how that could be done. For him, the rhetorical activity and tension within the classical text makes for its value and for his special interest in it. I call this interest the continuing literary perspective in Williams's interdisciplinary study of the past.

My example from current anti-imperialist criticism shows what happens when literary attention to the whole action of language within a text is abandoned in favor of selective looting of past language for incriminating pieces of evidence. In particular, I would point out how several of our leading critics of imperialism have seized on a single sentence, by repetition institutionalizing it into a self-incriminating formula of Victorian ideology. The sentence in question comes not from high literature but from *The Expansion of England*, by J. R. Seeley, the late Victorian imperialist historian: "We seem, as it were, to have conquered and peopled half the world in a fit of absence of mind" (8).

A striking and quotable sentence. Francis Hutchins, a perceptive historian of Victorian imperialism writing in the 1960s, found it a "paradoxical expression" (84, 140–41). Since then the literary critics have taken it over and smoothed it out: one calls it an idea "propagated" by Seeley (Said 9); another a "misleading dictum" of Seeley's (Brantlinger, *Rule* 7, 81); a third presents it as a "famous pronouncement" and quotes it on page 1 of a book about the Victorian novel that proposes to unmask Victorian repression of its expansionist culture (Perera 1). The chapter "The Nineteenth-Century Novel and Empire" in a major revisionary history of the British novel quotes the sentence yet again and now consolidates the embodiment of faulty consciousness in Seeley himself. What is called "Seeley's absentmindedness" becomes a synecdoche for a whole culture's denial of responsibility for imperial conquest (Brantlinger, "Nineteenth-Century Novel" 562).

When I came on repetitions of this sentence as a literary critic doing interdisciplinary work, what piqued my specifically literary curiosity was something oblique in it, something deliberately far-fetched and witty. The derivation of vast political power from so singular and personal an event as "a fit," the incongruity between the volition implied by "conquered and peopled" and the trivial unknowingness in "absence of mind"—this did not at all have the tone and style of a dictum or pronouncement. It was the stubbornness of my literary training that made me dig up Seeley's now despised and little-read book of 1883. What I found confirmed not only my literary intuition but also my dismay at how little tone and context have come to matter to critics who build political and cultural arguments on pieces of quoted language.

Far from being propagated as a dictum, Seeley's paradoxical sentence makes an ironic point in its context, which is the beginning of a lecture specifically about imperial expansion as "the great fact of modern English history" (12). Setting himself against rival Whig historians and the popular press, Seeley in 1883 was advertising the superior historical accuracy (and the greater interest) of his own Cambridge University course, which featured England's imperial competition with other European powers, especially France, during the preceding three hundred years, and especially in the eighteenth century. In other words, Seeley was making his own version of the cultural critique now being constructed at his expense.[1]

Except that Seeley's ironic tone gives a significantly different coloring to the point. He is deliberately exaggerating when he says, "We seem, as it were, to have conquered and peopled half the world in a fit of absence of mind." His caricature of popular Victorian indifference to imperial history is designed to make this posture look absurd. More specifically, Seeley is remarking a complex dissociation of the English popular imagination from the policies and goals of what he calls "the political community" (7).[2] He does not himself endorse or declare anew the alibi of unconsciousness but rather exposes through irony and other rhetorical devices its incompleteness as historical explanation. To misread his rhetoric as propagating or declaring an idea erases the entire purpose of his argument as well as the literary activity of his language. Although Seeley objects to some literary versions of history, he is at the same time a literary writer in the tradition of his hero, Burke. Thus his argument works through dramatic rhetorical shifts, to include irony, questioning, doubts, and exaggeration.

So what? One witty colleague, not overly impressed by my rehabilitation of Seeley, remarked, "Well, the Seeley family will be very grateful to you." Probably not, since my full reading of Seeley ends in seeing his defense of imperialism entangled in contradictions that his rhetoric cannot resolve. But the point of rereading Seeley for the tone and drama of his language is less to raise his individual reputation than to lower our own contemporary conceit of exclusive and superior consciousness.[3] Seeley's sentence has appealed to many recent critics because it seems so conveniently to fit the programmatic belittling of the past consciousness of writers, the belittling that now accompanies resistance to the written record. Irony is one of those rhetorical effects that often disrupt this program, because irony's doubleness enacts presence of mind where ideological critique posits absence.

Raymond Williams at his best admirably sustained the perception of tonal shifts and dramatic play in language that I identify here with literary reading. In his 1984 essay cited above, Williams refers to the valuable "habits of mind" that enable such perception (*What* 55). My point is that these so-called habits of mind are in actuality the learned and teachable skills of literary reading. They are as crucial to historical as to aesthetic investigation, and they are central to what our profession of language and literature has to offer students across disciplines and in interdisciplinary study. How ironic if we, in our own absence of mind, as it were, should not only discard those skills but even forget what they are.

Notes

[1]"It is thus that the great English Exodus is commonly regarded, as if it had happened in the most simple, inevitable manner, as if it were merely the unopposed occupation of empty countries by the nation which happened to have the greatest surplus population and the greatest maritime power. I shall show this to be a great mistake. I shall show that this Exodus makes a most ample and a most full and interesting chapter in English history. I shall venture to assert that during the eighteenth century it determines the whole course of affairs, that the main struggle of England from the time of Louis XIV to the time of Napoleon was for the possession of the New World, and that it is for want of perceiving this that most of us find that century of English history uninteresting" (13–14).

[2]"There is something very characteristic in the indifference which we show towards this mighty phenomenon of the diffusion of our race and the expansion of our state. We seem, as it were, to have conquered and peopled half the world in a fit of absence of mind. While we were doing it, that is, in the eighteenth century, we did not allow it to affect our imaginations or in any degree to change our ways of thinking; nor have we even now ceased to think of ourselves as simply a race inhabiting an island off the northern coast of the Continent of Europe. . . . This fixed way of thinking has influenced our historians. It causes them, I think, to miss the true point of view in describing the eighteenth century. . . . They do not perceive that in that century the history of England is not in England but in America and Asia" (8–9).

[3]Edward Said, in his *Culture and Imperialism*, recognizes Seeley as one of the "great rhetoricians" among imperial historians (107),

but this appreciation does not affect his posture of refuting the idea of absentmindedness "propagated" by Seeley. Said's own demonstration of "the consistency and density of continuous enterprise" in British and French imperial expansion (9–10) repeats rather than opposes Seeley's historical argument.

Works Cited

Brantlinger, Patrick. "The Nineteenth-Century Novel and Empire." *Columbia History of the British Novel*. Ed. John J. Richetti et al. New York: Columbia UP, 1994. 560–78.

———. *Rule of Darkness: British Literature and Imperialism: 1830–1914*. Ithaca: Cornell UP, 1988.

Donoghue, Denis. *The Old Moderns: Essays on Literature and Theory*. New York: Knopf, 1994.

Hutchins, Francis. *The Illusion of Permanence: British Imperialism in India*. Princeton: Princeton UP, 1967.

Leavis, F. R. *Education and the University: A Sketch for an "English School."* London: Chatto, 1943.

Levine, George. "Introduction: Reclaiming the Aesthetic." *Aesthetics and Ideology*. Ed. Levine. New Brunswick: Rutgers UP, 1994. 1–28.

Perera, Suvendrini. *Reaches of Empire: The English Novel from Edgeworth to Dickens*. New York: Columbia UP, 1991.

Said, Edward. *Culture and Imperialism*. New York: Knopf, 1993.

Seeley, J. R. *The Expansion of England*. Cambridge: Cambridge UP; Boston: Roberts, 1883.

Stanton, Domna C. "Editor's Column: What Is Literature?—1994." *PMLA* 109 (1994): 359–65.

Tredell, Nicholas, ed. *Conversations with Critics*. Manchester: Carcanet, 1994.

Williams, Raymond. *Politics and Letters: Interviews with* New Left Review. London: New Left, 1979.

———. *What I Came to Say*. London: Radius, 1989.

———. *Writing in Society*. London: Verso, 1983.

The Responsibility to Dream

Bryan Wolf

I begin my comments by trying to imagine what dreaming must look like to a young child first entering the educational system. I do so in part because we are all educators and because education, as I understand it, represents an institutionalized space for dreaming within our culture. I wish later in my paper to name that dreaming as a form of negative dialectics, a way of confronting and unthinking the various closures—formal, narrative, and ideological—that shape our lives. But for now I restrict the discussion to one image: a striking instance of conceptual art by the Chicana artist Celia Alvarez Muñoz. I invoke Muñoz's image *Which Came First? Enlightenment Series #4* for three reasons: because the narrative I wish to tell is linked to what we might term the history of perception in the United States; because Muñoz's image captures what it means to dream at the level of the body; and because this paper was first presented in San Diego, a city of border crossings and Proposition 187. All, I believe, are relevant to the theme In Dreams Begin Responsibilities.

That topic will carry us from contemporary art to early nineteenth-century painting to the remarkable exploits of P. T. Barnum. My remarks are divided into two parts, both concerned with the disappearance of the body in the modern world. The first part looks at the role of education in the effacement of the body; the second part briefly examines the relation of the body to professionalism, mass culture, and the university. I enlist your patience on this serendipitous journey, assuring you that all stops along the road represent way stations to the modern university.

To the art, then. Muñoz's image, the first of five panels that together constitute Enlightenment Series #4, invokes the experience of a Mexican American child growing up in mainstream America at the same time that it frames the experience within a specific cultural politics. The image is concerned with the relations among education, social assimilation, and cultural reproduction. I dwell on it because it takes the dreams of a young child down a twofold path: the disappearance of the body and the rise of mass culture.

If we were to take a strictly historical tack, we might connect Muñoz's image with early-twentieth-century experimental art. Marius de Zayas's visual poem *Mental Reactions*, published in Stieglitz's magazine *291* in 1915, scrambles Agnes Meyer's poem on feminine consciousness with imagery that is meant to suggest, among other things, a woman's breasts as seen by a male onlooker (the two prominent black triangles). The effect, like that of Muñoz's image, is to divide identity between personal experience and public constructions. De Zayas's image is at once an art of self-expression, a witty and modernist play on the materiality of the typographic surface, and a form of social criticism. Muñoz's art reiterates and racializes de Zayas's concerns in the context of the late twentieth century. Like many minority artists in postmodern America, Muñoz restages the formal claims of most canonical art as a series of political gestures. She is interested not in aesthetics but in ideology, and she links eggs, children, and writing into a single field of cultural production.

First the eggs. The economy of the upper part of the image invokes the world of 1950s commercial photography (Muñoz began her career, like Andy Warhol, as a commercial artist). Muñoz's eggs, neatly arranged in a row, slouch to the market to be born. They line up like items in a grocery display or like Levittown houses. In their message of order and conformity, they confirm corporate ideology of the postwar era, an attenuated

---

The author is Professor of American Studies and English at Yale University. A version of this paper was presented at the 1994 MLA convention in San Diego.

---

version of Enlightenment liberalism that produced children and suburbs in equal numbers.

Like modern works of art, Muñoz's eggs are both immaculate objects and consumable commodities. They sit on their field of gold like so many museum pieces mounted on a wall. Rather than provide us with a trope of birth, they provoke us with the opposite: they image a denaturalized visual territory where, to paraphrase Lévi-Strauss, eggs are "cooked" at birth, whisked from nature to the uncanny realm of culture. Culture is defined by Muñoz as a normalizing process, a logic that at its global level turns the reproductive habits of chickens into a metaphor for hegemony and at its more local level helps young brown bodies—Chicano and Chicana bodies—unlearn their differences from white ones. Nature, what we believe ourselves to be observing in the top panel, disappears, or rather it appears only in cooked form, as an educational by-product.

In the lines of text below, then, Muñoz converts an apparently innocent exercise in penmanship into a case study in Foucauldian politics. The cursive letters of a young child, bound visually by the taut lines of her writing tablet, mark the space within the image of bodily discipline. The child learns not to write but to write properly, internalizing a set of rules, a writing practice, that disallows expressions of difference. What

should be a site of personal expression, tied directly to hands and to the body's always eccentric identity, functions instead as a space of discipline, where self-expression is replaced by an impersonal writing code. The standardization of the child's cursive script repeats the regimentation of the eggs, and both together remind the viewer that this image is not only about writing but also about writing off. What is being written out of the image is the body, the world of nature, and with nature the ability to name bodily difference as anything more than a form of transgression, the tendency of unruly figures to cross clearly marked boundaries (whether those on a writing pad or between two nations).

Muñoz's image, then, is about renomination, the dream of a nameable body. It is about the politics of cutlure and the way that education intersects with bodies to deracialize them, to overwrite them with a set of cultural codes that do not so much deny difference as ignore it. This process of not-so-benign neglect disallows Muñoz's "primary grade" children the two skills Frederick Douglass insisted were necessary for racial survival: the ability to conceptualize one's situation and the ability to recover one's body—processes summarized in Douglass's description, in *Narrative of the Life*, of his quest for literacy and his physical defeat of the overseer Covey. Muñoz's agenda is to render visible the

Learning to speak English and understanding chickens were the hardest things for me during the primary grades.

1 The chicken will lay an egg today.

Celia Alvarez Muñoz. *Which Came First? Enlightenment Series #4*, 1982. Collection Museum of Contemporary Art, San Diego. Gift of the artist and Museum purchase with funds from the Elizabeth W. Russell Foundation.

processes of cultural invisibility. She wishes to understand how the body disappears in the politics of the nation-state and its acculturative machinery.

And that brings us to the forum topic. We might think of dreaming in Freudian terms, understanding the dream as a form of mental process, what Freud called the world of primary processes, where mental activity occurs unconsciously and in separation from the body's motor activities. Such dreaming bears striking resemblance to what in a rather different context we might term ideology, which is the unconscious mental map that habituates and reconciles us to our everyday experiences. The parallel between a Freudian hermeneutics and a more materialist notion of ideology, each looking to hidden or suppressed sources for the generation of meaning, in turn suggests two contradictory things. First, dreaming, as a social activity, does unpleasant cultural work. It overrides the body and substitutes for the body a fantasy of selfhood, a mode of identity constructed from imaginary rather than "real" relations.[1] These imaginary daydreams are the work of the nation-state, and they depend for their effect on our collusion, our willingness to live within the ideological closures that situate us relative to our history. And yet—second—such dreaming might also be understood as the space not where closure occurs but where it is known to occur, where it is named as closure. This type of dreaming works, as Freud insisted it must, only negatively. To extrapolate again from a Freudian hermeneutics to a mode of political critique that I believe emanates in revisionary fashion from Freud, such dreaming operates as a negative dialectics, a way of demystifying (from within) the illusion of wholeness so essential to our realm of already cooked eggs and proscribed borders.

Taking our cue from Muñoz, we might think of the first type of dreaming as Descartes's revenge, the disappearance of the body in the service not only of national ideologies but also of an impersonal and (by the nineteenth century) professionalized middle-class gaze. I take Descartes's good name in vain here not because I wish to sully an otherwise happy reputation but because Descartes's thought represents one of the earliest articulations I know of a new, and what I take to be modern, cultural logic. Cartesian thinking, by separating intellectual activity from the world of the body-machine, sets into motion a notion of personal life that develops over time into one of the central components of the middle-class formation. The division between *res cogitans* and *res extensa* (the thinking self and the material world) gets rescripted in the nineteenth century as

an agon between a managerial class flush with the prerogatives of its newly professionalized world and a working class affiliated with the cumbersome body of *res extensa*. And the central instrument of this professionalized class, as both Burton Bledstein and Gerald Graff have shown, is not Foucauldian forms of discipline but educational institutions. My purpose here is not to rehearse that history but rather to tether it to a parallel history of perception that is crucial for an understanding of a world still under Cartesian mandate. To inquire about dreaming in our culture, the spaces where we both enforce our collective identities and disentangle them, and to historicize that dreaming, we need to link the Great American Dream Machine to institutions of learning and the cultural work of seeing as they have evolved over the past two centuries.

Muñoz's image is interesting in this regard not just because it is winsome and witty but also because it connects the dream of the body to the acquisition of language, thus going beyond traditional forms of identity

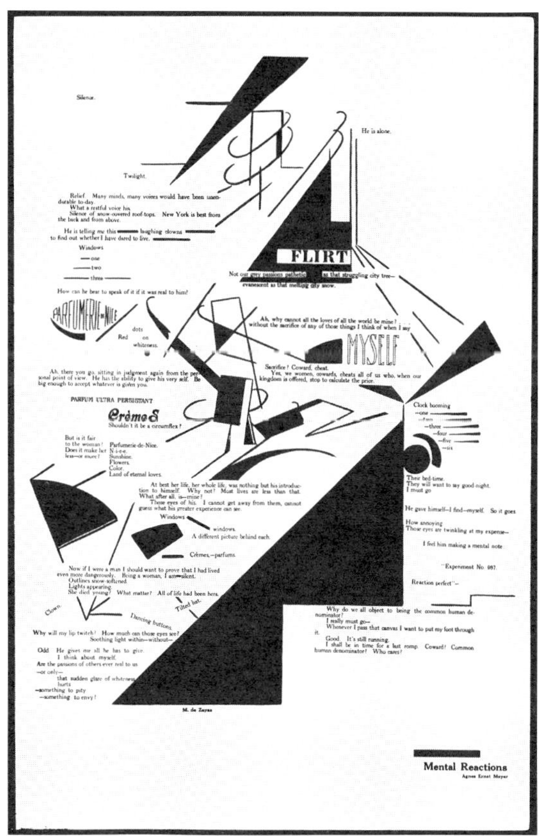

Marius de Zayas and Agnes E. Meyer. *Mental Reactions.* April 1915, pen and ink, from *291.* Yale Collection of American Literature, Beinecke Rare Book and Manuscript Library, Yale University.

politics. By identity politics I mean the making of group or ethnic categories based on a shared, racialized, and usually essentialized body. Muñoz's interest in the body cuts in other directions. She rejects the essentialism so often associated with body politics—the rather Emersonian notion that I am *me* first and a social creature only afterward—and turns the viewer's attention instead to a body so immersed in cultural processes that it is inseparable from them. "Which came first?" Muñoz asks, because she is interested in what moves are available to the body from within the language game we cannot help but inhabit. We know this from the image's middle line, where the artist laconically comments, "Learning to speak English and understanding chickens were the hardest things for me during the primary grades." That middle line, unlike the cursive script below, is an ironic piece of writing. It stands at a distance from the acculturative process it describes, and it does so as a form of critical commentary made available by the very print culture that the bottom line expresses in its most suffocating form.

The middle line, in other words, marks the space of negative dialectics in the picture. It is equivalent to Douglass's encounter with Sheridan's tracts on Catholic emancipation. It represents the one place in Muñoz's image where writing as a disciplinary practice is turned against itself, where the representational possibilities of the print culture produce neither Foucauldian subjects nor—the flip side of that coin—romanticized and self-expressive rebels but educated language-users whose goal is to create an alternative public sphere. By alternative public sphere I mean a place within the world of print and media where the body, like the lithe torso of Melville's Queequeg, is always already known as inscribed and the natural must forever be subjected to the politicizing and denaturalizing question, "Whose chicken, whose egg?"

What Muñoz's middle line of print reveals is that education is the only space in our culture where closure names itself. If we dream in Cartesian fashion to forget the body, we also dream to remember it. If we dream our way into class or racial ideologies, we can also dream our way not out, for that is never possible, but through them. We can, in Emersonian fashion, heap the horizon when it threatens to hem us in, even if what we encounter on the other side is only the exhilaration and threat of new horizons. In this narrative we become, by dreaming, not Emerson's "Representative Man" but—dare I say it?—the Frank Perdues of ideology. It takes a tough man to make a tender chicken, and it takes an even tougher person to break the eggs, to convert images of an imaginary wholeness—white, rounded, and disembodied—into yellow-and-white pools of liquid color, tasty, unstable, and likely to make a mess of any border. Breaking eggs might lead the French to omelettes, but it carries us toward education, which is the place where dreams occur.

I move from the issues Muñoz raises to a different form of social and educational enterprise. The question again concerns the body and its effacement, only this time I approach the issue not as a problem in education but as a prerequisite for mass culture. I examine the symmetry, the strange and fearful symmetry, between the modern university and forms of early mass culture. Both represent arenas of privileged symbolic action; both are aspects of public life or

Charles Willson Peale. *Exhumation of the Mastodon.* 1806. Oil on canvas. The Peale Museum, Baltimore City Life Museums.

public inquiry that occur through coded forms of discourse; and both occupy cultural spaces where intellectual activity intersects with the world of middle-class leisure. To make these abstruse claims concrete I take what may seem a circuitous route: hunting for mastodon bones, dallying over early American silver, and, at the end of our itinerary, dropping in on Emerson's chief rival and competitor for the national soul in the nineteenth century, P. T. Barnum. To state my argument in advance, I examine, in an all too brief sweep through nineteenth-century cultural history, how disembodied forms of vision underwrite early mass culture, and I then link that disembodied gaze to the history of professionalization and to the shape of the university. I invoke the ghost of Barnum to help us understand how the emergence of middle-class leisure and entertainment in the nineteenth century informs the cultural work of the university.

We begin this leg of our journey in 1806, when Charles Willson Peale, painter, patriot, and proprietor of one of the nation's earliest museums, recorded on canvas his efforts to excavate the remains of what turned out to be two mastodons found in the marl pit of a farm in upstate New York. What is interesting about Peale's *Exhumation of the Mastodon*—besides the way that Peale has included in the middle ground not only his self-portrait, with a banner of bones in hand, but also a portrait of his entire family, including his children Raphael, Rembrandt, and Titian and his two wives (one current, one dead)—what is interesting beyond the dynastic dimension of the painting is its social division of labor. The canvas is segregated into three planes: a foreground space of water, mud, and buried treasure, where the laborers that Peale hired dig; a narrow middle ground where the Peale family and assorted well-wishers observe; and a background upper region, where storm clouds on the right threaten the progress of the excavation on the left. The whole is united visually by Peale's ingenious device for removing water from the pit, a Rube Goldberg–like contraption that was connected to an enormous flywheel powered by a second set of laborers hired to run in it.

The key to the painting lies in the figure of Peale and the graph he holds in his hands. Peale is presented to us in his role as director of operations, a professional before the age of professionalization. His labor is intellectual, a form of headwork that contrasts not only with artisanal imagery, like that contained in John Singleton Copley's earlier portait of Paul Revere (1768), but also with the manual labor of the men in the pit. Copley, half a century before Peale, had converted

John Singleton Copley. *Paul Revere.* 1768. Oil on canvas. Gift of Joseph W. Revere, William B. Revere, and Edward H. R. Revere. Courtesy of the Museum of Fine Arts, Boston.

Revere, a silversmith long before he became a galloping patriot, into an idealized artisan-artist, a figure whose intellectual reflections were tethered to the dexterity of his craft. Headwork and handwork are held in balance in Copley's portrait; they are performed by the same person and understood as complementary aspects of a single work process.

Copley is playing a Cartesian game here. He has given up on Descartes's God as a sort of cosmic glue holding together body and mind; instead he turns to artisanal ideologies. His world is not only divided between head and hand like Descartes's, it is also self-conscious like the Cartesian cogito. And from the way that the painting puns on the notion of reflection, converting its many reflective surfaces into a trope of self-reflection, we know that Copley is working hard to disallow self-consciousness in its modern and alienated forms. Thinking, in Copley's utopian vision, is returned pragmatically to the world as an instrumental faculty. It produces teapots as well as self-awareness and for that reason resists the very solipsism it so closely approaches.

Peale's painting disavows Copley's unifying mythology. Peale pointedly places himself in the middle ground of the image, above the workers he superintends. He defines himself as a manager rather than as an artisan. He allows himself sole custody of the painting's intellectual capital and counterpoints his activities with those of the men laboring in the pit. The men lack Revere's power of self-reflection. They exist in Cartesian fashion as body-machines, pre-Taylorite figures who function as the flesh-and-blood counterparts to Peale's hulking machine. Like that splendid device, the men in the pit work not simply as physical extensions of Peale himself but as a form of labor split off from the figure of Peale. Peale defines himself in the painting as a holder of knowledge, and the ideological space that he occupies marks the beginning of a managerial-professional worldview distinguished by expertise. Peale has abstracted himself from the world of toil and the body, locating himself instead in a realm of symbolic actions (hence the graph in his hands). We witness here, at a moment earlier than the history books would have it, a specialization of labor based on intellectual skills and disembodied vision—a reminder of just how nostalgic Emerson's call for a representative man must have seemed by the late 1830s.

> *I suspect that the modern university and Barnum's museum are homologous institutions.*

The crucial step, then, as I understand the history of perception and its relation to the dreamwork of mass culture and the university, is not the embodiment of the eye, as Jonathan Crary recently suggested, but the contrary, its disembodiment by a professionalizing ethos underwritten by the specialization of work and the division between intellectual activity and de-skilled labor. Once seeing is set free from its bodily locus, once the seer is not also the doer, as in *Paul Revere*, then the artist-intellectual functions as a manager rather than as a craftsman, and perception is freed for other forms of social work. In particular we see the beginning of a spectatorial logic that is essential to nation-building (as the Muñoz image reveals) and to the modern university.

But to understand the modern university, we first need to understand P. T. Barnum. I propose that we examine his exploits for two reasons. I suspect that the modern university and Barnum's museum are homologous institutions. I also suspect that the differences between the two go back to the question of negative dialectics.

In August 1843, promising to bring a "Grand Buffalo Hunt, Free of Charge" to the citizens of Manhattan, Barnum transported a herd of mangy buffalo to Hoboken, New Jersey. The buffalo, it turned out, were too feeble and weakened to resist their enterprising "hunters." The best the animals could manage, on the day of the hunt, was to take refuge in a nearby swamp, putting a quick end to the afternoon's entertainment. Barnum, however, had advertised several stagings of the spectacle. When the tourists being ferried to New Jersey for the second showing heard what had happened from those returning from the first, they showed no visible disappointment. Rather, according to a witness, they "instantly gave three cheers for the author of the humbug, whoever he might be," and proceeded on to the wilds of Hoboken, where, one assumes, they meditated on the term *sucker* for the remainder of the day. The "author," in the meantime, had already profited handsomely from the event. Through an undisclosed arrangement with the ferryboat owners, Barnum received a percentage of the fares. His financial success had nothing to do with the buffalo's performance.[2]

In its appeal to the public's curiosity, the buffalo hunt helps explain the attraction of Barnum's Broadway Museum. The key to Barnum's success, as Neil Harris has brilliantly shown, lay in his willingness to exploit the public's urge to see for themselves. Whether the object was a bedraggled herd of buffalo or the torso of a monkey stitched invisibly to a fish and labeled the "Feejee mermaid," Barnum dared his public to detect the deception. Their evident assent to his hoaxes suggests something more than gullibility. Barnum succeeded by flattering his public: he confirmed their powers of judgment, offering endless opportunities for the museum goers to pit their wisdom against his deceit. He converted the public's anxiety about the world around them into a set of epistemological issues, a confidence game in which the players always won. For winning consisted not in proving Barnum wrong but in affirming each patron's right to be, in Emerson's term, MAN THINKING.

Barnum convinced his patrons that ordinary citizens like themselves, rather than "experts," ruled the world. His American Museum represented an antidote to the professionalized expertise of Peale's world. (Barnum, I should note, in one of history's more delicious ironies, bought Peale's museum from Peale's descendants and later incorporated its contents into his own.) "Who is to decide when *doctors* disagree?" Barnum asked in one advertisement. The answer, as both he and his audience understood, was the spectator, whose anxieties in a world of rapid social and technological change required the reassurance that Barnum provided: that each person possessed, as part of his or her native endowment, the ability to expose deception wherever it occurred.

Barnum's genius lay in recognizing the high cultural stakes attached to knowledge. He understood two things: that nineteenth-century sentimental culture placed a high premium on transparent forms of seeing, and that it would pay a great deal to enact—and reenact—the triumph of transparency over deception.

The promise of Barnum's museum was that large urban crowds, the masses of early industrial capitalism, could reclaim their individuality and their republican heritage by virtue of their native wit. He offered the wage earners and de-skilled artisans the opportunity to engage their five senses and become once again the masters of their fate. The trick lay in institutionalizing, within the symbolic spaces of the museum, the imperatives of republican ideology. For the price of admission (two bits), the museum goer could attempt to expose not only Barnum's hoaxes but also by implication all conspiracies, oligarchies, or cabals against freedom that loomed on the horizon.

Barnum's Broadway Museum thus assumes a professionalizing society in which power is tied intimately to questions of knowledge. Barnum's genius, his contribution to early mass culture, lay in the boldness with which he yoked leisure activity to cultural uplift and learning and then converted both into what Roland Barthes has called depoliticized speech. He understood the museum as an institution that replicated social anxieties as a mode of cultural theater. Barnum defined those anxieties in cognitive terms, challenging his audience to unravel his mysteries, see through his hoaxes, and thereby convince itself that the ordinary person was also privy to the secret of the skills of experts. He removed politics from the realm of history by converting it into a set of symbolic actions, creating in the process a fiction of control in a world afraid of spinning out of control.

What we see in Barnum, then, is the emergence of a new sort of public sphere: a space of middle-class leisure that functions indirectly as a form of political theater. Education and entertainment are linked here, not by coincidence, but because they share similar historical imperatives. Sometime between the middle of the eighteenth century and the close of the nineteenth, new institutions of middle-class leisure arose—from the pleasure gardens at Vaux Hall to Barnum's Museum—structured around discourse and symbolic display and shaped according to the dictates of a middle class happy to consume history as a commodity: well-packaged, easily digested, and freed from any disruptive or destabilizing tendencies.

The modern university is a stepchild of this process. It is an institution of cultural dreaming that we must understand as homologous to, as well as historically coeval with, early mass culture as represented by Barnum. The modern university is homologous to mass culture in that it serves as a socially sanctioned site for intellectual and disembodied forms of labor. And it is coeval with mass culture in that it springs from the same historical soil, an imperative borne by the professionalizing classes of the nineteenth century to resolve a crisis of authority and legitimation through discourses of knowledge and expertise. We cannot understand the university except as the ironic doppelgänger to Barnum's museum.

The difference lies in the willingness of the university to engage in forms of negative dialectics, egg breaking, that mass culture works most often to contain. I do not wish to sound here like a late representative of the Frankfurt school or a spokesperson for high modernist art criticism chastising mass culture for its ties to kitsch. I believe in kitsch and suspect that it can break eggs as well as the more canonical stuff can. But I also believe that the structural imperatives at work in mass culture cut against this possibility: what Barnum teaches us is that mass culture, because it honors its origins in the commodity form, tends historically toward closure, toward surrogate forms of symbolic action that efface history (and the body) by reducing them to sanitized dream states. What the university offers, when it is not acting in complicity with a culture of commodification, is the sound of eggs breaking. Strong readings, like strong educations, require, as Fredric Jameson reminds us, a theory of the unconscious, an ability to name closure by identifying the underlying mechanisms of mystification and repression and in the process unraveling the constricting narratives that we otherwise inhabit or assume.

Or, to conclude by switching metaphors in midstream, we might use Yeats, whose language has provided us with our topic, to understand our dilemma. Yeats tells us that we, linking mind to body, have pitched our tents in a place of excrement, a point reiterated most recently in the revisionary account of Yeats offered by former President George Bush, who affirms with Yeats that we are into Deep Do. Yeats—not Bush—means by this metaphor to suggest something about the relation of aesthetics to modern history. We can rephrase Yeats to make a point closer to what I am suggesting here: that the university has bedded down with, because it was never historically separate from, the institutions of mass culture. Thinking and dreaming occur most often in each as forms of depoliticized speech: they are disembodied states that make possible the nation-state.

The difference, then, between the university and mass culture is that the university, more often than Hollywood, takes seriously its claim to expose the little man in the booth as something less than a wizard, let alone the Great Oz. If we began with a little girl who introduced us, by her relation to chickens and to irony, to negative dialectics, a way of naming closure and thereby affirming the utopian dimension to discourse about the body, then let us conclude with another little girl, whose education climaxes when her scruffy dog pulls open a wizard's curtain. This moment, rather than Dorothy's subsequent return home, stands for me as the *Wizard of Oz*'s logical culmination. For what we learn here is not what audiences of the film discovered in 1939, that the pain of the Depression could be healed by the nuclear family and premodern agrarian relations, but that Oz, that ultimate egghead, is but the double of Muñoz's image. Enlightenment consists not in knowing which came first but in understanding how—and when—to pull open the curtain.

Notes

[1]I place the word *real* in quotation marks here, mindful of Fredric Jameson's injunction that the Real, as history, as that which really wounds, must always be represented as an absent cause.

[2]This account of Barnum is excerpted with modification from my essay "How the West Was Hung."

Works Cited

Bledstein, Burton. *The Culture of Professionalism: The Middle Class and the Development of Higher Education in America.* New York: Norton, 1976.

Copley, John Singleton. *Paul Revere.* 1768. Museum of Fine Arts, Boston.

Crary, Jonathan. *Techniques of the Observer: On Vision and Modernity in the Nineteenth Century.* Cambridge: MIT, 1990.

de Zayas, Marius, and Agnes E. Meyer. *Mental Reactions.* 1915. *291.* Beinecke Rare Book and Manuscript Lib., Yale Univ.

Douglass, Frederick. *Narrative of the Life of Frederick Douglass, An American Slave.* Ed. Benjamin Quarles. Cambridge: Harvard UP, 1960.

Graff, Gerald. *Professing Literature: An Institutional History.* Chicago: U of Chicago P, 1987.

Harris, Neil. *Humbug: The Art of P. T. Barnum.* Chicago: U of Chicago P, 1973.

Jameson, Fredric. *The Political Unconscious: Narrative as a Socially Symbolic Act.* Ithaca: Cornell UP, 1981.

Muñoz, Celia Alvarez. *Which Came First? Enlightenment Series #4.* 1982. Museum of Contemporary Art, San Diego.

Peale, Charles Willson. *Exhumation of the Mastodon.* 1806. Peale Museum, Baltimore.

Wolf, Bryan. "How the West Was Hung." *American Quarterly* 44 (1992): 418–38.

Statement on the Significance of Primary Records

Modern Language Association of America

The Modern Language Association of America applauds two developments aimed at ensuring the future accessibility of texts from the past. One is the organized effort to microfilm the texts of nineteenth- and twentieth-century books containing acidic paper that is now, or will become, brittle; the other is the systematic transference of printed and manuscript texts of all periods to electronic form. Everyone who cares about the past should be grateful to the library world for the way it has responded to the challenges of textual preservation. Frequently, however, discussions of these developments imply that, once reproductions exist, many of the artifacts from which they derive need no longer be consulted or saved. In this climate of opinion, the MLA believes that it is crucial for the future of humanistic study to make more widely understood the continuing value of the artifacts themselves for reading and research. The advantages of the new forms in which old texts can now be made available must not be allowed to obscure the fact that the new forms cannot fully substitute for the actual physical objects in which those earlier texts were embodied at particular times in the past.

Without broad public perception of the significance of this point, sizable portions of certain classes of textual artifacts face destruction. The MLA is expressing no opinion about the relative desirability of different forms of dissemination for future writing; rather, it is strictly focusing on the future study of texts that appeared in the past in handwritten or printed form on paper or parchment. By outlining the theoretical reasons for the importance of physical evidence in textual artifacts, the MLA wishes to promote awareness of the issues and to stimulate practical recommendations for taking action on them.

Texts are inevitably affected by the physical means of their transmission; the physical features of the artifacts conveying texts therefore play an integral role in the attempt to comprehend those texts. For this reason, the concept of a textual source must involve attention to the presentation of a text, not simply to the text as a disembodied group of words. All objects purporting to present the same text—whether finished manuscripts, first editions, later printings, or photocopies—are separate records with their own characteristics; they all carry different information, even if the words and punctuation are indeed identical, since each one reflects a different historical moment. Any such record may be a primary source, but an object that is primary as a source for one purpose is not necessarily so for another. A *primary record* can appropriately be defined as a physical object produced or used at the particular past time that one is concerned with in a given instance.

Physical evidence in manuscripts and printed matter is indispensable in two ways. First, physical clues (such as the structure of the folded sheets in a book) reveal facts about how an item was produced—facts that can in turn lead to the discovery of textual errors and contribute to a knowledge of contemporary textual, printing, and publishing practices. This kind of evidence has primarily been used by analytical bibliographers and scholarly editors. Second, elements of a book's physical design (such as paper quality, page size, textual layout, choice of letterforms, and arrangement of illustrations) can be significant indicators of how the text thus displayed was regarded by its producers and how it was interpreted by its readers. This category of evidence is currently being used by those investigating the history of reading and the social influence of books.

Not only do editions differ from one another, but also copies within an edition (of any period) often vary among themselves; as a result, every copy is a potential source for new physical evidence, and no copy is superfluous for studying an edition's production history. Furthermore, since the shape, feel, designs, and illustrations of books have affected, and continue to affect, readers' responses (some of which have been recorded in the margins of pages), access to the physical forms in which texts from the past have appeared is a fundamental part of informed reading and effective classroom teaching; if that access is to be as widespread as it can be, the number of available copies of past editions, held in libraries of all kinds, must be as large as possible. The existence of community libraries along with academic libraries has been, and will continue to be, essential for bringing historical embodiments of texts—and the sense of the past they impart—to a wide readership. The loss of any copy of any edition—from the earliest incunables to the latest paperback reprints (regardless of whether its text is considered interesting or consequential at the present time)—diminishes the body of evidence on which historical understanding depends.

There is an obvious practical consideration that also supports the retention of textual artifacts (handwritten as well as printed) after their texts have been copied: the fact that the accuracy and stability of reproductions can never be guaranteed. For this reason, the preservation of the sources of photographic or electronic reproductions would seem a prudent course even if those reproductions were the equals of the sources; but since they cannot possibly be, a concern for maintaining our inheritance of textual artifacts is not simply desirable but imperative.

It is clearly unrealistic to expect that all currently surviving manuscripts and printed books can be saved. They are subject to the same vicissitudes as every other physical object, and their survival depends both on the materials out of which they are made and on the nature of the events that befall them. But the attitudes that people hold about them can be instrumental in either mitigating or exacerbating the destructive effects of these factors. As more people come to see the impor-

tance of primary records, more use will be made of them in reading and teaching, and more constituencies will join together in the search for ways of financing artifactual preservation, storage, and access. More records will then be saved because there will be wider support for the allocation of resources to this purpose. Decisions about priorities for preservation will still have to be made, by individual as well as institutional owners of material, but those decisions will be reached in a framework that recognizes the artifactual value of every object. An appreciation of the significance of physical evidence also necessitates the adoption of standards for the creation and identification of reproductions, in order to minimize the damage done to primary records by the processes of reproduction and to maximize the usefulness of the reproductions.

Readers find themselves turning continually to reprints or reproductions of some kind. As they welcome the benefits conferred by new technology for creating reproductions, they must remember the distinctive limitations of every form of reproduction and the continuing need for the artifactual sources on which the reproductions are based. Not only do those artifacts provide the standard for judging the reproductions; they also contain, in their physicality, unreproducible evidence that readers (scholars, students, and the general public) need for analyzing and understanding, with as much historical context as possible, the writings that appeared and reappeared in them. If we approach the electronic future with these thoughts in mind, we will be more rigorous in our demands of new forms of textual presentation and more vigilant in our protection of the artifacts embodying the old forms. Both these actions are necessary to ensure the continuation of productive reading, teaching, and scholarship.

The Modern Language Association of America recommends that representatives of library, conservation, and scholarly organizations form a task group to promote continued thinking and cooperative activity leading toward (1) the maximum retention and preservation of textual artifacts, as well as a refining of the selection criteria necessarily entailed, and (2) the use of responsible procedures in the creation and identification of photographic and electronic reproductions based on those artifacts.

Introduction

G. Thomas Tanselle

I

The material gathered here results from the activities of the MLA Ad Hoc Committee on the Future of the Print Record, which during the past two years has considered how best to publicize the importance of preserving textual artifacts after the texts in them have been reproduced in microfilm, electronic, or any other form. The committee, which (despite its name) understands its charge to encompass manuscript as well as printed material, consists of Shelley Fisher Fishkin (English, University of Texas, Austin), Phyllis Franklin (ex officio, MLA), Everette E. Larson (Hispanic Division, Library of Congress), Philip E. Lewis (French, Cornell University), J. Hillis Miller (English, University of California, Irvine), Ruth Perry (English, Massachusetts Institute of Technology), Alice Schreyer (Rare Books, University of Chicago Library), Philip Stewart (French, Duke University), and G. Thomas Tanselle, chair (John Simon Guggenheim Memorial Foundation).

The origins of the committee go back to a paper that Phyllis Franklin, executive director of the MLA, read at the June 1992 convention of the American Library Association. In preparation for that paper, she took an informal survey of 319 people (members of the MLA and of other associations in the American Council of Learned Societies), asking them to comment on the widespread belief that reproductions of texts can supplant the originals. Of the 169 respondents, 94.5% affirmed the importance of preserving primary records, noting the inadequacy of reproductions for bibliographical and textual research and for studies that focus on the materiality of texts. In the light of this unambiguous response to her survey and of the interest aroused by her paper, she asked the Executive Council of the MLA to consider what the MLA might do to further the cause of the preservation of textual artifacts in an age that has seen considerable discarding and

deaccessioning of materials once they are reproduced. At its February 1993 meeting the council established an Ad Hoc Committee on the Future of the Print Record, charging it to develop an association statement on the subject and to determine other ways of publicizing the issues.

The main activity of the committee thus far has been to prepare the "Statement on the Significance of Primary Records" printed here, which is the product of four meetings (8 Oct. 1993, 4 Mar. and 14 Oct. 1994, and 31 Mar. 1995), correspondence and telephone conversations between meetings, and the consideration of many letters of suggestion from interested persons in the library and scholarly worlds. The draft of the statement that emerged from the 14 October 1994 meeting was given wide circulation on the Internet, by mail distribution to members and other interested persons, as handouts at the San Diego convention last December, and in the Spring 1995 *MLA Newsletter*. In addition, one of the three convention sessions held by the committee (sess. 499, on 29 Dec.) was an open hearing entirely devoted to discussion of the draft statement. The committee took all the responses to the draft into account and at its 31 March 1995 meeting produced a considerably revised document for submission to the MLA Executive Council. On 19 May 1995 the council formally adopted this version as an official statement of the association. Besides being printed here, the "Statement on the Significance of Primary Records" will be circulated widely to newspapers and magazines as well as to scholarly and library associations. The

The author is Vice President of the John Simon Guggenheim Memorial Foundation.

committee hopes that it will be endorsed by other groups or used by them as the basis for statements of their own and that it will thus serve to promote further discussion and action.

The pages that follow present a number of related papers stimulated by the committee. All but the last are drawn from two of the sessions that the committee sponsored at the 1994 convention to acquaint the MLA membership with the relevance of the committee's work to research and teaching. The first of these sessions was a forum entitled "The Importance and Challenge of Preserving Research Materials in Their Original Forms" (sess. 254, on 28 Dec.), which was divided into two parts. Part 1 consisted (after a brief introduction from me as chair of the committee) of two major papers: one by Paul Mosher, director of the University of Pennsylvania Library, on the electronic future as seen from a librarian's perspective, and the other by J. Hillis Miller, a former president of the MLA and a member of the committee. Miller's paper is printed here and provides an excellent illustration of how the physical presentation of a text affects reading and why a reprint can be a primary record for studying a critic's response.

Part 2 of the forum, organized by Ruth Perry under the title "Object Lessons," presented six speakers who offered personal testimony, with specific examples, regarding the way physical evidence has been important in their own work. Three were selected for inclusion here to represent the range of situations dealt with: Susan Staves, on the eighteenth-century playwright and novelist Elizabeth Griffith; Miriam Fuchs, on the diaries of Queen Liliʻuokalani; and Anthony R. Pugh, on Proust's manuscripts.

The second of the committee's sessions at the convention was entitled "Teaching in the Library: A Workshop on Using Primary Materials in the Classroom" (sess. 459, on 29 Dec.). Shelley Fisher Fishkin, who presided, had chosen ten short papers that described specific instances in which teachers put primary records to successful use in the classroom. As with part 2 of the earlier session, three of the papers have been chosen to reflect the rich diversity of that second session: Manon Anne Ress, on Diderot's *Encyclopédie*; Gregg Camfield, on Mark Twain; and Catherine Golden, on Victorian serialization.

The final piece is by Ruth Perry and entitled a postscript because it is an extension of a point made in the statement. Her paper calls attention to the essential role that public libraries play in intellectual and cultural life and to the fact that the existence of many libraries is currently threatened. The committee did not include this topic in the statement because it was focused on the role of primary records in understanding the past; the value of the intellectual exchange that has traditionally taken place in public libraries, though certainly a valid point, is a separate concern. (The committee, by the way, has emphasized throughout that it takes no position about whether printed or electronic forms are more desirable for the dissemination of new writing; its concern has been solely with the importance of artifacts in reading—the importance, that is, of reading texts in the physical forms they took at the historical moment one is studying.) The statement does, however, make clear that public as well as academic libraries have performed a great service in bringing the historical forms of texts to a broad public; and it is this point that the Perry paper builds on.

II

Because these papers focus on showing, through examples, the practical uses of primary records, it is perhaps in order here to provide—as background for the concisely expressed theoretical points in the "Statement on the Significance of Primary Records"—some of the comments I made at the opening of the 28 December forum. In pointing out that reproductions of texts cannot entirely supplant the original forms of those texts, the committee is not making any criticism of the current programs for microfilming brittle books or for creating databases of electronic texts. Obviously a microfilm of a book is better than no book at all, and electronic texts are searchable and manipulable in ways that printed texts are not. The committee's aim is not in the slightest to disparage new developments but simply to make more widely understood the fact that no reproduction of a text can ever be a fully adequate substitute for the original, since every reproduction necessarily leaves something unreproduced. Besides, there is always an uncertainty attaching to a reproduction; the user of one at any point may wonder whether the original was accurately rendered, and the only way to find out is to examine the original. The use of originals as the ultimate check on the accuracy of reproductions is simply an illustration of what it means to use primary evidence. Even if there were no other reason for needing access to originals, this one is sufficient.

But there are other reasons that are rooted in the significance of artifacts and the relation of form to content. All artifacts—not just books—can be studied as physical objects to discover two major classes of historical information that can influence the interpretation of any visual or verbal symbols present on the objects. One class relates to their production history, to the techniques of their manufacture; the other focuses on their postproduction history, on the implications of their physical appearance once the objects were created. Those scholars pursuing the first class of information examine objects for clues that reveal details about how the objects were made. In the study of printed books, this pursuit is called analytical bibliography, and it can provide information about typesetting, proofreading, and presswork—information that is essential not only to printing and publishing history but also to textual history and textual criticism (the genealogy of texts and the evaluation of their correctness, according to whatever standard of correctness is chosen). In the latter half of the twentieth century, an age of scholarly editing in many fields, editors have increasingly recognized that one of the foundations of their work is analytical bibliography—which in turn requires an understanding that printed books are like manuscripts in offering primary evidence for textual study and in regularly presenting variant texts, since even copies from a single edition can be expected to contain variations (a point that applies to books of all periods).

The second major approach to artifacts concentrates on the sensuous—primarily visual—characteristics of objects. Every object, whether or not it was intended by its producers to have a utilitarian function, can be looked at for whatever aesthetic value it may possess. The historically oriented form of this investigation, when applied to books, not only attempts to show how their visual and tactile features (such as typography, layout, leaf size, and binding) reflected cultural trends but also tries to understand how those features have affected the responses of readers over the years. Such research is clearly relevant to the history of reading and of the spread of ideas—that is, to the broad field often called *histoire du livre*, the history of the effect of printed books on society, which has attracted a great deal of attention in the last several decades.

Of the two approaches to books as artifacts, the first deals with hidden evidence, with details not normally noticed by readers; the second treats of features that readers were meant to notice and that do in fact influence, to one degree or another, their interpretations of what they have read. The first produces evidence for reconstructing the texts that authors (or others) intended; the second looks at the texts that actually appeared and their physical settings. (A discrepancy between intended and published texts—that is, between works and documents—is always to be expected, since the medium of verbal communication, language, is intangible and any tangible representation of it may distort what was intended, even in those instances where visual effects were part of what was intended.) The two approaches are thus complementary. Both illustrate the ways in which the reading of physical evidence is involved in the interpretation of texts; both show why the historical study of printed texts rests on the examination of the actual artifacts in which they have appeared.

It follows from these points that the books in existing book stacks should never be abandoned, because they will remain crucial as the original sources for future study of works transmitted in printed form. There can be no book in which the format and other physical features are unrelated to the process of reading and understanding the book's text. But a recognition of this fact does not stand in the way of an enthusiastic acceptance of the developing technology for the electronic dissemination of texts. After all, even those scholars who understand that microfilm and xerographic copies do not fully substitute for originals have gladly used them as convenient interim tools. The availability of printed texts in electronic form is an advance greater in degree but not different in kind: it accomplishes in a far more sophisticated way the same function that xerography has fulfilled, making texts widely accessible and more easily manipulable at the price of removing them from their original physical contexts. All scholars should welcome the day when they can sit in their studies and call up on their terminals an enormous array of texts without the cumbersome process of interlibrary loan or the ordering of xerographic copies. But they should also realize what evidence they are thereby missing and why recourse to the originals can never be rendered irrelevant, however inconvenient it may happen to be. Many discussions of the future of libraries speak of access replacing ownership; but when it is understood that access to physical evidence is an essential kind of access and that printed books must therefore be preserved in multiple copies, the questions of ownership and care remain significant.

The theoretical content of the "Statement on the Significance of Primary Records," in short, is that texts and their settings are not separable; that all the characteristics of the artifacts conveying texts are potentially relevant to the act of careful reading; that those characteristics can differ even among copies of individual editions; and that there is a consequent need to preserve as many copies of printed editions as possible in order to maximize both the quantity of evidence available and the access to that evidence. The usefulness of textual reproductions is not in question, but it has no bearing on the rationale for the preservation of artifacts.

III

Those who wish to read further on this topic might turn to several of the papers in the published proceedings of the Houghton Library fiftieth-anniversary symposium (ed. Wendorf), especially the papers by Nicolas Barker, Werner Gundersheimer, Alexandra Mason, David McKitterick, Ruth Perry, and me (my comments are largely reprinted in section 2 above). Other useful readings are Elizabeth Witherell's presidential address to the Association for Documentary Editing, D. F. McKenzie's concluding remarks at the Elvetham Hall conference on humanistic scholarship and technology, and my "Reproductions and Scholarship" (which contains many references to related material, as does a forthcoming article of mine entitled "The Future of Primary Records").

The committee hopes that the present addition to the literature of this subject—in the form of the statement and the articles offered below—will arouse further interest in the cause of preserving textual artifacts. By the end of 1995, various members of the committee will have spoken on this subject at the New York Public Library, the University of Kansas, and meetings of the American Library Association, the American Institute for Conservation, the College Language Association, the National Council of Teachers of English, and the Rare Book School of the University of Virginia. The committee has also scheduled two sessions at the 1995 MLA convention in Chicago, one to be presided over by Philip Lewis, on decision making in libraries, and the other to be chaired by Alice Schreyer, on shared decision making. A sharing of ideas and discussion among relevant professional organizations (many of which have already given thought to these questions) is the heart of the recommendation made at the end of the statement, and the proposed task group would provide a way for all interested parties to pursue the issues together. The MLA can usefully act as a catalyst in setting this joint activity in motion; it has taken the first step in implementing the committee's recommendation by accepting an invitation from the Preservation of Library Materials Committee of the Association of Research Libraries to form a joint working group. In this spirit of cooperative action, the committee encourages members of the MLA to distribute the statement to persons who might not see it otherwise and to bring it to the attention of other organizations with which they are connected. The MLA office welcomes letters from members reporting on such initiatives or commenting on related matters.

Works Cited

Franklin, Phyllis. "Scholars, Librarians, and the Future of Primary Records." *College and Research Libraries* 54 (1993): 397–406.

McKenzie, D. F. "Computers and the Humanities: A Personal Synthesis of Conference Issues." *Scholarship and Technology in the Humanities: Proceedings of a Conference at Elvetham Hall, Hampshire, UK, 9th–12th May 1990.* Ed. May Katzen. London: Bowker-Saur, 1991. 157–69.

Tanselle, G. Thomas. "The Future of Primary Records." *Encyclopedia of Library and Information Science.* Vol. 58. Ed. Allen Kent. New York: Dekker, 1996. Forthcoming.

———. "Reproductions and Scholarship." *Studies in Bibliography* 42 (1989): 25–54.

Wendorf, Richard, ed. *Rare Book and Manuscript Libraries in the Twenty-First Century.* Proc. of Houghton Library Fiftieth-Anniversary Symposium, Sept. 1992. Cambridge: Harvard U Lib., 1993. Also printed as *Harvard Library Bulletin* ns 4.1 and 4.2 (1993).

Witherell, Elizabeth Hall. "ADE Presidential Address." *Documentary Editing* 16 (1994): 1–2, 20.

What Is the Future of the Print Record?

J. Hillis Miller

It is a great honor and a great responsibility to be a member of the MLA Ad Hoc Committee on the Future of the Print Record. The future of the print record is jeopardized in two quite different ways these days. The first threat: approximately one hundred million books and other materials in United States libraries printed on acid paper will become unusable during the next several decades. They are oxidizing, slowly burning up, becoming brittle, crumbling away, and becoming unreadable. Second threat to the print record: new electronic communication technologies are bringing about a revolution as great as was the shift from manuscript culture to print culture. Books and other materials printed on paper will become, indeed have already become, less and less important in the new electronic culture we are rapidly entering. Computers, e-mail, faxes, the Internet, electronic books, and multimedia materials are already decisively transforming research and teaching in the humanities. They are doing this in ways we have hardly begun to understand fully, since we are in the midst of the revolution. Books will be with us for a long time, decisive in the lives of many for the foreseeable future, but already the sensibilities, the ethos, the politics, the sense of personal identity of many of our citizens, including college students and faculty members, are determined more by television, cinema, and video than by printed books.

Both these changes are, for better or worse, irreversible. Those brittle books are going to fall apart. The electronic revolution has already, to a considerable degree, occurred. It joins the end of the Cold War and the globalization of university research (which means that universities more and more serve transnational corporations rather than the nation-state) as one of the three major factors that are rapidly transforming American higher education.

In preparing these remarks, I have asked myself what I really do think about the use of original materials. One thing is clear to me. The first obligation of the MLA is to support vigorously those efforts in textual preservation, now funded to a large degree by the NEH, that will at best be able to save only twenty-five or thirty percent of the titles printed on acid paper.

The second obligation: the MLA needs to make every effort to study the effects of the electronic revolution, along with those of the globalization that goes with it, and to make sure that it happens in ways that will be beneficial to our interests. To study this revolution means supporting the radically new graduate training that will make our young scholars and teachers appropriately educated for the study of many cultures (as in, for example, global literature in English or United States literature in languages other than English) as well as for the study of those media that mix language with other visual and auditory materials, media such as cinema, television, and video, which have such influence on our lives today. To make sure the electronic revolution proceeds in ways beneficial to our interests means resisting the rapid commercialization of the Internet that is at this moment occurring. It means also doing our best to make sure that electronic storage of printed materials carries as much as possible of the history that is embodied in the physical artifacts: for example, all the illustrations in Victorian novels and all the information in the dust jackets, title pages,

The author is Distinguished Professor of English and Comparative Literature at the University of California, Irvine. A version of this paper was presented at the 1994 MLA convention in San Diego.

end pages, and so on of physical books in general that electronic books now characteristically leave out but could easily include. We need to ensure the preservation of full bibliographical information about the originals when books are electronically or photographically stored. We need to urge care in the choice of exemplars to be copied. We need to urge those who prepare electronic transcriptions to follow the guidelines of the Text Encoding Initiative.

The third obligation is to attend closely to the uses of original materials and to save as many of those artifacts as possible. I strongly urge that the MLA appoint a joint working group with the Association of Research Libraries to make decisions about preserving original materials where the artifactual value is questionable. In urging that this joint group be formed, I join Betty G. Bengtson, chair of the ARL Preservation of Library Materials Committee. In her recent letter to Phyllis Franklin she said: "The issue of cost is critical, given the magnitude of the preservation problem and the vast number of endangered research materials. In a context where choices will be made, it is vital to distinguish between materials that have significant artifactual value and those for which surrogates can be created through electronic, photographic, or other means."

The difficulties will come in trying to make such distinctions. Let me give a little example. Last summer on Deer Isle, Maine, where I spend my summers, I was rereading a novel by Anthony Trollope, *Ayala's Angel* (1881). I brought with me my old copy of the Oxford World's Classics reprint of this novel. Originally published in 1929, this reprint was reissued several times thereafter (my copy is dated 1960) as part of a more or less comprehensive edition of Trollope's novels. They were included over fifty years ago in the World's Classics series (in which *Ayala's Angel* was number 342), long before personal computers were invented. A note at the end of the book tells me it was "set in Great Britain at the University Press, Oxford, and Printed by J. W. Arrowsmith Ltd, Bristol." It cost "10s 6d. net in U.K. only," and I bought it in London in the late 1960s. I first read the novel in this edition. It is a quasi-sacred object for me, one with which I have a long personal association. I have carried it from place to place as part of my library. My relation to this object is an example of the way so many readers of my generation and many generations before mine have participated in a reasonably benign fetishism of the book.

Ayala's Angel, however, was also available to me on Deer Isle in another way: as an electronic book, part of the Oxford Text Archive collection of such books. I had access to that by way of my laptop computer and

the modem that connected me by courtesy to the Internet server at Colby College. What is the difference between reading *Ayala's Angel* in book form and reading it in electronic text form? I have stressed the physical embodiment of *Ayala's Angel* in the World's Classics edition. Not only is the text of the novel caught in the materiality of the book, it is also tied by way of the book's paper, cardboard, ink, and glue to the historical and economic conditions of its production and distribution. The edition was part of a moment in English publishing history when one of the great academic-commercial English publishers made classic books of Western literature available in inexpensive form. This moment was preceded by earlier moments, first by the initial publication of the book in 1881, then by subsequent cheap editions. Many of Trollope's novels were reprinted as yellow-bound paperbacks sold in railway stations in the late nineteenth century. The twentieth-century World's Classics version was thus a later stage in English publishing history. It depended on the existence of a large literate middle-class reading public in Britain. It also depended to some degree on the fact that television was not yet available.

The Oxford University Press in the twentieth century has been, moreover, an international operation. Its books have been marketed all over the world, but especially in cities in what were once British colonies or parts of the British Empire. The globalization of the English language did not occur by accident or because of some intrinsic superiority of that language. The list of cities—printed on the page facing the title page—where the Oxford University Press in 1960 asserted itself as located reads like a litany of sites associated with British colonialism and imperialism: Glasgow, New York, Toronto, Melbourne, Wellington, Bombay, Calcutta, Madras, Karachi, Kuala Lumpur, Cape Town, Ibadan, Nairobi, Accra. The sun never sets on the Oxford University Press. In all these ways, and in others space does not allow me to specify, the little book that I hold in my hand is embedded in history, embodies that history in material form, and gives me access to that history.

The electronic text version of *Ayala's Angel* is cut off from all signs of historical context. Or, rather, it is given a strange new historical placement in the cyberspace of today. A date of original publication is indicated, and that is about all. The novel exists not as embodied in material form, or at least not material in the fixed way of a printed book. It exists as a large number of bits of information, zeroes and ones inscribed as magnetic differences on a hard disk or on magnetic tape or as minute scratches on an optical disk or as electrical pulses on the wired and wireless transmissions of the Internet. *Ayala's Angel* as an electronic book takes on a new meaning when it is placed in this new context, when it floats in cyberspace. It is detached from its local historical context and becomes a text in the context of an enormous and incoherent abundance of works of all kinds—verbal, pictorial, and auditory—on the Internet. As such it might now become the object of a globalized "cultural studies" by scholars who are themselves more and more transformed—in part by their use of the computer and by their inhabitation of cyberspace—in their relation to the culture of the book. This transformation is occurring even though it is still a primary goal of literary history and literary criticism in the modern languages to understand and interpret that culture of the book.

To show the difficulties involved in deciding which original materials to preserve and which not, I have deliberately chosen an example, *Ayala's Angel* in the Oxford World's Classics edition, that is not original in the ordinary sense. A well-known essay by R. W. Chapman long ago demonstrated how unreliable as texts the Oxford World's Classics editions of Trollope's novels are. Probably this edition of *Ayala's Angel* would not qualify as a book worth saving in its original form for its artifactual value, whereas a first edition of *Ayala's Angel* might conceivably do so. My example is meant to show, however, that much can be learned about history, even with such secondary or tertiary editions, from close attention to the materiality of the book, its binding, dust jacket, title page, and so on. My example is also meant to show how difficult it is, in practice, to distinguish between the book as artifact and the book as the bearer of pure verbal information, data that might be transcribed unchanged and without loss into any form, including electronic, just as it might be translated, without loss, into another language. This does not weaken my allegiance to the three obligations I began by identifying, or the hierarchy in which I placed them, but it does indicate the extreme difficulty of deciding which books to save in their original form for their artifactual value, as they cannot all be saved. Nevertheless, we must decide. I hope the MLA will play an important role in that process.

Works Cited

Bengtson, Betty G. Letter to Phyllis Frankin. 7 Dec. 1994.

Chapman, R. W. "The Text of Trollope's Novels." *Review of English Studies* 17 (1941) 322–31.

Trollope, Anthony. *Ayala's Angel*. 1881. World's Classics 342. Oxford: UP, 1929. Online. Oxford Text Archive. World Wide Web. August 1994. Available FTP: black.ox.ac.uk./ota/english/Trollope/ayala.1873.

Discussion

Traces of a Lost Woman

Susan Staves, Brandeis University

Elizabeth Griffith was the author of six plays, three novels, and a variety of other works published between 1757 and 1782. With her husband, Richard Griffith, she also published six volumes of *A Series of Genuine Letters between Henry and Frances*. Although we do not know to what extent the letters have been edited since the manuscript letters have not survived, these nevertheless do seem to be genuine letters between Richard, writing as Henry, and Elizabeth, writing as Frances. The letters chronicle first a seduction attempt resisted, then a marriage, and finally many happy years in which the two share love and common literary interests (see Tompkins 1–40).

Until recently, scholars were inclined to dismiss Griffith as unworthy of serious inquiry. They contented themselves with fleeting mention of her works in comprehensive literary histories of the drama or the novel or produced perfunctory notes explaining who she was in cases where she or her works were mentioned in the texts of canonical writers. Not surprisingly, the low level of scrutiny she was thought to deserve accounts for a significant amount of disinformation in reference works. For instance, in *Bibliotheca Britannica* the title of Griffith's play *A Wife in the Right* is transformed—whether through the accident of a printing error or by a Freudian slip on the part of the nonfeminist compiler—into *A Wife in the Night*.[1]

Now, of course, critics and scholars are very interested in refinding, researching, and reevaluating the works of women writers of many historical periods and many countries. Some early women writers have been profoundly lost, with no trace of their works apparently remaining; others only relatively lost, as in the case where we have copies of at least some works and reason to suspect the existence of more.[2] Three facts pose particular difficulties for those compiling lists of the works of early women writers we are now trying to rediscover. First, many women circulated their works in the form of unsigned manuscripts or published them anonymously or with formulas like "By a Lady" instead of the author's name. Second, some women wrote kinds of texts scorned by collectors and libraries, like children's books. And, third, most women changed their names on marriage, and some women were married more than once.

The truism we do not know what we do not know is especially relevant to the study of neglected women writers. Let us suppose that we replace the surviving printed copies of Griffith's works with reformatted versions, anything from microfilm to electronic text. What sorts of information present in the existing paper documents might disappear in the reformattings?

Much, of course, depends upon the principles of selection used. Suppose that our reformatting program decides to select "good copies" of first editions of original works—a frequent and unsurprising choice. We then lose evidence of subsequent authorial revision, and, in Griffith's case, sometimes more important, the evidence contained in preliminary matter to later editions. For instance, in the second edition of volume 1 of *Genuine Letters* Griffith added a new dedication, "To my Sex." (For comments on the significance of this and other variations between different editions, see Bernstein.)

No one, after all, can really tell what a good copy is without collating it with others. The value of the textual critic's maxim that every copy is unique until proven otherwise is amply demonstrated by the work on Griffith that Brandeis graduate students and I have done (see Staves, "Revising the Pedagogy"). Horace Walpole's copy of her first performed play, *The Platonic Wife*, has pasted into it a printed announcement with the heading "To the PUBLIC from the Author of the PLATONIC WIFE," an attempted defense of herself against charges of "Indelicacy" in the play. This looks like it was clipped from a contemporary newspaper, but we have not been able to find this text in any surviving newspaper.

One copy of the Dublin second edition of volumes 1 and 2 of *Genuine Letters* (currently at the Beinecke Library of Yale University) is quite imperfect, missing many pages, and, as the librarians say, "mutilated" in various ways by marginalia and crossings out of words and passages. The mutilation, however, seems to have been done by Griffith herself, who used this particular printed copy as a base text for making revisions intended for a future edition (although these revisions were not incorporated in later editions). Many of the deletions are of low phrases, descriptions of Elizabeth's poor health, references to money, or references to Richard's passions—all revisions designed to make the text more genteel and more belletristic. Griffith also decides to excise a playful early threat that she will publish Richard's letters, presumably because it makes her appear too aggressive, too poor, and too mercenary: "[I]f I am reduced, I vow, I will print your Letters— I think they will keep me in Tea, clean Linen, and Plays. . . ." The printed letter is signed "Your affectionate Pauper," but "Pauper" is crossed out and replaced with the more decorous "Frances" (55). Richard's wish for the "Enjoyment" of her "Person" is transmuted into a chaster hope for the "certainty" of her "Love" (122). His willingness to marry her is made less casual and more eager. Instead of forming "a Sort of vague Determination in his Mind, to marry her," he forms "a Determination" and the caveat that "he had not resolved with himself on the Time" is stricken (163). When she writes with the direct question of whether he intends ever to make her his wife, a deleted passage unromantically explains that he deferred a reply until he saw her, "for he did not chuse to give any thing under his Hand, which might be construed into a Contract" (268).

Among versions of texts "of no authority" likely to be ignored in reproduction programs designed to preserve "intellectual content" are translations.[3] Translations are also likely to get short shrift in reproduction programs supported by government funds and designed to preserve particular national heritages. Yet translation has long been an important literary medium for women writers, and earlier norms of translation practice often made less of a distinction between translation and adaptation than we do now. Griffith did a number of book-length translations from the French, which on inspection add considerably to our knowledge of her ideas. She believed that translators had a right to comment on the texts they translated, so her translations characteristically contain interpolated, even on occasion feminist, commentary. Despite her English literary persona as a champion of sentimental virtue, she translated some French libertine texts, notably *The Memoirs of Ninon de L'Enclos* and Claude Joseph Dorat's *The Fatal Effects of Inconstancy*.[4] When one of Dorat's libertine protagonists discusses women's incapacity for disinterested resistance to seducers, Griffith retorts in a note:

> Such is the artful and insidious manner of arguing, with all libertine wits; but 'tis certainly most unphilosophic. They seem to speak of Women, not only as of a different gender, but of a different species, too, from Men. There is no distinction of Sexes in virtue or vice; and whatever has been once determined to be the point of honour, in man or woman, will be equally defended, by each. (9–10)

Who would have guessed a hundred years ago that in 1995 roughly half the new professors of literature would be women or that so many of them would want to study women's writing? Not only do we now not know what we do not know, we cannot predict what scholars or what society will want to know a hundred years from now. But we certainly can proceed to let decay or to destroy the printed texts that could support the inquiries of 2095.

Notes

[1] A less amusing example in a more recent work attributes the novel *The Gordian Knot* to Elizabeth Griffith, though it was in fact written by her husband Richard (Martin, Mylne, and Frautschi). That this error should arise is not startling, since Elizabeth and Richard together published *Two Novels: In Letters. By the Authors of Henry and Frances*, the set containing one novel by her, *The Delicate Distress*, and another by him, *The Gordian Knot*.

[2] For example, we know that Ann Masterman, Griffith's contemporary, was the author of one novel that survives, *The Old Maid*, but contemporary sources say she wrote more than this. We have not yet found another title that can be attributed to her. See Staves, "Matrimonial Discord."

[3] For the phrase "intellectual content," see United States 6.

[4] For a discussion of the significance of Griffith's involvement with libertine texts and details about her interventions in *Memoirs of Ninon*, see Staves, "French Fire."

Works Cited

Bernstein, Susan David. "Ambivalence and Writing: Elizabeth and Richard Griffith's *A Series of Genuine Letters between Henry and Frances*." *Eighteenth-Century Women and the Arts*. Ed. Frederick M. Keener and Susan E. Lorsch. New York: Greenwood, 1988. 269–76.

Bibliotheca Britannica; or, A General Index to British and Foreign Literature. 4 vols. 1824. New York: Franklin, n.d. S.v. "Griffith, Elizabeth" and "wife."

Griffith, Elizabeth, trans. *The Fatal Effects of Inconstancy; or, Letters of the Marchioness de Syrcé, the Count de Mirbelle, and Others.* By Claude Joseph Dorat. Vol. 1. London, 1774.

Griffith, Elizabeth, and Richard Griffith. *A Series of Genuine Letters between Henry and Frances. The Second Edition, Revised, Corrected, Enlarged, and Improved. By the Authors.* Vol. 1. Dublin, 1760.

Martin, Angus, Vivienne G. Mylne, and Richard Frautschi. *Bibliographie du genre romanesque français, 1751–1800.* London and Paris: Mansell and France Expansion, 1977.

Staves, Susan. "French Fire, English Asbestos: Ninon de Lenclos and Elizabeth Griffith." *Studies on Voltaire and the Eighteenth Century* 314 (1993): 193–205.

———. "Matrimonial Discord in Fiction and in Court: The Case of Ann Masterman." *Fettered or Free? Collected Essays on Eighteenth-Century Women Novelists in England, 1670–1815.* Ed. Cecilia Macheski and Mary Anne Schofield. Athens: Ohio UP, 1986. 169–87.

———. "Revising the Pedagogy of the Traditional Scholarly Methods Course: The Brandeis Elizabeth Griffith Collective." *Eighteenth-Century Women and the Arts.* Ed. Frederick M. Keener and Susan E. Lorsch. New York: Greenwood, 1988. 255–62.

Tompkins, J. M. S. *The Polite Marriage.* Cambridge: UP, 1938.

United States. Commission on Preservation and Access. *Preserving the Intellectual Heritage: A Report on the Bellagio Conference, June 7–10, 1993.* Washington: Comm. on Preservation and Access, 1993.

The Diaries of Queen Liliʻuokalani

Miriam Fuchs, University of Hawaii, Manoa

Many factors in Hawaii work against the preservation of print media. They include Hawaii's semitropical climate—high humidity and frequent rain—and long tradition of the open-window system of air cooling, which takes advantage of the trade winds. State and university buildings that house important documents are usually air-conditioned but not always in all rooms, and the conversion to air conditioning has been gradual and slow. For example, only one floor of the undergraduate library at the University of Hawaii at Manoa is currently air-conditioned; my office still waits. Rooms used by the English department were only recently converted, putting an end to such dramas as classroom windstorms and visits by local birds. Sunlight, even when filtered through windows on the opposite side of a room, has a quick, devastating effect on print media. Books lose their color, and the writing fades. Hardbound covers attract a type of mildew that leaves them soft and with a slightly furry surface. Paper clips oxidize and leave documents with brown imprints. Paper stays soggy, and as the ocean salt works its way into expensive machinery, printers jam and computer innards begin to corrode. Cockroaches eat the glue of bindings until books come apart. What the cockroaches neglect, the bookworms undertake. They burrow their way through the text and leave behind them pin-size tunnels, sometimes from cover to cover.

Manuscripts and records are therefore guarded with vigilance, and they are not always easy to gain access to. In particular, eighteenth- and nineteenth-century documents from the time when Hawaii was a monarchy and, as such, a Pacific island nation tend to be kept out of sight in restricted sections of library collections, state archives, and museums, so cool that one might think they were refrigerated. But as sovereignty for Hawaiians has become a pressing ethnic and political issue, interest in Hawaiian language, history, and culture has gained momentum, and increasing numbers of people are requesting access to print materials that once were of interest primarily to scholars and historians. Among these documents are memoirs, official reports, and newspaper accounts containing information about the 1898 annexation of Hawaii to the United States as well as about Hawaii's last reigning monarch, Liliʻuokalani. The year 1993 marked the hundredth anniversary of her overthrow and 1995 the hundredth anniversary of her formal statement of abdication. These landmark dates and numerous commemorative activities continue to generate interest in Liliʻuokalani, who could readily serve as a rallying symbol for the Hawaiian sovereignty movement.

Interested in Liliʻuokalani myself, I did research on the book *Hawaii's Story by Hawaii's Queen*, which Liliʻuokalani wrote from late 1896 through 1897 and which is widely known and read in Hawaii. Published in the United States only months before Congress was to vote for or against the annexation of Hawaii, the book was Liliʻuokalani's final effort to intervene in the political process, from which she had been removed by her overthrow, forced abdication, trial, and imprisonment in her own palace (which now stands restored in the middle of Honolulu). In the book, Liliʻuokalani argues and pleads with the American people not to take over her country. She declares "absolute authority" in saying that "the native people of Hawaii are entirely faithful to their own chiefs, and are deeply attached to their own customs and mode of government; that they either do not understand, or bitterly oppose, the scheme of annexation" (370). *Hawaii's Story by Hawaii's Queen* is rich in Hawaiian history and will undoubtedly be cited in future debates on the contested history and status of indigenous Hawaiians and of their land and political rights.

The question that arose in my research on Queen Lili'uokalani resulted from my willingness to rely on photocopies of her transcribed diaries from 1878 through 1906. The original volumes are not readily available to the public, but I anticipated no particular problems in using the photocopied versions, which are conveniently shelved in the Hawaiian and Pacific Collection at the University of Hawaii. I offer the following paragraphs as a cautionary tale to illustrate the dangers of not using original documents, dangers that unfortunately become apparent only when researchers decide for some reason to examine the original documents. Reproducing primary materials by any method—even simple ones such as transcription and photocopying—may have the effect of distorting the original text.

Using typed copies of the diaries seemed altogether reasonable to me—that is, until I began to think, very surprisingly, that Lili'uokalani may not have written *Hawaii's Story by Hawaii's Queen*. It was not my intention to discredit her authorship of a book that is so widely known. Still, rumors of a ghostwriter or of a very liberal collaboration with the man who served for a time as Lili'uokalani's secretary have existed at least since the 1930s, when Lorrin A. Thurston, a grandson of missionaries and a leader of the pro-annexationist party, declared Lili'uokalani's authorship of *Hawaii's Story by Hawaii's Queen* a sham. In his own memoir of the overthrow of the monarchy, Thurston uses Lili'uo kalani's diaries to support his embittered accusations against the queen, who had worked so hard to thwart his plans for a Hawaii that would be tied politically and permanently to the United States. After his political party confiscated the diaries and other personal papers from the queen, Thurston, who had a law degree from Columbia University, examined them. Certain passages turned up in the case against the queen when a military tribunal of the Provisional Government put her on trial for treason. She was found guilty of misprision of treason and sentenced to five years of hard labor and a $5,000 fine. The sentence was commuted to imprisonment, and when it was over, she had spent eight months confined to one room of her palace, five months under house arrest in her private residence, and for another eight months she was forbidden to leave the island of Oahu (Allen 341). In *Memoirs of the Hawaiian Revolution* (1936), Thurston discredits the queen's authorship even though,

while imprisoned in 1895, she worked on the first English translation of *The Kumulipo*, a Hawaiian poem and chant of the Creation, which she published in 1897 with her own introduction. (She was also one of Hawaii's most talented and prolific composers.) Thurston insists, however, that there is too large a disparity between the style of the diaries and that of *Hawaii's Story by Hawaii's Queen*. "I have checked the record in various sources," he writes, and "[t]he English of the book, as compared with that of the diary, is evidence of my statement. Lili'uokalani personally was incapable of using such clear-cut English as that published" (175, 180).

To my regret, the typed copies seemed at first to confirm Thurston's charge: the entries were often short and oddly fragmented or elliptical, with a pattern of abbreviations and errors. Lili'uokalani seemed also to write on standard-size paper, but strangely she ignored its horizontal dimension; her sentences were foreshortened and rarely came close to the right-hand margin. There were many oddities in the diaries that I read for the years 1878, 1885, and 1898 and many inconsistencies from diary to diary. Deciding it was necessary to view the original volumes, I learned that some were sequestered in the State of Hawaii Archives Building and others in the Bishop Museum, both in Honolulu. I went to the Bishop Museum, which stores thousands of documents and artifacts from pre- and post-Contact Hawaii, and consulted with an archivist there. He agreed to remove the diaries from a room that is dehumidified and air-conditioned twenty-four hours a day, which I was not allowed to enter. Returning to another room in which I waited, the archivist handled the diaries with spotless white gloves and carefully placed one volume, then another, and then another on a table before me, and he patiently turned down each fragile page for me to examine but not to touch. I then discovered something that surprised me even more than had my initial skepticism of Lili'uokalani's authorship, something I would never have discovered had I not seen the original entries.

Utterly absent from the photocopied transcripts and utterly obvious in the originals was the way in which the physical dimensions of each diary determined the odd style of its entries. Only by viewing the originals did I realize that the diaries, in contrast to the photocopied versions, come in a variety of shapes and sizes. Furthermore, nearly all the diaries are very small. For example, the 1886 diary is 3 by 4½ inches, the 1898 diary 3 by 5 inches, and the 1906 diary 2¾ by 5½ inches. Some of the diaries are so small they are more accurately described as appointment books with space only for quick, hasty entries. The materials that I had examined earlier were physically identical, all the standard 8½ by 11 inches, all in bound notebooks the size of academic theses. Also, and again in contrast to the photocopied texts, the original diaries do not generally have conspicuous gaps between the text and the edges of the paper. In fact, the original diaries show what the typed copies camouflage, that Lili'uokalani's handwriting often goes to the very edge of the page, leaving no space whatever. In the smaller diaries the queen's handwriting is very cramped with occasional additions even written upside down, providing evidence that she worked hard to utilize all the space available to her and was thus expressive rather than reticent.

The conclusion I drew from even a cursory study of the original documents was the opposite of the impression I first received from the photocopied version: Queen Lili'uokalani was more than capable of writing *Hawaii's Story by Hawaii's Queen*. Many of the supposed errors and idiosyncrasies of her prose are a natural and logical result of writing in what she considered a private genre and in the physical books she chose for her diaries. The typed copies that are available throughout Hawaii give the impression that Lili'uokalani used standard American notebook paper, which she collected and bound as a manuscript. They also suggest obvious improbabilities—that, for example, she typed some of the entries or that when she wrote in Hawaiian, she also translated those sentences. In retrospect, I see that the insufficiencies of the copies are embarrassingly evident, and yet I was slow to recognize them. They corrupt the originals in ways that led me, at least for a few days, to divest Lili'uokalani of authorship of her important *Hawaii's Story by Hawaii's Queen*.

Although without systematic study it is difficult to generalize about the textual corruptions from one year's diary to another, I think it fair to say that the duplicating process and the preparation of fragile materials for undergoing that process create significant problems. In fact, they produce "copies" that are dangerously unfaithful to the original. The decision, for instance, to photocopy typed versions of handwritten diary entries produces odd differences and dislocations. The decision concerning the relation between text and page tends to magnify minor errors so that they appear glaring. Without sufficient editorial apparatus, copies that aren't really copies emphasize qualities of Lili'uokalani's prose that seem idiosyncratic on a standard page but are absolutely appropriate to the cramped format of the actual diaries. Lili'uokalani's prose, removed from its original context, is thus stripped of its history.

Thurston, who read the original diaries, surely understood that the fragments and elliptical constructions were the result of the dimensions of the diaries. Given Hawaii's benign climate, which is anything but benign for the preservation of print, and given Hawaii's volatile politics, perhaps he believed that the diaries would not survive but that his accusations would. The crucial diary of 1897, which Lili'uokalani must have written in while she worked on *Hawaii's Story by Hawaii's Queen* and which would probably corroborate her authorship and offer details of the drafting process, has never been found. In view of the history of Lili'uokalani's confiscated possessions, I suspect that it never will be found.

Thurston proclaims Lili'uokalani incapable of writing her own book. I conclude that Hawaii's last indigenous ruler not only wrote her own book but also was someone for whom writing was imperative. Using those pocket-size diaries was very practical. Lili'uokalani was able to keep one or two of them hidden in the folds of her late Victorian dresses and write the instant she felt the urge to write. Symbolically, if not in fact, she was protecting the record of her life from those who she feared might gain political ascendancy and who eventually did. They were the same people who imprisoned her, ransacked her private rooms, and confiscated every diary and personal and official paper they could find, allowing her to keep only one document, her last will and testament. We are uncertain why some of the diaries still have not surfaced and why others show evidence of tampering and erasures, but we know this much: Lili'uokalani could not be stopped from writing. Not only are the diaries written in English and Hawaiian, but in later years, after Hawaii became a Territory of the United States, Lili'uokalani began to use a private numerical code that was not broken until 1971 and occasionally a personal shorthand. It seems certain that *Hawaii's Story by Hawaii's Queen* was indeed written by Hawaii's queen, and it is ironic that the original diaries, but not their typed copies, offer strong support for this conclusion.

Note

My thanks to DeSoto Brown, an archivist at Bishop Museum, Honolulu, Hawaii, for his helpful reading of this paper.

Works Cited

Allen, Helena G. *The Betrayal of Liliuokalani: Last Queen of Hawaii, 1838–1917*. Honolulu: Mutual, 1982.

Lili'uokalani. *An Account of the Creation of the World according to Hawaiian Tradition*. Boston: Lee and Shepard, 1897.

———. *Hawaii's Story by Hawaii's Queen*. 1898. Honolulu: Mutual, 1990.

Thurston, Lorrin A. *Memoirs of the Hawaiian Revolution*. Ed. Andrew Farrell. Honolulu: Advertiser, 1936.

Manuscripts on Microfilm:
The Disturbing Case of Proust

Anthony R. Pugh, University of New Brunswick

I have three anecdotes, three for the price of one: together they indicate that there is more than one aspect to the business of manuscript versus microfilm. One of the anecdotes even suggests that we should be happy that some manuscripts have been preserved on film.

For the last ten years or so I have been working on the manuscripts of Marcel Proust, trying to establish the chronological sequence of everything that he wrote in preparation for his great novel *A la recherche du temps perdu*, from 1909 (when it first took shape, and the pillars were set down) through 1911 (when Proust completed a first draft) to 1913 (when a typescript of half the novel was ready for a publisher; half this typescript was set in proof and half the proof published). My examples come from the first book of the novel, *Du côté de chez Swann*, the part entitled "Combray"; from the central portion, *Le côté de Guermantes*; and from the last part, now *La fugitive* or *Albertine disparue*.

The "manuscripts" are essentially exercise books, with the addition of a few episodes written on loose sheets and of a seven-hundred-page typescript that covers about half the novel as it was envisaged in 1911. Proust wrote on the recto pages of his exercise books, frequently passing from one book to another, and maybe another, and back again to the first; he used his verso pages for subsequent additions. Occasionally he saved himself the trouble of recopying by giving a whimsical cross-reference (a sketch of a boat, or a butterfly, for instance), but generally, as he refined his prose and reorganized his episodes, he rewrote the whole text.

This material was all in private hands until the early sixties, when the Bibliothèque Nationale in Paris acquired the lion's share (other exercise books have come into the library since then). It was not in good order, with exercise books falling apart, and so the books were all "restored," which means essentially that they were rebound, with the loose pages firmly fixed in place. A practical method of classification was devised, assigning each rebound exercise book to the part of the novel to which it seemed most closely related; thus the books that work on the overture were numbered 1–7, the books on "Combray" 8–14, the books on "Un amour de Swann" 15–19, and so forth.

For twenty years scholars had a field day with this material, gradually analyzing the contents, identifying problems, proposing solutions. But the day came, inevitably, when it was decided that too many fingers in the Proustian pie were having a destructive effect on the precious pages and that henceforth consultation would be done on microfilm, in order to preserve the manuscript. It is not impossible to obtain permission to see the originals, but all routine work has to be done first under glass. In the process, things can get overlooked.

One disadvantage of microfilms, as everyone who has used them knows, is that all sense of the physical reality of the book disappears. A microfilm is like a black-and-white reproduction of an oil painting. The words are there, but everything has become intellectualized, distant. For the scholar in search not only of evidence but also of suggestions, some clues are no longer discernible—the color of the ink, for example. Ten years ago I realized that the first part of the "1911" typescript, including nearly all of "Combray," must have been made toward the end of 1909, and I asked a young Japanese doctoral student, Akio Wada, who was writing a thesis on the evolution of "Combray," if he had considered that possibility. "Yes," he replied, "and, what is more, I can prove it." His proof, which he would not disclose at the time but which became public knowledge once his thesis had been defended, was that a note in Proust's personal *carnet*, which we can certainly date December 1909 or January 1910, indicates in red ink that there were passages added on certain pages. On the typescript all these pages have marginal additions, and they are all in red ink. Red ink is very rare in Proust. Luckily Wada noticed the red ink in time, before the manuscripts were taken from him.

With microfilms you proceed one dreary page at a time, without the sense of the whole, which you get physically from the exercise books themselves. My second anecdote suggests that the mechanical process of microfilm reading encourages laziness. It was always said that there was a gap in the manuscript version of the central portion of Proust's novel, *Le côté de Guermantes*. The manuscript version is found in exercise books 39–43 and 49 of the Bibliothèque Nationale collection. The last page of 43 ends in mid-sentence, and the first page of 49 begins in mid-sentence, and they are not the same sentence. The assumption, never questioned, was that we were in the presence of two different versions, the first version missing only its last exercise book, the second version known only through its last exercise book. Or maybe it was the other way around; there was some dispute about which was the first version and which the second. But nobody doubted that there were two distinct versions. We were, however, in the presence of a modern-day "golden tooth." The gap between 43 and 49 is of only a few lines, as we see if we compare the draft with the published text, and it seemed to me unlikely that 43 and 49 did not belong together. That the remaining portions of two different versions should fit almost exactly was too much of a coincidence. Evidently a few lines, perhaps one manuscript page, was missing. Could the missing text be found? More easily than I had imagined; for when I looked at the microfilm of book 43, I realized that when Proust had got to the end of his last page (writing, as usual, on the recto), he continued on the facing verso. But once again he reached the end of the page without finishing his sentence, and he picked up a new book (our 49) and completed it there. The scholars who had studied *Guermantes* had evidently not thought to wind back the reel to the previous image. It can get quite hot and soporific in the microfilm room, but even so. . . . Can you really afford not to bother to read the verso pages of a crucial manuscript?

My third example comes from later in the novel, the part that never made it to the 1911–12 typescript. Here we find that the microfilm, far from obscuring the evidence, actually leads us to the truth about the original version. This part of the novel, reworked by Proust during the war, is one of the rare instances where he simply cut out pages and included them, without recopying them, in his new manuscript. Another Japanese scholar, Jo Yoshida, had spotted and identified five such pages. When I was trying to reconstitute the original 1911 version, using the microfilm, I noticed a sixth page, of which only the margin (which was empty) remained in the original exercise book; the rest of the page had been pasted into the wartime exercise book. But in 1911 Proust had written something on the back as well, going of course all the way to the right-hand edge of the page, so when he cut along the margin line of the recto, which was the text he wished to reuse, the writing on the verso was divided about one inch from the end of each line. The text could be reconstituted by putting together the two portions of the divided page, but this is quite unpractical on microfilm, even if one could for a few minutes use two adjacent readers. So I preferred to add this question to the list of questions I needed access to the originals to answer. Imagine my surprise when I had the original 1911 exercise book in my hand and could find no trace whatever of the page I wanted to see. I can only assume that the one-inch margin was "tidied up" when the exercise books were rebound and that fortunately this tidying up occurred after the microfilm was made. I have no proof of this, however. It shows why the Japanese scholar counted only five such pages: in the early eighties, he was working straight from the originals. It also presents a horrendous prospect to the conscientious scholar, who would have to compare every page of the originals with every page of the microfilms to be really sure that nothing was missed. This is impossible, practically speaking, but it shows just how careful one has to be.

This final anecdote leads to another conclusion. Scholars are responsible for their evaluation of the evidence put before them. The onus is on libraries to give very complete bibliographical descriptions of their manuscripts and to suppress no evidence, however untidy it may be. Scholars need to contemplate the mess and work it out for themselves. The assumptions of librarians and archivists may not be beyond reproach, and it is dangerous to present assumptions as facts and tidy up the evidence.

Twentieth-Century Undergraduates and an Eighteenth-Century Edition of Diderot's *Encyclopédie*

Manon Anne Ress, Temple University

Undergraduates come to my course on French civilization with a variety of backgrounds and with different ideas of what studying civilization is all about. The shape the course takes depends to a great degree on the interests and needs of the students. However, a basic goal shared by all students is the discovery of connections among such areas as history, art, music, literature, and religion. Students are introduced to major events in French history and to works of art produced in France from the Middle Ages to the present. Since we have only fourteen weeks to cover such a large amount of material, we select a few works of art to illustrate each period we study. Students participate in the choice by deciding together what event or work of art they will discuss more in depth in class or in their written work. Conducted entirely in French, the course is primarily a discussion class where students are expected to learn how to express their opinions about French civilization. By the end of the course they should be able to describe several French institutions, historical events. They should also be able to recognize and define basic concepts of French society in terms of its social and political structures and literary and artistic movements.

This year Diderot's *Encyclopédie* was the document selected to start a discussion on the French Enlightenment. The short extract in the textbook could of course not represent fairly the huge compilation that took twenty-nine years to publish in full and eventually ran to twenty-one volumes of text, twelve plates, and two indexes. The complexity of the document and its place in French eighteenth-century society are best investigated using the document's original form. After a class during which we discussed the background of this formidable work and its effect on French culture, the students were given specific assignments to be carried out in the university library. They were to meet in small groups in the rare books collection and then report back to the class about a variety of issues. We had agreed on the entries they would check, such as "autorité politique," "guerre," "peuple," or "droits féodaux." Two students chose to focus on the famous illustrations of the *Encyclopédie*. All the students reported their findings with enthusiasm and had many

interesting observations. They were struck by the number of volumes (thirty-five) and their size and by the names of the numerous intellectuals who participated in Diderot's project. The look and feel of the document were also discussed in class—by students who had never seen or touched an eighteenth-century edition. The calligraphy and spelling interested them. The rare books collection itself was an important discovery for them. Most had never been in that part of the library and found the experience fascinating, though the rare-books librarian did not seem to have enjoyed their visit much. Some students were reprimanded for writing on pieces of paper placed directly on the eighteenth-century edition. With humor, they told different anecdotes of their first contact with the rare books and with the librarian there.

The discussion of the different entries they looked up was very informative. They had discovered, on their own, through the difficulty of consulting the original work, some of the subtlety of the *Encyclopédie*. We spoke, for example, about censorship and self-censorship. I am convinced that, in many ways, students have gained more from working with an eighteenth-century edition of the *Encyclopédie* than they ever did from working with a textbook reproduction of an *Encyclopédie* article or two. For example, the students raised interesting questions about the cost of such an edition and about the number of readers who were able to acquire these huge volumes at the time.

Looking at, touching, and reading the *Encyclopédie* is a wonderful way to put oneself into the mind-set of eighteenth-century France, to grasp what was considered so sensational, shocking, and revolutionary then. The hundreds of engraved illustrations that show people at work making all manner of industrial products definitely helped my students understand why the *Encyclopédie* embodies the Enlightenment and is one of the most important documents on eighteenth-century France in general.

I asked the students to evaluate our pedagogical experiment. Most were very positive even when they had encountered difficulties. Many students told me that using an eighteenth-century edition had changed their conception of what a research project could be. One student I met later told me that she had just got a good grade on a research project about Frederick Douglass (in a journalism course) because her use of Douglass's articles instead of the course's compilation of secondary sources had helped her shape a personal and creative approach. She laughed as she was telling me about the difficulties of finding his articles in various libraries and about her perseverance. She struggled with the libraries' catalogs and the texts themselves but eventually learned a lot. At the end of our brief conversation the student, young but a scholar indeed, mentioned that she is still thinking of trying to find original copies of *The North Star* and maybe even some of Douglass's manuscripts.

On the Importance of Judging Books by Their Covers

Gregg Camfield, University of Pennsylvania

Any proposal to make an exclusively electronic library is predicated ultimately on an extreme idealism, an idealism crudely but accurately expressed by the axiom "You can't judge a book by its cover." This axiom implies that the words alone count and that if we could simply pour them unmediated into our brains, we would best be able to judge books. According to this principle—by which we teach our classes out of cheap paperback reprints of authors' words—the medium doesn't count at all. Get the words right and the student can read them off microfilm, a VDT, or even listen to them on audiotape.

But as the amount of money publishers spend on covers suggests, we can—indeed we usually do—judge books by their covers. The Harlequin romances at the checkout counter in the supermarket have covers that tell us not only what but also how we will read. Leather-bound, gilt-edged volumes also tell us how to read: reverentially in the face of transcendent genius, which we have the good taste to purchase and display ostentatiously. My point is simple and obvious: the physical presentation of a piece of literature gives us essential clues about how we are intended to read it and gives us further clues about the means of its production and the social role it plays. In my classes on nineteenth-century literature, I insist that the students take the physical book into account as a part of their reading experience. For that I need libraries to have early editions of the books I assign.

Let me give an example. In my class on Mark Twain, I want my students to understand what risks Twain ran and what benefits he sought in publishing his books by subscription. I refer to his own words to describe his sense of his business, but these words themselves refer to the physical artifacts quite concretely:

> There is one discomfort which I fear a man must put up with when he publishes by subscription, and that is wretched paper & vile engravings. I fancy the publisher don't make a very large pile when he pays his author 10 p.c. You notice that the Gilded Age is rather a rubbishy looking book; well, the sale has now reached about 50,000 copies—so the royalty now due the authorship is about $18,000. (81)

Twain traded aesthetic pleasure for economic power, but what that tradeoff meant is not fully obvious to late-twentieth-century readers.

To show what the tradeoff meant, I have my students study the physical copies of books that span much of Twain's career, from the early days when he did not control the presentation of his books to the days when he took control by publishing his books himself. Using copies of *The Innocents Abroad*, *Roughing It*, and *The Gilded Age* as examples of Twain's earlier works, I have my students take note of the gaudy covers; the cheap woodcuts; the brittle, thin, yellowing paper; the thin cardboard covers; the crude typesetting; and the simple heft of the books. These details concretely show that the books were relatively inexpensive. They suggest further that such books were directed to an audience not used to buying books, an audience buying books not for status but rather for entertainment, an audience wanting as much as possible for the price and willing to trade quality for bulk. When I add to this an example or two of subscription book prospectuses, my students see all the more clearly the economic conditions of subscription publishing and the audience expectations that to a large extent determined the range of content of the books.

Thus, reading the material artifacts helps my students read the content, especially when they turn to those books that Twain published himself. Their new insight into the entertainment value of Twain's early subscription books allows them to see how having control over the production of *Adventures of Huckleberry Finn* put Twain in something of a bind. He wanted the book to sell as a typical subscription book, but he had written a biting satire. Rather than alienate an audience that expected simple entertainment, he hired an artist to draw conventional comic illustrations, essentially muzzling the biting prose with silly pictures.

When my students examine the beautiful book that is *Connecticut Yankee*, they can see how Twain tried to extend the range of meaning available to a subscription book by changing its material circumstances. The cover is sturdier, and its ornamentation is more tasteful. Inside, the paper is relatively slick, allowing for crisp printing of both text and illustrations. The illustrations are beautiful and expensive, even though Twain hired a previously unknown illustrator in order to hold costs down. The careful layout of each page to integrate words and illustration into one visual whole hints at the effects soon to be exploited by popular magazines of the twentieth century after typesetting costs diminished with the development both of the Morganthaler typesetter and of several less expensive techniques for reproducing graphics. But in *Connecticut Yankee*, the typesetting was done by hand, and the cost was high. Not surprisingly, Twain never made much money on the book, in part because his desire to expand the range of the subscription book outran the technology available to him.

As the book's presentation suggests in yet another important way, Twain may not have cared about profitability. Unlike in *Adventures of Huckleberry Finn*, in *Connecticut Yankee* he made no attempt to hide his political intentions behind benign illustrations of harmless clowns. On the contrary, he gave his illustrator, Dan Beard, free rein to highlight the book's satire. Beard penned biting political cartoons, most of which pointedly attacked abuses of political or economic power. He brought to the fore the novel's allegorical significance by depicting contemporary political and literary celebrities in his illustrations. To make illustration explicitly serve purposes other than ornamentation is a notable departure from the formula for success in subscription publishing. This and the other merely aesthetic departures from the conventions of subscription publishing suggest that Twain meant his work to have enduring artistic and political value as opposed to ephemeral entertainment value. All of this is suggested not so much by the words as by the book itself. Thus, the material artifact helps students understand authorial intention as well as the book's social and economic circumstances.

I do not know how I could make such points real to my students without the physical copies of the books. I understand the difficulties of making nineteenth-century subscription books available. They are by nature fragile, and their fragility makes them increasingly rare. Rebinding robs them of some of their usefulness, but restoring old bindings is difficult and expensive. Yet in spite of these difficulties, the benefits of maintaining a multifaceted understanding of our cultural history are worth the trouble and expense. If we wish to give our students a truly usable past, we must give them a realistic rather than a purely idealistic sense of the past.

Work Cited

Clemens, Samuel. *Mark Twain's Letters to His Publishers*. Ed. Hamlin Hill. Berkeley: U of California P, 1967.

Rekindling the Reading Experience of the Victorian Age

Catherine Golden, Skidmore College

I confess that part of the mystique of visiting the rare book room at Skidmore College lies in its location; even graduating seniors are as surprised of its existence as Mary Lennox is surprised, in *The Secret Garden*, when she discovers her cousin Colin in a forbidden wing of Misselthwaite Manor. Like Mary's visits to the forbidden wing, visits to the rare book room unlock a world: the world of Victorian literature and culture. Thus I regularly bring students in my nineteenth-century literature courses to the rare book room in the Lucy Scribner Library of Skidmore College. Together we examine works in the Hannah M. Adler Collection, which features illustrated nineteenth-century periodicals, part issues, books, and multivolume works by leading and popular writers.

Undergraduates reading nineteenth-century novels often marvel at the length of works by Dickens, Thackeray, and Eliot. Seeing long novels in their original installments, however, shows how these texts appeared to the Victorians who read them as multivolume works, as parts of works published independently, or as serials in the leading weekly and monthly journals of the day. Examining pivotal texts and periodicals—Eliot's *Middlemarch* (1871), *Master Humphrey's Clock*, and *Bentley's Miscellany*[1]—rekindles the reading experience of the Victorian age. A first edition of *Middlemarch* in eight slim volumes shows how reading a long novel, a challenge for many of my students, was in 1871 a far more manageable task than that of absorbing the fat paperbacks we assign today. A more dramatic point is made when we examine serial publication in the collected volumes of *Bentley's Miscellany* and in the unbound part issues of *Master Humphrey's Clock*, which have their original blue-green paper wrappers, an artifact of Victorian publishing. As Linda Hughes and Michael Lund point out in *The Victorian Serial*, it is well known that serialization brought forth some of the best literature of the age, but the experience of reading a novel over a period of two years (or longer), as the Victorians typically did, is foreign to our students, who are given approximately two weeks to read the same work. The installments of Dickens's *The Old Curiosity Shop* and *Barnaby Rudge* in the part issues of *Master Humphrey's Clock* encourage students to ask themselves how reading lengthy novels one segment at a time, with breaks between reading periods, affected the ways Victorian audiences responded to and created meaning from these works as well as the ways in which Victorian authors and artists created fiction. Students today can thumb ahead to discover a mystery's conclusion; the serial reader could not. Learning the story's outcome thus was postponed, gratification delayed. Moreover, when students actually see from the publishing format that illustrated serial novels unfolded over months and years, they more readily understand how the illustrations provided continuity between installments and an aid to memory. Illustrations, a vital part of the reading experience even of sophisticated Victorians, were studied, as author-illustrator George Du Maurier has put it, "with passionate interest before reading the story, and after, and between" (350).

The monthly installments of *Oliver Twist* from February 1837 to April 1839 (omitting June 1837, October 1837, and September 1838) in *Bentley's Miscellany* dramatize the benefit of using primary materials to teach about illustrated Victorian fiction. Dickens's novels unfolded through and with pictures, though modern editions typically eliminate all or most of the original illustrations. The monthly numbers of *Oliver Twist* in *Bentley's Miscellany* show students all twenty-four illustrations, allowing them to understand why many Victorian readers considered the memorable characters in *Twist* more Cruikshank's than Dickens's. Cruikshank was known for his caricature art. In his illustrations, the body of Fagin, who lures Oliver into his den of crime, shrivels in emaciation, while the overweight forms of Mr. Bumble and Mrs. Corney, parish beadle and workhouse matron, call attention to the fact that, unlike thin Oliver and the backdrop of famished children, those who oversee the workhouse have no need to ask for more. Pictures integral to plot and character development, such as "Monks and the Jew," have been dropped from modern editions,[2] and even the best reproductions available today do not capture the nuance of detail and shading so vital to illustrations like "Fagin in the Condemned Cell," where the stippled effect on the cell wall calls attention to Fagin's circular, glazed eyes and crazed manner. Seeing all twenty-four images reveals that the story of *Oliver Twist* is told through Cruikshank's pencil as well as Dickens's pen and adds credibility to Cruikshank's grand claims, in his book *The Artist and the Author*, for authorship in his collaborations with Dickens and William Harrison Ainsworth.[3]

The novels we typically read in my Victorian literature classes are all now part of the canon of British literature. However, viewing these texts in their originally published format in the rare book room demythologizes the aura of classic that now surrounds them. *Oliver Twist*, collected in volumes 1–5 of *Bentley's Miscellany*, demonstrates how a new serial was often started alongside a successful one nearing completion to entice established readers to keep purchasing the periodical. In volumes 1 and 2 (each volume contains six monthly numbers), the installments of the new serial *Oliver Twist* follow *Songs of the Month*, by Ainsworth, Samuel Lover, and other authors now forgotten but then more established than Dickens. The placement of *Twist* indicates the publisher's lack of certainty about the success of this new serial, even though Cruikshank was quite popular in the 1830s and Dickens, then better known as a journalist than as an author, still had enjoyed success with *The Posthumous Papers of the Pickwick Club* (1837), which popularized serial fiction in the first place. Not surprisingly, *Oliver Twist* rises to the lead position in the table of contents of volumes 3 and 4 of *Bentley's*. But despite the enormous popularity of *Twist*, the final four installments drop to the sixteenth position in the table of contents for volume 5.[4] Instead, Ainsworth's *Jack Sheppard* has first billing, which reveals the publisher's desire to excite his readership with the escapades of another Newgate novel.

Extending the boundaries of the classroom into the rare book room of a library is more than a field trip to view dusty artifacts. Seeing novels in the very publishing format the Victorians once saw them in makes Victorian cultural constructs accessible to students. The rare book room thus becomes a window into Victorian culture as well as into the best literature of the age.

Notes

[1]*Master Humphrey's Clock* was a weekly periodical written wholly by Dickens to carry installments of his full-length novels *The Old Curiosity Shop* (1840–41) and *Barnaby Rudge* (1841). *Bentley's Miscellany* was a distinguished monthly periodical including important contributions by William Harrison Ainsworth and by Dickens, who was also the first editor of *Bentley's*.

[2]Many paperback editions that retain illustrations do so only erratically. For example, following Dickens's own later selection of illustrations, the Oxford edition of *Oliver Twist* retains only eight of Cruikshank's original illustrations, which editor Kathleen Tillotson numbers as twenty-five to include an illustration Dickens rejected. "Fagin in the Condemned Cell" and "Oliver Asking for More" are retained; but other, less memorable illustrations, such as "Sikes and His Dog," are included rather than, for instance, "The Last Chance" or "Mr. Bumble and Mrs. Corney Taking Tea." Similarly, the Signet edition of Thackeray's *Vanity Fair* retains some of the inset capital designs and an occasional woodcut. Recently, there has been a trend to include illustrations in modern editions, and the complete illustrations of *Vanity Fair*, for example, are printed in the 1994 Norton Critical Edition as well as in the Oxford University Press edition of that novel. Furthermore, the Norton Critical Edition of *David Copperfield* also includes all of Phiz's illustrations. These are but a few examples of the revaluation of Victorian illustrations in recent paperback editions.

[3]Cruikshank's career ended in controversy over his exaggerated claims that his illustrations had altered Dickens's original concept of *Oliver Twist* and had inspired Ainsworth's *The Miser's Daughter* and *The Tower of London*. His struggles over authority ended his collaboration with Dickens in 1841 and with Ainsworth in 1844.

[4]Other factors may have influenced this decision. The final magazine installments of *Twist* appeared serially after the three-volume publication of *Twist* and after Dickens had resigned the editorship of *Bentley's*. Also, Ainsworth, the subsequent editor, may have been eager to showcase his own fiction, *Jack Sheppard* (1839).

Works Cited

Cruikshank, George. *The Artist and the Author*. London: George Bell, 1870.

Du Maurier, George. "The Illustrating of Books from the Serious Artist's Point of View." *Magazine of Art*. Aug.–Sept. 1890: 349+.

Hughes, Linda K. and Michael Lund. *The Victorian Serial*. Charlottesville: U of Virginia P, 1991.

Postscript about the Public Libraries

Ruth Perry

The MLA "Statement on the Significance of Primary Records" is part of a wider professional response from the library and scholarly communities to problems of funding and space that they are encountering in their efforts to preserve the print record. The conservation of damaged or deteriorating books and the creation and distribution of adequate reproductions of manuscripts and printed texts for scholars and students without access to originals are two issues that concern those responsible for transmitting to the next generation our cultural and intellectual heritage. Less well understood and publicized but also crucial to the future of our culture is the threat posed to local public libraries by cutbacks in public spending. The closing of even small neighborhood branch libraries, with the loss of their collections, means that the public suffers an irreplaceable loss of a wide variety of books, many dating back to earlier eras and containing material as well as intellectual evidence of cultural history. Furthermore, while these closings may not directly affect the lives of academic professionals with their university library cards, specialized private collections, and online computer texts, they accelerate our society's alienation from books and reading culture and thus in the long run undermine the work we do and the textual history we value. Most important, the defunding of public libraries stymies the taste for books and reading in those who are poor and less mobile and cuts off their access to a quiet, non-commercial place of respite and imaginative renewal.

Every state in this country has seen branch libraries close or cut back their hours in the last decade. Operating with reduced staffs, many small branch libraries stay open only a few hours a week, often when people working nine-to-five cannot get to them. Cutbacks in federal funding in combination with the diminishing tax base for many state budgets (a function of disappearing industry and declining property taxes) are making it impossible to keep libraries open at times and in neighborhoods most convenient for the people who most need libraries. Meanwhile Buck-a-Book stores are springing up in many shopping malls, and large chain bookstores flourish, testifying to a newly structured mass market for books and a new level of commodification of literacy and reading.

In California this year there is a statewide library crisis because of the reallocation of local property taxes from library budgets to school districts. It is an expressive double bind—to promote either public libraries or schools, either public ownership of books or institutional selection of reading materials, either autonomous browsing or regulated learning, either book culture or textbook culture, but not both. Although the California case has a special poignancy, libraries everywhere have been in trouble since at least 1990, given their shrinking resources to maintain collections and pay expert staff.

Some larger public libraries, forced to raise money and save space, have been selling their older, out-of-print books to private dealers. Used book dealers will tell you that the market in rare books is picking up again as libraries quietly deaccession to make ends meet. But the cheapest way to dispose of books when they are beyond repair or when bulging shelves need relief is simply to throw them away. Susan Koppelman, known for her anthologies of nineteenth-century women's stories, was

The author is Professor of Literature at the Massachusetts Institute of Technology.

dismayed to learn, on repeatedly submitting call slips for nineteenth-century American women's novels and collections of short stories in the Saint Louis Public Library, that many rare and important volumes were permanently unavailable because they had ended up in a landfill. Indeed, according to Koppelman, many of the sources from which she gleaned her first short story collection, *Old Maids* (1984), have been fatally deaccessioned. It has been reported that the works of Langston Hughes and Edmund Wilson were removed from some New England municipal libraries, probably because of the poor condition of the books, but the libraries apparently had no funding to replace them.

Built long ago as a public resource funded by taxpayers' money, the network of public libraries in this country belongs to everyone and to no one in particular. These public buildings with their irreplaceable collections of books are our common property, like parks and beaches and highways. They are not a phenomenon of the market; not much money changes hands for the service they provide. The current Congress is less inclined to support public enterprises than to privatize them, but while some private service industries, like the mail businesses, are turning a profit, so far no one has figured out how to turn a profit from the public libraries. Still, there is clearly more money to be made from selling books than from lending them, and library collections, of no obvious fiscal advantage to anyone, are being allowed quietly to run down, despite the dedication of many library workers and managers and the needs of the public.

Yet public libraries are the very cornerstone of a true democracy. They provide access to information and ideas about everything a thinking citizen might want to know to make a reasoned judgment, cast a vote, or register an opinion. Democratic access to knowledge is essential to the free play of ideas, a concept originating in the Enlightenment and very much conditioned by the rise and spread of print culture. Books provide literary art and entertainment. They support productive aims as well and are the resource of inventors and dreamers. They supply information on everything from building machines and filing patents to fertilizing gardens and raising children. A free society needs free public libraries.

In our century, public libraries have also been an important wellspring of serious literary production. Many of our best writers educated themselves in public libraries, browsing the open shelves, absorbing influences, coming upon unknown authors long out of print, following the trail of sudden interest and inspira-

tion. Libraries thus represent our literary future as well as our literary heritage. Where will the poets and citizens of the future make their unexpected discoveries? Where will they roam uncalculatingly among writers out of fashion and not to be found in any undergraduate syllabus? Aspiring writers cannot buy everything they need to read. And how many poets can afford computer access to online texts—even if screen reading were the same as hand-held book reading? Democratic access to books in our thousands of public libraries will not soon be replaced by any electronic or market mechanisms. Professors of literature in particular should be aware of the cultural cost of the erosion of this public resource.

A letter written by the author Helena Maria Viramontes in 1993 as part of a campaign to save a local library makes the case eloquently:

> Several weeks ago I was informed that a branch library in the city of Orange [California], appropriately called "The Friendly Stop / La Parada De Amistad," is being shut down. This deeply concerns me. I have been involved with the library which is a trailer situated in the barrio of West-Central Orange. The one room library is constantly visited by Latina/os primarily, mostly teens, who have found the library a comfortable reprieve from the streets. They read, receive homework assistance, or become involved in the many bilingual activities the library has to offer. . . .
>
> How many of us Chicana/o-Latina/o writers grew up in bookless homes? How many of us found solace and rapture in being able to attend the library, sit in a quiet place and read or have the right to exercise our imaginations? I, for one, made an office of a library chair and a piece of table where I would sit for hours and read, conduct meetings, write in my journal, dream, even nap. In a house with eleven people, this library space was my private heaven. It was a space filled with floating answers, infinite questions, and the quiet time for meditation. It was a space for me like no other and we simply can't sit by and let this experience be ripped away from our youth who so very much need it AND want it.

Viramontes speaks for thousands of intellectuals and writers who rely on such oases in our speedy and materialistic world. More, she speaks for the poor and on behalf of the young at risk.

Free public space is in increasingly short supply in this country; there are few places to go any more and few things to do that do not cost money. Public libraries are among the last places left where all people are welcome, qualified for admittance merely by their humanity, curiosity, and literacy. Public libraries symbolize the commitment of our society to something other than commercial exchange. They provide democratic access to books and knowledge for a broad cross section of our population including the elderly, the self-educated, immigrants, children, the poor. It is extremely shortsighted for academics to ignore the current defunding of public libraries and the real and symbolic threats it poses to the reading public and to extracurricular book culture. We need to defend our public libraries for the sake of an informed citizenry and for our children's children, the readers and writers of the future. Our art and our politics depend on the fullest possible access to the cultural record. If we do not make the effort to keep our librar-

ies intact during these lean years, we will jeopardize for all time what is best in our society.

Works Cited

Koppelman, Susan. Telephone conversations with the author. 25 and 27 Apr. 1995.

Viramontes, Helena Maria. Fax to the author. 3 May 1995.

Young and Highly Educated in the 1990s: Job Prospects in the Professional Labor Market

Lori G. Kletzer

We live in a world characterized by increasing job insecurity and income inequality. Twenty years ago, college graduates could look forward to putting on suits and going to work for the same companies for fifteen to twenty years. The picture was much the same for those less educated and working in goods-producing industries: long-term jobs were the norm (see, e.g., Hall). Income inequality also looked different twenty years ago. From the onset of the Great Depression through the early 1950s, earnings inequality declined sharply. For the next thirty years (through the 1970s), it rose slightly (see Levy and Murnane).

Today the picture is very different. Earnings inequality began a sharp acceleration in 1979, and now a number of labor market trends provide workers with ample reason to worry about job security. Millions of workers have been displaced by changes in technology, by changes in the composition of demand, and by increasing foreign competition. Permanent job loss has spread into the white-collar ranks as firms downsize and restructure to meet the demands of an increasingly competitive marketplace (see Kletzer). More and more, long-term employment relationships are replaced by contingent (temporary) employment. In the business and popular press, articles and editorials about job insecurity have become common. Here is one example:

> When Karl Marx described an increasingly miserable and exploited working class, he never imagined that his oppressed workers might someday include Ivy League M.B.A.'s tossed out of $200,000-a-year jobs.
>
> But a changing economy is gradually linking highly educated managers and technicians with high-school trained assembly-line workers and office clerks. The link is in their common place in an increasingly competitive economy that no longer values workers as much as it once did. What they share, public opinion polls show, are feelings of uncertainty, insecurity and anxiety about their jobs and their incomes.   (Uchitelle)

The purpose of my paper is to describe the broad outlines of the college-educated professional labor market. To do that, I try to answer two big questions: What are the key characteristics of this labor market? What are the prospects for employment and earnings over the next ten years? The Bureau of Labor Statistics of the US Department of Labor monitors current conditions and trends in the labor market, and its employment projections are the main source of my comments here.

But first I want to describe briefly another labor market, the market for individuals with a high school diploma or less—not because this market is directly relevant to the professional one, but because there are important and troubling societal questions raised by recent changes in it. I believe that knowledge of this market, and of the trends in American labor markets in general, will help put the professional labor market—and perhaps the employment concerns of humanities PhDs—in perspective.

Much has been written and said about the 1980s rise in income inequality. (For an excellent survey, see Levy and Murnane; see also Juhn, Murphy, and Pierce; Katz and Murphy.) Between 1979 and 1987, the proportion of men earning more than $40,000 increased, as did the proportion of men earning less than $20,000, in 1988 dollars (see Levy and Murnane).[1] Rising inequality is best understood by considering the entire distribution of earnings. Real hourly wages for male workers at the median of the distribution were 5% lower in 1989 than in 1970. Wages at the ninetieth percentile

The author is Assistant Professor of Economics at the University of California, Santa Cruz. A version of this paper was presented at the 1994 MLA convention in San Diego.

were 15% higher in 1989 than in 1970, and wages at the tenth percentile were 25% lower (Juhn, Murphy, and Pierce).[2] In other words, men of less education and lower skills were earning less in 1989 than in 1970, while men of greater education and higher skills were earning more.

Increasing returns to skill, where skill is measured by educational attainment or work experience or both, is one factor accounting for the rise in inequality. This pattern is often indicated by the differential between college graduate and high school graduate earnings. In 1971, among male full-time workers aged 25–34, college graduates earned 22% more than high school graduates on average (for women the difference was 41%). But during the 1970s, with the entry into the labor force of many college-educated baby boomers, the earnings premium associated with college fell. In 1979, young male college graduates earned 13% more, on average, than young male high school graduates, and female college graduates earned 23% more, on average, than female high school graduates. By 1987, however, the earnings premium for college graduation had risen to 38% for young men and 45% for young women (see Levy and Murnane, table 5).

While college graduates gained relative to high school graduates, there was also a large increase in income inequality within each educational group. High school graduates in the bottom 10% of the hourly wage distribution lost 15% in real dollars between 1964 and 1988, while high school graduates in the top 10% of the distribution gained about 9%. The bottom 10% of college graduates earned 5% less in 1988 than in 1964, while the top 10% earned 25% more (see Juhn, Murphy, and Pierce).[3] For workers at the top, the college-educated labor market has never looked better.

It is now well documented that the bottom has fallen out of the labor market for those with a high school education or less. Only the top 30% of male high school graduates have had real earnings gains since 1964; the bottom 40% earn 10% to 17% less than corresponding workers in 1964. An important part of this precipitous decline for less-educated men is the reduction in full-time work.[4]

What I have just described is the most important labor market development of the past fifteen years. As we turn our focus to the professional labor market, it is important to note that the rise in the earnings premium for a college education has coincided with the increase in the supply of college graduates. College enrollment rates have been steadily growing across groups. The rise in the returns to skill has occurred because the demand for skill has increased faster than its supply. (For more

on demand-and-supply factors accounting for changes in relative wages, see Katz and Murphy.)

The future of the professional labor market looks relatively bright. That is how I interpret the projections made by the Bureau of Labor Statistics. The BLS issues workforce projections every two years, and the most recent cover the period 1992–2005. These projections can perhaps be better understood with a very abbreviated consideration of past trends in the United States economy, particularly labor market developments. (Kutscher provides a framework for my discussion here about historical trends in the economy.) These trends help explain why I am guardedly optimistic about the professional labor market. The American labor force grew by 74% between 1950 and 1980, an increase of 44 million workers. More than half that growth, 24 million, occurred during the 1970s with the entry into the labor force of the baby boomers and with the increased participation of women. From 1980 to 1990, growth was slower, when 18 million entered the labor force.

Table 1

Growth in Selected Service Industries, As Projected by BLS for 1992–2005[a]

	Jobs Added	Percent Change
Business services	3,000,000	3.6
Personnel supply (temp. agencies)	932,000	3.5
Computer and data processing	795,000	5.3
Photocopying, commercial art, photofinishing	101,000	3.4
Health services	4,000,000	3.0
Medical and dental labs, home health care, specialty outpatient	744,000	5.0
Educational services	462,000	1.9
Elementary and secondary schools	149,000	2.2
Colleges and universities	211,000	1.5
Libraries and other schools	102,000	3.1
Social services	1,700,000	5.0
Individual and family	459,000	3.9
Child day care	328,000	4.3
Residential care	800,000	7.3

Source: List adapted from Franklin.

[a]These numbers should be used with caution. Growth rates can be large because sectors are starting from a small base. Many slower-growing industries and occupations will add large numbers of jobs but have low growth rates because of a large employment base.

The personal consumption component of the gross domestic product (GDP) was 67% in 1992, as compared with 61.6% in 1950 (the other components are investment, government expenditures, and net exports). This increase reflects growth in personal income as a share of national income, and it reflects a long-term decline in the personal savings rate (i.e., on the whole, consumers have more income to spend and they are saving less of it). Purchases of services within consumption spending rose to 36.5% in 1992 from 26.7% in 1950, and much of that increase is due to escalating health care expenditures. The United States economy has become more open to the rest of the world, and exports and imports have grown as a share of the GDP. The trend away from employment in goods-producing industries and toward employment in the production of services has been in place for decades. Service industries accounted for 26.8% of nonfarm employment in 1992, up from 16.2% in 1970. Manufacturing industries accounted for 16.6% of nonfarm employment in 1992, down from 27.3% in 1970. Between 1980 and 1992, service industry employment increased by 11 million jobs, and much of that growth was in health care and business services. Managerial, professional speciality, and technical occupations all had a steady increase in employment share, as a group going to 30% in 1992 from 21% in 1972.

There are several factors to keep in mind when thinking about the future of professional jobs (or any jobs). Some projection about growth in the overall economy (productivity, labor force, the federal budget, total demand) is required. I am basing my remarks on the BLS's moderate growth scenario.[5] Demographics are also important, particularly the aging of the baby boomers. Personal consumption expenditures are expected to continue to increase as a share of spending.

Service industries are expected to add 13 million jobs from 1992 to 2005, which is about half the projected 25 million new jobs in the nonfarm workforce. Many of these new service jobs will be in business and health care industries. Table 1 shows projected growth for a selection of the fastest growing service industries.

Though service occupations, many of which require little formal education, will have the largest share of the labor market by 2005, occupations that require a bachelor's degree or other postsecondary education or training are expected to have faster than average rates of growth. Professional specialty occupations (the college labor market) are expected to grow by 37.4% from 1992 to 2005. Six million new jobs in this category will increase its share of nonfarm employment to 15.5%, up from 13.7% in 1992. Professional jobs will increase even

in manufacturing, an industrial sector where employment is expected to decline by 518,000. Other fast-growing occupations include technicians and technical support, expected to grow 32.2% for 1992–2005, as compared to 57.6% for 1979–92; executives, administrative and managerial, expected to grow 25.9% for 1992–2005, as compared to 50.4% for 1979–1992. The slowdown in the growth rate of executive and managerial employment is likely due to restructuring and downsizing, particularly in manufacturing.

The college-trained labor force is most closely identified with professional specialty occupations, which account for the vast majority of jobs requiring a college or more advanced degree. Table 2 shows projected growth in some of these occupations.

Although many occupations will provide more new jobs than the ones listed in table 2, they will have slower growth rates because of their large employment base. Most new jobs will be in these occupations: retail salesperson, registered nurse, cashier, general office clerk, truck driver, waiter, nursing aide or orderly, food preparation worker. Each of these occupations is projected to add 500,000 to 700,000 new jobs from 1992 to 2005 (Silvestri).

Table 2
Growth in Selected Professional Specialty Occupations, As Projected by BLS for 1992–2005

	Jobs Added	Percent Change
Engineers	306,000	23
Life scientists	40,000	22
Medical scientists	12,000	31
Computer, mathematical, and operations research occupations	772,000	102
Social scientists	95,000	37
Economists	13,000	25
Psychologists	69,000	48
College and university faculty members	214,000	26
Secondary school teachers	462,000	37
Special education teachers	267,000	74
Chiropractors	16,000	36
Writers, editors, and technical writers	66,000	23
Reporters and correspondents	15,000	26
Public relations specialists and publicity writers	26,000	26

Source: List adapted from Silvestri.

Another important aspect to consider is replacement hiring. Even in declining occupations, employers continually need to replace workers who quit, retire, or are discharged. In skilled blue-collar occupations, net replacements are expected to exceed job growth by 88%, while in the professions there will be half as many openings because of replacement as because of job growth (Silvestri).

What do these projected job growth rates mean for earnings? Many of the fastest-growing occupations have above-average median weekly earnings, while many of the occupations projected to provide most of the new jobs have below-average median weekly earnings. This situation is likely to leave the income distribution relatively unchanged.

As the numbers illustrate, jobs that require a college or more advanced degree will grow faster than jobs that do not. Put simply, workers with higher levels of education will be better prepared for future labor market opportunities. Does this mean that all college graduates and those with advanced degrees will be assured of success? No. Even an advanced degree will not guarantee a job that exactly matches one's training. Under various scenarios for the 1992–2005 period, the supply of college graduates will exceed demand (Shelley). However, those with four or more years of college will have significantly higher earnings than high school graduates will, and they will experience less unemployment. This view is a continuation of current trends. As Thomas Amirault reports, of all BA-degree holders in 1992, 23% were employed in non-college-level jobs and 4% were unemployed (see also Hecker). Of MA-degree holders, 10% were similarly underemployed and 3% were unemployed. Of PhDs, 4% were underemployed and 1% were unemployed. Median earnings for BA-degree holders in 1992 were $34,385. That median was 62% more than the median for high school graduates, $21,241. For MA-degree holders, median earnings were $40,666, and for PhD-degree holders, median earnings were $52,403.[6]

The future is likely to involve income and job insecurity for many. At the same time, people with high levels of education will earn more than those with little education, and they are likely to be better situated to handle labor market uncertainty. Competition for jobs will be keen. People with exceptional skills (achieved through hard work, ability, good schools) and good luck will find well-paying jobs. Others with less exceptional skills may need to be more flexible in their job selections, or they may experience some underemployment before they find satisfactory positions.

I have described here a healthy labor market for people with high levels of educational attainment. A good education earns a good return in the market. One may need to think creatively about how to use one's skills, but the returns are there. As college graduates and advanced degree holders cope with the anxieties of the academic market, a market that perhaps looks grimmer than anticipated, they should remember that they have high levels of skill and that skill is valuable. Millions of workers in our economy face an alternative, low levels of skill, that is worse. That alternative is, and will remain, an important policy concern.

Notes

[1]The trend was the same for women, although in their case increases in hours worked slowed the rise in inequality. Because the inequality rise was sharper for men, they are the focus of my comments.

[2]The median of a distribution is the point where 50% of observations lie above and 50% lie below. The ninetieth percentile is the top 10% of observations (the highest earners) and the tenth percentile is the bottom 10% of observations (the lowest earners).

[3]Greater reward for hard-to-measure, unobserved (by scholars) skills may be one factor accounting for the rise of income inequality within groups.

[4]Through the 1970s, 68% of male high school dropouts (15% of the male workforce) worked full-time and year-round in eight out of ten years. By 1989, the fraction working steadily had dropped to 51% (Nasar).

[5]Moderate growth is the alternative that the BLS chooses to discuss in depth. It makes this choice to ease presentation, not to suggest that moderate economic growth is more likely than low or high. In this scenario, labor force growth will be somewhat slower than currently, the trade balance and federal budget balance will improve, and labor productivity growth will rise modestly from its current rate. See Saunders.

[6]These numbers should be interpreted with some caution, as they are for one year only. The earnings medians are for annual earnings for full-time, full-year workers.

Works Cited

Amirault, Thomas A. "Job Market Profile of College Graduates in 1992: A Focus on Earnings and Jobs." *Occupational Outlook Quarterly* 38 (1994): 21–28.

Franklin, James C. "Industry Output and Employment." *Monthly Labor Review* Nov. 1993: 41–57.

Hall, Robert E. "The Importance of Lifetime Jobs in the U.S. Economy." *American Economic Review* 72 (1982): 716–24.

Hecker, Daniel E. "Reconciling Conflicting Data on Jobs for College Graduates." *Monthly Labor Review* July 1992: 3–12.

Juhn, Chinhui, Kevin M. Murphy, and Brooks Pierce. "Wage Inequality and the Rise in Returns to Skill." *Journal of Political Economy* 101 (1993): 410–42.

Katz, Lawrence F., and Kevin M. Murphy. "Changes in Relative Wages, 1963–1987: Supply and Demand Factors." *Quarterly Journal of Economics* 107 (1992): 35–78.

Kletzer, Lori G. "White Collar Job Displacement, 1983–91." *Proceedings of the Forty-Seventh Annual Meeting of the Industrial Relations Research Association, Refereed Papers Competition, January 1995*. Madison: Industrial Relations Research Assn., forthcoming.

Kutscher, Ronald E. "Historical Trends, 1950–92, and Current Uncertainties." *Monthly Labor Review* Nov. 1993: 3–10.

Levy, Frank, and Richard J. Murnane. "U.S. Earnings Levels and Earnings Inequality: A Review of Recent Trends and Proposed Explanations." *Journal of Economic Literature* 30 (1992): 1333–81.

Nasar, Sylvia. "More Men in Prime of Life Spend Less Time Working." *New York Times* 1 Dec. 1994: A1.

Saunders, Norman C. "The U.S. Economy to 2005: Framework for BLS Projections." *Monthly Labor Review* Nov. 1993: 11–30.

Shelley, Kristina J. "The Future of Jobs for College Graduates." *Monthly Labor Review* July 1992: 13–21.

Silvestri, George T. "Occupational Employment: Wide Variations in Growth." *Monthly Labor Review* Nov. 1993: 58–86.

Uchitelle, Louis. "The Rise of the Losing Class." *New York Times* 20 Nov. 1994, sec. 4: 1.

Speculating about the Labor Market for Academic Humanists: "Once More unto the Breach"

Jack H. Schuster

Prophesying what the academic labor market holds in store, even for the relatively near future—say five or eight years downstream—is a hazardous undertaking. The odds that projections beyond eight or so years will prove to be reliable probably fall somewhere between exceedingly long, as in predicting precisely when the next sizable earthquake will rip through California, and not very good, as in Don't bet next year's travel allowance on any of your first three guesses who the next Nobel laureate in literature will be.

Put another way, the track record of the "experts" does not exactly inspire cult worship. As one of those persons associated with a previous forecast—a projection that foresaw that by the mid-1990s the academic marketplace would turn around—I can now, ten years later, only offer a propitiary mea culpa and sigh that at least I've traveled that mine-strewn path with some pretty distinguished company. But being a slow learner, I've agreed to return to my heavily bandaged crystal ball and attempt once more to discern the outlines of the future.

Moving beyond self-flagellation to razor-sharp analysis, I first try to explain why the much awaited faculty shortfall failed to arrive on schedule. Indeed, that train, long overdue, has not yet become visible as we peer expectantly down miles of empty track.

Second, I attempt, before your very eyes, the amazingly bold feat—some may call it stupid—of proclaiming just what the future holds, albeit hedging in a variety of ways.

And finally I establish what I think it all means for prospective graduate students in the humanities, current graduate students in the humanities, and the current faculty in the humanities.

My strategy does not entail making actual projections of demand and supply. In my view, so many new factors are shaping the academic marketplace that the kinds of projections attempted from time to time in the past would today be particularly foolhardy. Rather, I try to identify and describe the basic forces at play, venture conclusions, and prepare the way for some educated guesses about what job seekers and their advocates can expect.

The Question to Be Addressed

The central question is, What will be the demand for, and the supply of, persons qualified to be faculty members at American colleges and universities in the proximate and intermediate future? That is a far from simple question; in fact, it is immensely complex, and convincing answers are arguably more elusive than ever. While substantial studies have been undertaken in recent years to project academic labor market conditions, higher education realities have shifted so rapidly in just the past few years that an entirely fresh look at the marketplace is needed. Will the sizeable faculty shortages projected by several major studies in the not-so-distant past materialize after all, albeit well behind the schedule that those studies anticipated? (See Bowen and Schus-

The author is Professor of Education and Public Policy at the Claremont Graduate School. A version of this paper was presented at the 1994 MLA convention in San Diego.

ter; Bowen and Sosa.) Or do new conditions that have emerged or that we can foresee call into question the basic assumptions that have informed the studies previously undertaken?

A Conceptual Frame

At least eight factors have converged—or are converging—to reshape the academic marketplace. Some are relatively new; some are not new but escalating. These factors are connected and crosscutting. Some will stimulate demand, others will depress demand, and still others will shape supply. Considered together, they mandate a new assessment of marketplace forces.

Before considering these eight elements, we should contemplate the probable effects of two huge and inexorable demographic forces on future faculty demand: replacement needs and enrollment increases. These two vectors are so fundamental to any analysis of the future academic marketplace that they must be understood to be the framework within which the other elements operate.

First, let us consider *replacement-driven demand*. With the average age of faculty members now at about forty-nine, it is clear that scores of thousands of them will soon need to be replaced. The most recent estimate (fall 1992) places the total number of full-time faculty at 595,000 (National Center 10–11, tables 2 and 3).[1] We can assume that 45% to 48% of those now aged fifty and over will retire in the next fifteen years or so. Such an assumption is based on previous experience. By about the year 2008, the total number of vacancies created by retirement would be 267,000 to 285,000. Although considerably less than a hundred percent of those positions are likely to be filled—for reasons to be discussed—the number of replacements will nonetheless be very large.

Let's now turn to the other demographic inevitability, *enrollment-driven demand*. The number of eighteen-year-olds, in decline for two decades, has just bottomed out, and a powerful wave of new college-going applicants is building. The number of eighteen-year-olds can be fairly easily estimated for some years into the future; after all, that cohort has already been born. But will college-going rates grow, fall, or remain stable? Enrollment projections vary depending on underlying assumptions, but one reasonable guess, emanating from the United States Department of Education, holds that between 1994 and 2004 total higher education enrollments will increase by nearly a million. That constitutes a 6.7% increase in full-time equivalent students over

current postsecondary enrollments—and an expanding age cohort is expected subsequently to swell college enrollments even more.[2]

A number of important questions have a bearing on future enrollments. For example, will the proportion of future students who seek full-time enrollment be comparable to the proportion of students who have attended full-time in recent years? If the trend in attending college part-time continues to increase, fewer new faculty members will be employed. Also crucial are the shifts in student interests that undoubtedly will occur from one field to another. Such shifts underscore the importance of disaggregating demand rather than fashioning policies based on projected aggregated demand. In sum, while it is unlikely that enrollment increases will trigger proportionate expansions of instructional staff, those increases, even when discounted, will create a considerable demand for new faculty members.

A Volatile New Environment

The confluence of these two demographic forces will exert a very strong upward pressure on the demand curve. Put another way, replacement-driven demand and enrollment-driven demand constitute the fundamental factors that will shape the future academic marketplace.

The question remains, Are there other factors in play that may substantially temper the projection of steeply increasing demand, a projection that would be incontrovertible if based solely on replacement needs and enrollments? The answer is *yes*, and here is where those eight factors mentioned previously enter the equation and where the analysis gets complicated. Some of those factors will have a dampening effect on faculty demand; others a mixed effect. Let us consider them one by one.

1. *Economic and political conditions.* The national economic downturn, more acute in some regions than in others, has squeezed budgets throughout higher education, especially the budgets of public institutions. Intertwined with the national economic condition is the uncertain capacity (and political will) in many states to maintain levels of support for public higher education. This is especially evident as the needs of other human service sectors—elementary and secondary education, health care, and penal corrections among them—grow more severe and typically are assigned higher priorities. While the economy shows unmistakable signs of recovery, the postelection momentum for fiscally conservative

public funding policies suggests that constrained budgets for postsecondary education will prevail for the foreseeable future. Will research and development funds available to higher education shrivel? Will nonvital federally supported fellowships atrophy? Will a recommitment to a stronger military establishment fuel basic research, displacing research and development funds for health, environmental research, and the pittance that still remains for education? The questions are endless.

Yet whatever details emerge, this political-economic factor will undercut—likely to a considerable degree—the demand created by both replacement and enrollment needs. That is to say, anxiety about resources will almost surely persuade institutions not to replace retiring faculty members on a one-for-one basis. Similarly, the anxiety will deter them from hiring additional faculty members in proportion to increasing enrollments, thereby allowing student-to-faculty ratios to drift upward. We do not know just how much to discount faculty demand because of economic and political realities, but most colleges and universities, given the current depressing environment, will probably behave very conservatively in authorizing new hires.

2. *Early retirement.* In the face of the economic imperative to trim operating costs and to increase administrative flexibility, many institutions (particularly some large public multicampus systems) have offered attractive retirement incentives to faculty members. This strategy has resulted in thousands—maybe tens of thousands—of early exits from the academy. By making room for new hires, these retirements boost demand, at least in theory. (To complicate matters, this phenomenon simultaneously adds at least marginally to faculty supply, as early retirees become available to teach at other campuses.) To my knowledge, no one has yet calculated the number of such early retirements and, therefore, the extent to which future replacement needs may ease.

3. *The end of mandatory retirement.* Arguably the most obvious of the eight factors is the end of mandatory retirement—the so-called uncapping that took effect 1 January 1994. A number of important studies have addressed the probable consequences of putting an end to a university's ability to require retirement by a certain age. The consensus to date appears to be that uncapping will lead to an increase of one to two years in the average age of retirement. But the actual effects of uncapping have not been tested under current conditions, nor have longer-term implications for the academic marketplace been assessed. In all, earlier

apprehensions that large numbers of faculty members would opt to stay on well beyond age sixty-five seem unfounded. Thus, future demand is not likely to be softened by the option newly available to faculty members to remain at their lecterns beyond the usual age of retirement.

4. *Immigration and internationalization issues.* The United States Immigration Act of 1990 (P.L. 101–649, sec. 121) allows large numbers of "outstanding professors and researchers"—up to forty thousand—to immigrate to the United States above and beyond the "levels" (i.e., quotas) fixed for each country by federal law. This act may have a quite significant effect on the supply of faculty members from abroad, especially as American higher education (and, more generally, the national interest) becomes more internationally oriented. The recent enactment of the North American Free Trade Agreement and the bold extension of the General Agreement on Tariffs and Trade, giving rise to the World Trade Organization, are among the initiatives fueling internationalization and likely to make magnets of educational institutions in the United States. The marginal economic conditions for higher education prevailing in many countries—the former Soviet republics, for example—make a move to the United States all the more attractive to foreign academics. At present there are few faculty openings here, but when openings do materialize, it is safe to assume that nationals from other countries will compete for those positions.[3] This phenomenon may be less prevalent in the humanities than, say, in the natural sciences, but internationalization will nonetheless be a factor that adds to supply.

5. *The need for flexibility in staffing.* Interwoven with the other factors, particularly with the factor of financial constraints, is the administrative imperative to maintain flexibility in instructional staffing in a time of considerable uncertainty. This priority has powerfully influenced staffing patterns over the past two decades as increasing numbers of academic appointments have circumvented the tenure track (Gappa and Leslie; Pratt). Looking ahead, administrators cannot help but wonder whether student curricular preferences will be so volatile in the future that colleges and universities will be persuaded to continue to place a high premium on flexibility in instructional staffing, possibly relying even more heavily on non-tenure-track appointments than they have in the past. Note that the proportion of part-time faculty members has already mushroomed to nearly 40% and that other types of full-time nontenured appointments abound (Gappa and Leslie). But can the number and propor-

tion of "nonregular" academic appointments, already at such extraordinarily high levels, continue to rise without seriously jeopardizing quality? What are the implications for future staffing? Those questions cannot be answered confidently now, but meanwhile the perceived need for flexibility exerts a steady downward pull on the demand curve.

6. *A reemphasis on teaching.* This is a more subtle factor. The powerful assessment movement that has focused policy makers' attention on undergraduate education (and on teaching in particular) also affects the marketplace. Assessment pressures, coupled with regional accreditors' increasing insistence that campuses demonstrate value added, may have motivated many an institution to reallocate faculty resources, at least at the margin, away from research activities in order to support better its undergraduate teaching mission. How much of this reallocation has taken place, or will take place, is unclear. The development will presumably increase the demand for teaching, although an institution's teaching requirements might be met partially from within—perhaps by nonteaching professionals who do not hold faculty status. The pressure to improve teaching will likely be felt most acutely by those institutions that were relatively late in adopting a serious research mission at the expense of their historic teaching mission. Moreover, debate abounds over the need to define scholarship more broadly. Will the movement to reconceptualize what constitutes legitimate scholarship affect the type of graduate training deemed desirable in the marketplace? Will there be a diminished emphasis on conventional dissertations? What will be the net result? This development relates more to the kind of graduate student preparation than it does to the quantity of graduate students to be prepared, but it is a factor that must be taken into account.

7. *Quality and "the competition."* While many studies focus on quantity, that is, on the numbers in the labor market, we should not forget that the quality of job candidates is arguably at least as important. The academy's ability to attract its fair share of highly capable young persons—those with the mobility to choose among desirable careers—depends on higher education's appeal relative to other professions. The question arises: How will perceptions of the competition affect the career choosers? Some professions have become saturated (law), some are becoming less lucrative (medicine), and some are being affected by substantial downsizing (management). Faced with fewer attractive career options, talented undergraduates may increasingly gravitate to graduate study in the arts and sciences, including the humanities, and thereby begin to enter the academic pipeline in numbers even greater than before—leading to an even greater glut in the marketplace.

8. *Technology.* Hovering over the entire future academic marketplace is the biggest x factor of all: technology. A spectacular technological revolution overarches all the aforementioned developments. It is widely perceived as having profound implications for academic staffing in the future. The technological revolution may sharply reduce the demand for faculty. The downstream consequences are difficult to gauge, however. Institutions that for economic reasons must rely increasingly on distance learning will not share the fate of those "elite" institutions that can afford to maintain normal student-to-faculty ratios *and* acquire glittering technologies. The information revolution is of course ever-evolving, but it seems that the immense possibilities of extended learning and interactive communication modes are only now being seen as a not-so-distant reality. In any event, technology is destined to change the role of higher education teaching in substantial ways. Just when technologies will come online to an extent sufficient to affect staffing decisions is hard to foresee—and very different scenarios are plausible. But the technology factor, combined with economic constraints and the managerial imperative to maintain flexibility, militates strongly in the direction of diluting the demand for faculty.

Big Stakes and Urgent Timing

Another observer might highlight more than these eight vectors, but surely each of them compels some reassessment of the labor market's future direction. Taken together, these developments appear to undermine both the willingness and financial ability of institutions to replace departing faculty members and maintain current student-to-faculty ratios. (Fig. 1 is a rough depiction of the probable effects of the factors discussed above.) Yet, in view of the underlying fundamentals—the escalating replacement-driven and enrollment-driven demands—the net demand for faculty members seems destined to rise significantly. For what it may be worth, a recent Department of Labor projection shows the total number of college and university faculty members growing from 812,000 in 1992 to 1,026,000 in 2005, an increase of 214,000 jobs or 26%. The total number of job openings foreseen for that same period is 505,000: 291,000 for replacement purposes and 214,000 due to growth (Silvestri).[4] But, again, how much should these basic demographic factors that drive demand be discounted by the emerging developments outlined above?

All of this is to say that conditions have changed abruptly (compared with the usual rate of change in higher education), and the time has come to assess anew what the implications of these changes are likely to be for faculty demand and supply.[5]

A great deal hinges on whether colleges and universities will need to hire more or fewer faculty members in the foreseeable future. Public policies (both federal and state), institutional policies, and foundation priorities all influence the supply-demand equation by stimulating (or not stimulating) supply and, less directly, by creating additional demand—for example, through expanded research and development funding. Such policies need to be modulated according to perceived levels of need for new faculty members. Should existing programs designed to stimulate supply be allowed to expire or should they be expanded? Much is at stake.

Most important is the human factor. Over the past twenty years, incalculable damage has been inflicted on thousands of aspiring academics as the academic pipeline continues to disgorge people into a marketplace saturated in most fields. Preventing such dysfunctional imbalances in the future should have a high priority in the making of national, state, and institutional policies (Schuster 93–106, 162–63, 169, 178–82).

And, in view of the time it normally takes to earn a doctorate—the total elapsed time between baccalaureate and doctoral degrees, across fields, has averaged about ten years—decisions made today will affect the labor market for years to come, when current conditions undoubtedly will have changed significantly.

What Does All This Mean for the Humanities?

Now comes the hard part. It's one thing to identify the variables that are inducing change; it's another to try to calculate what they mean "on the ground" for job seekers and those who are still wondering whether it makes sense to opt for an academic career. So here is what I think the answers are:

Question: Should faculty members in languages, literature, and related fields encourage strong undergraduate students to pursue an academic career?

Answer: A cautious yes. The market *will* improve. It certainly cannot get much worse than it has been, and positive signs are coming into view. If, however, faculty members routinely encourage their students to go on to graduate school, the risk of saturation will remain. If they are more discriminating and encourage only their best students to pursue an academic career, that risk will be lessened. So the indicators suggest that one *should* encourage excellent undergraduates. By the time they have completed doctoral programs, there will likely be openings for them.

Question: What advice is appropriate for advanced graduate students about their prospects for regular academic appointment?

Answer: Well, here's the toughest part. Though the market is beginning to change, particularly as retirements accumulate, the change is not yet significant in most fields. I believe, for the reasons cited above, that greater transformation is coming soon. Wholesale change will not occur within the next several years—but it will occur. Accordingly, while there is considerable cause for optimism, the ability to tread water for another five years or so would help. That is perhaps asking too much of many aspirants, but such a strategy reflects the hard reality.

Question: Will the number of humanists with doctorates who thus far have been unable to secure regular faculty appointment constitute so large a supply pool that many if not most vacancies will be snapped up by them?

Figure 1
Anticipated Effects of Emerging Factors on the Academic Labor Market

	Demand		Supply	
	+	−	+	−
1. Economic and political constraints		↓		
2. Early retirement	↑		↑	
3. "Uncapping" (mandatory retirement)		↓		
4. Internationalization (including immigration)			↑	
5. Staffing flexibility		↓		
6. Reemphasis on teaching		↓		
7. Problems affecting "the competition"			↑	
8. Technology and distance learning		↓		

Answer: This cohort of would-be regular faculty members will be viewed differently by different types of institutions. The relatively few institutions that can afford to be choosy in hiring new faculty members after the market turnaround will have little interest in the cohort of nonregular faculty members. They were not interested before; they won't be in the future. Many institutions, however, will look to that cohort to supplement the normal sources that consist of new graduates and faculty members at other institutions.

Question: What about women and ethnic minorities?

Answer: The data show that women in large numbers have succeeded in obtaining initial appointments throughout the humanities. That does not mean that the issues of discrimination have been solved; but progress has been made.

Less progress has been made, however, in regard to prospective faculty members of color. One can debate long and hard about the relative influence of pipeline supply issues versus the effects of continuing discrimination. Whatever weight is assigned to those factors, I am persuaded that the demand for racial minority humanists is strong now and will continue to grow.

Question: What should faculty aspirants do now to better position themselves in the forthcoming marketplace?

Answer: Here my counsel must be general. The beginning of wisdom is to appreciate that there is no one academic labor market but rather a great many submarkets. I do not pretend to know the distinctions at present between the outlook for, say, specialists in nineteenth-century Russian novels and hermeneutics, or between contemporary South African literature and semiotics. An individual should seek the best possible advice from those able to view his or her specialty in a somewhat broader context. Beyond that elementary suggestion, I would advise prospective faculty members to develop their teaching experience and extend their technological skills as much as possible.

The academic labor market is on the verge of a transformation. The features of the past will give way—slowly and unevenly—to new realities. The timing of the turnaround will be propitious for some but will continue to frustrate others. There is hope.

Notes

[1] The 1993 National Study of Postsecondary Faculty has just been released in part. The survey calculates the number of full-time faculty and instructional staff for fall 1992 to be 594,941 (not including 291,855 part-time faculty and instructional staff).

[2] According to the Department of Education's "middle alternative forecast" (i.e., the department's best guess), total college enrollments will build from a 1994 base of 15.01 million (8.31 million full-time, 6.69 million part-time, 10.73 million FTE) in ten years to 15.89 million (9.07 million full-time, 6.81 million part-time, 11.54 million FTE), an increase of 5.9% (9.3% full-time, 1.7% part-time, 6.7% FTE). In those same ten years the number of high school graduates is seen as increasing by 23.6%, from 2.53 million to 3.12 million. Note, too, that the percentage of eighteen-to-twenty-four-year-olds enrolled in college has grown sharply over the past decade, from 26.6% in 1982 to 34.4% in 1992 (of all high school graduates, from 33.0% to 41.9%).

[3] Ronald G. Ehrenberg's analysis establishes that before P.L. 101–649 American research universities have generally managed to obtain permission to employ foreign nationals. But the numbers to date have been relatively small.

[4] For faculty employment the low and high projections respectively are 164,000 (a 20% increase) and 253,000 (a 31% increase). Note that the increase in the number of secondary school teachers (the "moderate" projection) is more than double that for college and university faculty members: 462,000 (37%). The estimated growth for other teacher groups: elementary school teachers, 311,000 (a 21% increase); special education teachers, 267,000 (a 74% increase). From Silvestri 62 (table 2), 80 (table 8).

[5] To better understand the emerging factors that are affecting the academic marketplace, the author is currently directing a study, The Academic Labor Market: New Realities and Policy Implications for Higher Education and Government, that is supported by TIAA-CREF, the Lilly Endowment, and the Spencer Foundation and is co-sponsored by the American Council on Education and the University of California. The project is examining the probable effects of the variables identified in this article. A report is scheduled for fall 1996.

Works Cited

Bowen, Howard R., and Jack H. Schuster. *American Professors: A National Resource Imperiled.* Oxford: Oxford UP, 1986.

Bowen, William G., and Julie Ann Sosa. *Prospects for Faculty in the Arts and Sciences: A Study of Factors Affecting Demand and Supply, 1987 to 2012.* Princeton: Princeton UP, 1989.

Ehrenberg, Ronald G. "Should Policies Be Pursued to Increase the Flow of New Doctorates?" *Economic Challenges in Higher Education.* By Charles T. Clotfelter, Ronald G. Ehrenberg, Malcolm Getz, and John J. Siegfried. Chicago: U of Chicago P, 1991. 233–58.

Gappa, Judith M., and David W. Leslie. *The Invisible Faculty: Improving the Status of Part-Timers in Higher Education.* San Francisco: Jossey-Bass, 1993.

National Center for Educational Statistics. *Faculty and Instructional Staff: Who Are They and What Do They Do?* NCES Report 94–346. Washington: US Dept. of Educ., Office of Educ. Research and Improvement, 1994.

Pratt, Linda Ray, et al. "Report on the Status of Non-Tenure-Track Faculty." *Academe* Nov.–Dec. 1992: 39–48.

Schuster, Jack H. *Preparing Business Faculty for a New Era: The Academic Labor Market and Beyond.* Saint Louis: Amer. Assembly of Collegiate Schools of Business, 1994.

Silvestri, George T. "Occupational Employment: Wide Variations in Growth." *Monthly Labor Review* Nov. 1993: 58–86.

Graduate Programs and Job Training

Seth R. Katz

In *Profession 94*, Erik D. Curren writes, "Graduate study is more than simply job training; its excitement and challenges are intellectual rewards in themselves" (57). Curren's assumption makes me angry: while my PhD program was loaded with excitement and challenges that were innately intellectually rewarding, it did not do as much as it might have to train me for a job, or perhaps I was not ready to hear the advice. I am finishing my third year in a tenurable position in a medium-sized English department. Over these three years, my anger has grown as I have watched friends work on dissertations, enter the market, interview, and join the profession. Their experience has generally been the same as mine: little guidance in or education about the profession. I have begun to read applications for positions in the department in which I teach and to participate in interviewing candidates. Candidates who present themselves poorly, whether in their letters and vitae or in interviews, often seem to do so because they lack basic knowledge about the profession.

A little research has shown me that there is a body of useful literature on the profession—literature that answers most of the questions about the profession that I should have asked as a graduate student. This literature discusses finding a job, the kinds of institutions and jobs there are, and the kinds of duties an academic must perform. However, there is important information about the profession that this literature does not provide. I would like to try to fill some of the gaps.

All the topics I am concerned with here are interrelated, and while I start out talking about looking for a job, I find that it is difficult and in some ways dishonest to try too hard to tease the topics apart. Graduate programs typically do students a disservice by making it seem as if the profession is just about doing research in one's field. Getting a job that affords the opportunity of doing research—that is, being the kind of candidate a department is looking for—is intimately bound up with the type and size of the institution; the depart-ment's immediate teaching needs; the ways in which the institution values teaching, research, and publication; the institution's enrollment history and projections; the fiscal health of the institution; and many other factors.

The best brief bibliography of works on the profession appears in the October 1994 MLA *Job Information List* (iii; the prefatory material in the *JIL* is also extremely useful). All graduate students in English should read the items in the bibliography early in their graduate careers, as they finish course work or work on a dissertation proposal. This reading, as well as much discussion with professors and advisers at students' home institutions and with professors, scholars, and graduate students at other institutions (at conferences, through e-mail, or in online discussion groups such as E-Grad and discipline- or field-specific lists), would help students see how what they do in their PhD programs relates to and positions them for the job market and the profession. Trudelle Thomas advises viewing the job search "as a research project" (312). This advice holds true for learning about the profession more generally.

Among the works in the *JIL* bibliography, the best overall discussion of the profession is in A. Leigh Deneef, Craufurd D. Goodwin, and Ellen Stern McCrate's *The Academic's Handbook*, an anthology of articles based on talks given to graduate students at Duke. English Showalter's *A Career Guide for PhDs and PhD Candidates in English and Foreign Languages* and Thomas's "Demystifying the Job Search: A Guide for Candidates" provide the best discussions of and advice about job hunting. As a graduate student on the market from 1987 to 1991, I did not know, but I wish I had known,

The author is Assistant Professor of English at Bradley University.

that such works existed; it never occurred to me to ask, and no one suggested that I should. I also did not know that I should familiarize myself with professional issues and trends by regularly reading such periodicals as *Profession*, the *ADE Bulletin*, the *Chronicle of Higher Education*, *CCC*, and the *MLA Newsletter*.

Finding a Job

The job search can easily absorb a lot of psychic energy—energy that is much better spent on finishing the dissertation, writing to publish, and teaching. Applicants should treat the job search mechanically, making it a routine and trying not to become obsessed about such uncontrollable details as whether or not they have received an acknowledgment for each letter sent or what the meaning of each inscrutable form letter might be. Applicants should read the job postings religiously and apply for every opening they could reasonably fill. I found it useful to write a brief passage about each of my research and teaching fields, then to construct my application letters and vitae by editing those passages together in varying ways depending on the order and emphasis of the job postings I responded to. Similarly, I had a generic vita that included all the information about my activities that might be useful, and I rearranged and edited it to make it fit the requirements of each posting as closely as possible.

Several works provide excellent advice about writing application letters, creating vitae, and preparing for interviews (see esp. Showalter; Thomas; Neel; Wilbur; and Shetty). I would like to emphasize two points that these authors make:

1. In preparing for interviews, do a lot of research on the school and its location, on the department and its course offerings and members, and particularly on the people who will interview you—find out what they teach and what they have published. Get the school's catalog, and be prepared to talk about which classes you could teach and how you might teach them. Spend some time working up descriptions, outlines, and even syllabi for courses you could teach, and have copies of these plans to offer to interviewers: this exercise shows that you understand not only the mechanics of constructing a class but the department's needs as well. The day-to-day business of an English department is teaching; candidates should show that they can logically and easily fit into that routine. Thomas discusses research and preparation for interviews as well.

2. Bring a printed list of questions to each interview and, as they are answered, take notes for later review.

Again, Thomas provides an excellent list of questions that, at the least, can guide candidates in the kinds of things they will want to ask about. Thomas also provides a valuable list of questions the candidate should expect to have to answer (319–22).

The Pressure on Graduate Students to Publish

It is a commonplace in academia that publications make a candidate more attractive to a search committee. Candidates must, of course, at least show potential for publication: they should mention their research activities in a letter and vita and should also prepare a written "research statement" that describes their current and projected research activities. In interviews, candidates should be ready to talk glibly about specific projects they plan to work on over the next three to five years (understanding that other things will come up along the way); they should be able to sketch out, say, three articles, two conference papers, and a book-length project that they plan to work on or are currently working on and should be able to name specific conferences, journals, and publishers that might be interested in this work. If a project will require doing research in a particular place, candidates should be able to suggest where they might get grant money to support the research. Projects may overlap substantially: "I anticipate that when I deliver this conference paper, the ensuing discussion will help me find additional resources to turn it into two chapters in the book." This sort of talk shows coherence in the research plan and demonstrates that the candidate understands how the game works. When reviewing a junior faculty member's progress toward tenure each year, senior faculty members expect to hear about their colleague's ongoing research, current and projected work, and potential and actual publications.

However, at my school and, I suspect, at many other non-PhD-granting institutions (that is, at much of the overwhelming majority of colleges and universities), teaching experience carries more weight than publication does. Despite all the talk about research and publication, the primary emphasis in most jobs is on teaching; and while one may be hired to teach a course in one's field, most of the teaching load will consist of composition and introductory literature courses for nonmajors. In the current market, candidates fare best who (1) have experience teaching first-year composition, business and technical writing, and general introduction-to-literature courses; (2) can speak articulately about the structure and organization of their versions of those courses and justify the texts and approaches they use;

(3) can talk about how they would teach a course in their field; and (4) can discuss the relation between their research interests and their teaching. The recent pressure on graduate students to publish is damaging to both them and the profession (see Spacks). Institutions not already emphasizing teaching will soon have to stress it because of the pressure for assessment of student learning. Parents want to know how rising tuition costs help their children learn better. State legislatures are pressing for a better accounting of how tax dollars are spent by colleges and universities (both public and private—private institutions receive public funds for various purposes), which leads to greater pressures on professors to document their time and productivity. As a result, at institutions of higher learning throughout the country, the emphasis on effective teaching will continue to increase (see Harris).

Kinds of Jobs

PhD programs assume that their graduates will all go on to teach at research-oriented, PhD-granting institutions. A moment's thought shows the falsity of this premise: PhD-granting institutions constitute less than ten percent of the profession (Neel 37). Robert F. Gleckner and Jasper Neel both present taxonomies and descriptions of different sorts of institutions; these discussions make it graphically clear that graduate students have to expect to find jobs in "non-elite private colleges," "regional public institutions," and community colleges (Neel 37). Graduate students should start with such a taxonomy when researching the kind of place they might want to work at; Ann Bugliani offers a variety of criteria for making this decision (39). Linda Ching Sledge and Roger H. Garrison in particular discuss working at a community college.

Bugliani also touches on the role of faculty members in bringing students into a department: "A smaller department may well expect you to show great versatility and, because enrollments are usually low, to attract new students to the program. Since enrollments mean jobs, this responsibility is serious business" (39). That is, the more demand there is for a department's classes, the more jobs there may be in the department. Increased enrollments in a department's classes also mean that the department is bringing in more revenue to the institution. And if more students take classes in a department, the department carries more responsibility for retaining students at the institution—and as a result may wield more power in the institution. Tuition dollars fund the day-to-day operations of a college or university. The whole academic industry is shrinking, and so the competition for students and their tuition money is fierce. At an institution that has suffered or is suffering a financial crisis, retention of students is crucial to the survival of the school and of individual programs and departments and even to the continuation of individual jobs. Once this economic reality is explained, it is obvious: it is little different from the competition among lecturers for students at medieval universities (fortunately, these days professors are less likely to use physical violence against one another to protect their tuition base). It is, however, an important bit of the profession that students are rarely privy to.

Research and Publication; Teaching; and Service

The traditional duties of academic professionals fall into three major categories: research and publication; teaching; and service. As a graduate student, I never heard these words uttered together; now, halfway to my tenure decision, I am beginning to understand what they mean. Different institutions give different value to research and publication and to teaching in making hiring and tenure decisions, though these two criteria are always more important than service. At a "research institution"—a school that may keep teaching loads at one or two courses a semester to allow more time for research—publication will be the first and most heavily weighted criterion for tenuring. However, even at a "teaching institution"—a school where teaching loads may be as high as four or five courses a semester and where, ostensibly, teaching is the first and most heavily weighted criterion for tenuring—publication still carries great weight. Though a school's mission and tenuring criteria may explicitly rank teaching first and research second, "teaching effectiveness" is much harder to measure than successful publishing. Criteria for assessing teaching (beyond student evaluations) are being developed and debated, particularly in response to the same calls for accountability that are leading to "outcomes assessment." At the same time, the power of publication remains strong throughout the profession.

Kinds of Publications

Louis J. Budd talks about the problem of ranking publications by quality (207): writing a book oneself versus editing an anthology; publishing in *PMLA* versus publishing in *Exercise Exchange*. In general, single-author print publication remains the most highly regarded form, even though more and more interesting and productive work is being done collaboratively. Budd gives an excellent account of the process of having a journal article published, including a range of dos and don'ts. Richard C. Rowson gives similar guidance.

Online Publishing and Other Online Academic Activities

An area of growing importance not dealt with in the literature is the relation of online academic activities to more traditional research, publication, and teaching. There has been a good deal of deliberation on such online discussion groups as the Alliance for Computers and Writing list (ACW-L) and the computers-and-writing list Megabyte University (MBU-L) about how institutions should evaluate the growing range of online publishing options. The general consensus seems to be that aspiring academics who spend a lot of time online should participate in the creation of criteria to evaluate their activities; at the same time, they should also continue to see to their print publications.

There are several issues involved in evaluating online publishing and online academic activities more generally. Some members of the profession remain at worst technophobic and at best skeptical of the capacity of computer-related technology to improve or expand what we already do and can do in research, publication, and teaching. Thus, even an online journal with a strong editorial board and a rigorous editorial policy may not be regarded as a serious publication, because it is free and in a digital rather than a paper format. Online conference papers cause even larger problems: if a paper is reviewed for, accepted by, and posted for up to several months to an online conference, where any participant in the conference can read it and write comments on it, is it more like a print publication or a paper delivered orally? What if the conference papers are then publicly archived online? Is this comparable to having one's paper published in a volume of conference proceedings?

And what about participation in online discussion groups? On the one hand, this is a kind of publishing, in that one writes one's ideas down and submits them for judgment and response to an audience of fellow academics; on the other hand, the atmosphere of online discussions ranges from that of a serious roundtable to that of a congenial gathering at a bar. Whatever the atmosphere, a great deal of public work with academic ideas and issues takes place in these new forums; and, like physical conferences, online conferences and discussion groups provide chances to meet other academics and develop future research, publication, and teaching opportunities. And when one participates in such online arenas, one still represents and advertises one's home institution—contributing to its prestige and public presence in the profession—just as much as one does through traditional forms of academic exchange. Online activities may even bring more public relations benefit to the institution than the traditional kind do, since they often reach more people more immediately and more frequently. The tenuring process does not yet have standard criteria for adequately measuring collaborative work and online activities; these criteria are gradually evolving.

The same holds true for teaching activities involving computer technology: because the academy does not yet know how to categorize such efforts, one may receive little or no particular credit in hiring and tenuring decisions for developing useful course software or creating effective lessons and syllabi that incorporate the use of locally networked microcomputers or the facilities of the Internet. The graduate students and pretenure faculty members who apply new technology in their projects have to help develop criteria for the evaluation of such work. At the least, they have to be prepared to explain how activities in new media fall within and extend the traditional meanings of research, publication, and teaching.

> *Even at a "teaching institution" publication still carries great weight; "teaching effectiveness" is much harder to measure than successful publishing.*

Teaching

Many graduate programs provide their students with some experience and training in teaching. Others, unfortunately, do not. Graduate students thus receive varying degrees of preparation for working in a college classroom. Even in programs where they have the opportunity to teach, the amount of training in teaching that they receive may be negligible. To anyone outside the academy, this lack of consistent, thorough instruction in how to be a teacher is astounding: after all, teaching is the most time-consuming activity in the overwhelming majority of academic jobs.

A strong, common subtext of graduate education is that teaching is not what academics do by choice; rather, it is a sort of necessary evil (Spacks). As a student, I never thought to ask my professors about how they taught or why they taught the way they did. Reflecting back, I realize that most, if not all, of them ran traditional lecture-discussion classes. Had I asked—and I should have—I am sure that some of them would have willingly talked about how to put together a lecture, how to construct a syllabus, how to choose and order textbooks, how to write an exam or a paper assignment, and how to choose grading criteria for exams, papers, and other kinds of exercises. Since leaving graduate school, I have come to regard teaching as a subject for research in itself and so have discovered the enormous and rich literature on the theory and practice of teaching English literature, language, and composition. I have also gotten many useful ideas from my wife, Barb, a high school social studies teacher, who uses a lot of innovative, student-centered teaching activities; and I have benefited from discussions about teaching in conference sessions and online, especially on ACW-L and MBU-L. As I observe above, teaching is in many places the first criterion in hiring and tenure decisions, and the assessment of teaching will become a larger and larger part of academic professional life over the next few years.

> *I never thought to ask my professors about how they taught.*

Service

For graduate students, service is the least apparent aspect of the academic's trade. Service primarily involves being a member of some of the committees that make decisions about how most aspects of the institution are run. Most administrators are typically chosen from the faculty by vote of the faculty members. Faculty committees, whose members are elected or appointed by faculty members, make decisions about faculty hiring, tenure, and promotion; these committees construct the curriculum and decide what classes will be offered and what goals the classes will have. Faculty committees or their appointees administer special facilities, such as computer classrooms and departmental libraries. Faculty committees make budget proposals for all academic departments of the institution (and for many nonacademic functions as well) and decide how funding will be allotted (see Pye; Colton).

All faculty members can thus expect to have to carry their share of the load of running the institution, maintaining its programs, and deciding how the programs will evolve. When I was a graduate student, all these mechanisms were invisible to me. It might be helpful for students to see how the institution works so that they better understand what part they will play in it. It might even be useful for students to take on some more formal role in the governance of the institution. At some schools, students already sit on search committees and serve as nonvoting members of other bodies, such as a university senate. Certainly, more exposure to the workings of the institution will help graduate students to be better colleagues.

In "Caveat Emptor; or, How Not to Get Hired at DePaul," James S. Malek writes:

> PhD-granting departments could perform a useful service for their students by learning more about conditions and expectations in a range of English departments in MA- and BA-granting institutions and community colleges. There is little evidence that most departments are doing any more to arm Candide for his adventures in the academic world's outposts now than they were fifteen years ago, even in the face of a depressed job market. (35)

Graduate programs do well at teaching students to appreciate the intellectual rewards of academic research. Typically, though, graduate programs do not train students to be professional academics. That lack of preparation weakens graduate students' performance as job candidates and, subsequently, makes the transition to college faculty member more difficult.

A recent special issue of *U.S. News and World Report* on America's best graduate schools included an article, "Gypsy Profs," on temporary English instructors who hold limited-term appointments simultaneously on more than one campus and who must regularly change jobs (Hardigg, Mulrine, and Sanoff). The article quotes Jacquelyn Kahn, a PhD from the University of Illinois who had to give up a three-year appointment at Iowa State after one year because "she simply wearied of the 800-mile round trip each week from her home in Champaign, IL," where her husband (a seventh-grade teacher) and children lived. Kahn states, "I am happy I got a PhD, but I do wish I had been a little more realistic going through it. I wish I had thought more about making myself more marketable." Part of the problem about the job market is just that: PhD programs do not teach students how to make themselves marketable enough. The programs are typically run as though their purpose were to provide an intellectual exercise rather than to prepare students for a job. An academic position is exciting and intellectually rewarding, yes; but still it is a job.

Works Cited

Budd, Louis J. "On Writing Scholarly Articles." Deneef, Goodwin, and McCrate 201–15.

Bugliani, Ann. "The MLA Job Interview: What Candidates Should Know." *ADFL Bulletin* 24.1 (1992): 38–39.

Colton, Joel. "The Role of the Department in the Groves of Academe." Deneef, Goodwin, and McCrate 261–81.

Curren, Erik D. "No Openings at This Time: Job Market Collapse and Graduate Education." *Profession 94*. New York: MLA, 1994. 57–61.

Deneef, A. Leigh, Craufurd D. Goodwin, and Ellen Stern McCrate, eds. *The Academic's Handbook*. Durham: Duke UP, 1988.

Garrison, Roger H. *Teaching in a Junior College: A Brief Professional Orientation*. Washington: Amer. Assn. of Junior Colls., 1968.

Gleckner, Robert F. "A Taxonomy of Colleges and Universities." Deneef, Goodwin, and McCrate 4–18.

Hardigg, Viva, Anna Mulrine, and Geoffrey Sanoff. "Gypsy Profs." *U.S. News and World Report* 20 Mar. 1995: 106.

Harris, Charles B. "Mandated Testing and the Postsecondary English Department." *Profession 93*. New York: MLA, 1993. 59–67.

Malek, James S. "Caveat Emptor; or, How Not to Get Hired at DePaul." *ADE Bulletin* 92 (1989): 33–36.

Neel, Jasper. "On Job Seeking in 1987." *ADE Bulletin* 87 (1987): 33–39.

Pye, A. Kenneth. "University Governance and Autonomy—Who Decides What in the University." Deneef, Goodwin, and McCrate 241–59.

Rowson, Richard C. "The Scholar and the Art of Publishing." Deneef, Goodwin, and McCrate 226–37.

Shetty, Sudhir. "The Job Market—an Overview." Deneef, Goodwin, and McCrate 77–85.

Showalter, English. *A Career Guide for PhDs and PhD Candidates in English and Foreign Languages*. New York: MLA, 1985.

Sledge, Linda Ching. "The Community College Scholar." *ADE Bulletin* 83 (1986): 9–11.

Spacks, Patricia Meyer. "The Academic Marketplace: Who Pays Its Costs?" *MLA Newsletter* 26.2 (1994): 3.

Thomas, Trudelle. "Demystifying the Job Search: A Guide for Candidates." *CCC* 40 (1989): 312–27.

Wilbur, Henry M. "On Getting a Job." Deneef, Goodwin, and McCrate 63–76.

Burning In / Burning Out

H. L. Hertz

I remember asking someone, fifteen years ago, when I was buying my first computer, what the term *burning in* meant; I had heard computers ought to be burned in for twenty-four hours, but the precise effects of burning in were never clear to me. I vaguely supposed electricity was turned on and circuits or pathways were burned into memory so they would work with less resistance and the machine would remember more easily. Only now, either because I have been using a computer or because I have been thinking about a problem that involves memory, have the words *burning in* unexpectedly returned to me. Or perhaps they were suggested by the words *burning out*—frightening words, though I have chosen to include them in the title of this essay. In any case, the explanation of "burning in" that I was given, or that I remember, was obviously wrong or wrongly understood; memory chips, after all, need testing but do not require channels of memory to be "burned in" to reduce "resistance." I must have transferred to the memory of the machine qualities I sensed or believed to be in myself. Don't some habits of thought or association seem more readily available to us than others? Doesn't the current of memory flow more easily in certain familiar, "burned-in" channels?

But if I was thinking of my own memory while imagining, ignorant of how the electronic kind worked, special channels with less resistance in silicon chips, perhaps I was only anticipating the problem that has given rise to this essay: the meaning of habit and repetition in instruction and in the mental lives of instructors. I have spent the last twenty years teaching English in a community college, and this issue of repetition in teaching has become, perhaps, easier for me to identify.

Habits that develop over the years are naturally less visible at the start; so for beginning teachers (regardless of age) repetition may not seem to be a problem at all. On the contrary, after five years or so on the job, habits and their accompanying relaxations are welcome. The rhythm of the academic term, of lectures and assignments, becomes familiar, comforting. Commonly, as we learn the job of teaching, we find it grows easier

and we think we become more effective. A collection of useful materials is gathered—and they aren't only written notes and assignments but also ideas, words and phrases used again and again because they work with students or because we think they work. No wonder that in my fifth year or so, when I was buying my first computer, I associated "burning in" with a more serviceable memory and ease of operation!

Last night, at an open house held at the elementary school our children attend, we listened for a moment to our oldest child's instructor, a kindly man, something of an art collector and connoisseur as well as a fifth-grade teacher, as he summed up our child's performance and behavior. It was all quite positive; and yet, while I listened, a teacher myself, I couldn't help sensing an entirely mechanical and habitual method in his approach to us, as if his sincere and well-chosen observations flowed smoothly in long-established channels of which he himself seemed unaware. No doubt it was because the talk was about my child and because I unconsciously desired a special consideration from him—an effort to break through the accretion of years of similar evaluations—that I glimpsed in myself, through the lens of my disappointment, what otherwise would have been concealed from me. His performance illuminated what self-regard had encouraged me to ignore in my own classroom practice.

Age and its corollary for a teacher, repetition, have had, among other effects on me, this one: as months have become semesters and semesters years, patterns of association (including the telltale repetition of jokes) have become mechanical. That is, in small ways and in larger, I have developed not only habits in teaching but the additional habit of ignoring and forgetting these

---

The author is Professor of English at Pasadena City College, California.

habits. Maybe, since as teachers we instruct ourselves as well as our students, I've only discovered a way of forgetting what I've already said, enabling me to learn (from myself) afresh the next time. Or if I can't keep learning, then maybe habit has worked in the classroom much as it operates in my daily commute between home and school. I no longer notice streets through which I steer my automobile or the facades of buildings I have seen for decades. Nor can I regularly distinguish today's drive from thousands of nearly identical journeys.

The fifth-grade teacher's words and kindly intentions, perhaps not so different from my own, dramatized for me an underlying fixity, one that had been burned into me as well as into him.

Of course the thought that first occurred to me and what my colleagues at work first said when I told them about this teacher was that in elementary school teachers, and in high school teachers too, habitual responses are bound to be more dominant than in college instructors like us. A convincing objection to that argument is that we ourselves may be seen by four-year-college instructors and university teachers in much the same light as we sometimes see K–12 teachers. And any teacher might be so viewed by someone outside the profession. In fact, community college teachers, having heavy class loads (15–24 hours a week) and often teaching—for good reason—many sections of the same course each semester and from semester to semester, work under conditions that are not so different from those of the secondary or primary level. It is not surprising that this faculty, which is not required or much encouraged to do research or show intellectual development (in spite of the ubiquitous phrase "professional development," which is used quite mechanically, by the way, and which the faculty must periodically "sign on to"), generally perceives conferences, sabbaticals, and summers as opportunities for recuperation, not development. Indeed, serious thought is rarely given to the kinds of development that community college teachers might need. In practice, for those among us who are more ambitious (or more desperate to shed the burden of classroom hours), development often consists in efforts to escape laborious and repetitive tasks. English teachers emigrate into reading-skills classes, for example, which require no essays to mark, or, better yet, they go into administration, which combines release from the classroom with the novelty and satisfaction of a more elevated status. Yet having taught in four-year schools and universities myself, I have seen that teachers at those levels also rehearse phrases and enjoy the repertoire in which they have become most comfortable; in short, they too often fly on automatic pilot.

So perhaps, eventually, teaching at any level or long practice in any profession or line of work is bound to become habitual and mechanical to an extent. This isn't necessarily bad; after all, habit may burden and deaden, but it is also essential. Without the regularities imposed by habit in personal as well as professional life, the stability that prevents us from going mad would disappear. In this sense, repetition, which seems to preclude development, is also its precondition. And the fact that lessons and ideas must be explained many times, either to the same or different audiences, does not necessarily mean that our explanations remain the same; they may change in all sorts of ways. With practice, there is an embroidering and elaboration of methods and concepts in some cases, a simplification and clarification of them in others. If we allow some material to become more automatic in expression, our energy and attention can be focused on material that is new or unexplored. Such an evolution, impossible without practice and repetition, that is, without the formation of habit, permits a refinement of instruction even while teachers may rightly feel that in some respects they parrot themselves.

> *Anything worth teaching is worth repeating.*

Moreover, isn't repetition as necessary for learning as for teaching? Unless what we have to say is trivial or already familiar to students, can we expect instant assimilation? Anything worth teaching is worth repeating.

Even the obvious is sometimes worth repeating. In the story "The Teacher of Literature," Chekhov portrays a geography teacher, Ippolit Ippolitich(!), who insists that his students repeatedly fill in maps with names and memorize important dates and who gives advice to the romantic if fuddled and slightly silly teacher of the story's title. But the literature teacher doesn't want to listen. Ippolit Ippolitich's advice, he says, is only stuff that "everyone already knows." Likewise, the geography teacher's classroom instruction is what "everyone already knows." But though everyone knows it, everyone does not know it really. So, for example, when Ippolit Ippolitich remarks to the young literature teacher (who is preparing to marry disastrously) that getting married is a serious step and that one ought to think about it before taking the plunge, the young man replies, in essence, "Yes, yes, of course!" The geography teacher, who dies before the literature teacher is able to learn what he needs from him, is developed by Chekhov not only as a model of a virtuous and so foolish-seeming teacher but also as the kind of poet or artist who explains, at personal risk, our "geography" and inevitably repeats himself and wants us to learn the most important lessons "by heart." So in this way teaching shares with other arts, with athletics, with the sciences, and with physical and psychological therapies the necessity for repetition.

Why, then, when I heard my child's fifth-grade teacher, was I so shocked by the fixities I observed in myself? Apparently (though how could this surprise?) teaching had engrossed me. A plumber's brusqueness or a salesperson's impulse to please, over time, gradually becomes a feature exhibited not only on the job but also in family life and on vacation; either the feature is absorbed into the self through a kind of osmosis or it results from the release in the self of a potential, among many, that gradually pushes aside competing possibilities. In the same way, the repetition inherent in the act of teaching, probably reinforced by the dramatic element so necessary to instruction, with time produces in the fifth-grade teacher—and in others, like me—a life of iterated performance that is not left behind when the class hour comes to an end. Being a teacher spills over. Now, for instance, when I read a book, I habitually ask myself not only what it has to say and whether it is intrinsically interesting but also whether I can use it in a class. I am offended and shocked by my own instrumental thinking, which over the years has become as mechanical as the way my child's teacher speaks to the parents of his students at an open house.

Indeed, not only do we grow into the role of teacher; the role grows into us. We *become* teachers.

This truism, of which I had somehow remained happily unaware, struck me all the more at the elementary school, accompanied as it was by a forcing sense of loss. The pain was familiar enough, felt since childhood, in school and out, and later in personal and romantic, political and professional life. This feeling of loss is a kind of sinking ache—but an ache tied vaguely to a thought or to the start of a thought. My painful sense of loss at the open house was only the emotional correspondent of learning, a subtractive process, one teachers as well as students naturally resist.

I reflected later that all I had learned about was loss. But in this I was mistaken. In the same erroneous way I had imagined memory being burned into a computer chip, only because that image conformed to my half-perceived needs at the time and to their context of experience. I wrongly saw only one side of habitual

thought and was appalled, considering repetition only in its most negative aspect, identifying it as burnout. In the mechanical responses of another teacher I could see an exhaustion that I experienced in myself. When I described what I had seen, my professional colleagues, fellow teachers, also saw burnout and its symptoms, though they preferred to restrict such automatic behavior to teachers at lower grade levels.

Unfortunately, I was also encouraged in this line of thought when I considered repetition from the standpoint of instinctual life. Didn't instincts express themselves precisely through repetition—and, if so, didn't the mechanization of response signify a loss of conscious direction, an abridgment of ourselves? Didn't such involuntary reactions (verbal but unthinking) undermine our most serious efforts in behalf of our students, namely, to get them to think? It was not hard to conclude that, like certain reluctant teachers Jonathan Kozol describes in *Savage Inequalities*, we also were doing—if unintentionally—more harm than good. Furthermore, as this behavior was nourished by the most deeply rooted impulses, we were helpless to stop it and, precisely because it was habitual, were largely unaware of it—until, by accident, something (a fifth-grade teacher, for example) enforced our attention. As I thought of Freud, a final and particularly distressing idea presented itself: I recalled from one of his later texts the thesis that alongside the instinct aiming toward pleasure (and life) was an ultimately stronger drive, one that expressed an even more vital biopsychological reality. Organic life was always trying to return to an earlier, inorganic state, that is, to reiterate a phase of existence prior to life itself. This built-in second instinct, toward death, at times might reinforce other instincts but finally overcame them all. So the burnout evident in repetition, which was bound to grow more insistent with time, signified a movement not only toward the end of a teaching career but also toward the end of the life on the back of which that career was borne.

Habit in any case must be too deeply embedded in the self for our practice as teachers to be independent of it. Perhaps, I mused, that was why so many in our profession searched so hard for new techniques of teaching, as if by altering the method of presentation we could avoid the repetitions that the complementary acts of instruction and learning demand. What did need to change, with the development of our various fields, was the subject matter, the content of our classes. Yet despite the search for novel approaches, there was a reluctance to alter content, not only because of the skepticism that usually greets the new, good or bad, and professional and personal investment in the older content, but also because the fondness in which we hold our present tastes and beliefs has itself become habitual—and nothing strengthens affection more than habit.

Even though now, on second thought, the necessary and creative aspects of repetition for teaching had become manifest, and the equation of burnout with habit no longer convinced, there remained the strength of automatic response and its capacity to overwhelm everything, including the introduction of new content. In addition, I could ignore neither the pain I'd experienced at the open house nor the feelings revealed on the faces of my fellow teachers when they heard my description of it. They had all been there, and more than once. There was a link between burning in and burning out, but the fear of the latter had led me to exaggerate the former and think of it in too one-sided a way.

It seemed to me that some element in my picture of the situation of teachers and of me as a teacher was missing. What did it mean to become exhausted *as a teacher*? If it wasn't merely that we repeated ourselves in classrooms—which we had to do, ought to do and which we certainly had been doing (if we were honest with ourselves) for years before we felt exhausted— then what did burning out mean?

While theoretically determined to track this meaning, I felt there was a kind of embarrassment attached to writing about exhaustion, as if the subject might be taken as a personal admission of failing powers. Would an administrator at my college view this essay as an oblique confession of professional inadequacy? Or, if burnout always pursues teachers into their second decade of professional work, would those with whom our representatives negotiate our contracts propose our salaries be discounted rather than raised with increased experience on the job? Then, too, my fellow teachers might object that writing about the subject of repetition could reinforce the prejudice of those in the public (and in school management) who secretly or openly believe that teachers don't really think, don't really work, and are uncreative. The voices in my imagination may have raised frivolous objections, but they nevertheless produced a certain resistance against which my thinking had to contend. At the same time, they suggested that the problem of repetition and burnout, while first appearing in a subjective register, could be viewed also from a broadly social or even economic standpoint.

I return to my experience in the fifth-grade classroom, which was so telling and from which I had learned so much already. The social material that had been obscure now appeared with skylike clarity. When I had described the performance of my child's teacher to my colleagues, they understood the problem immediately. Like laborers who work on the same project but who rarely meet, forgetting their commonality not only for that reason but also because of snobbishness (widespread in our profession, stratified as it is by educational levels), we easily overlook what we share. The only medium in which our labors combine is the students whom we share and who, in turn, share what they learn from us among themselves. But since we do not clearly see how our work is integrated within students into a deepening practice and sense of the world—an integration made possible only by the largely invisible efforts of many teachers (professional and otherwise)— the usefulness of that work often remains concealed from us.

The joint ideas of the usefulness of our individual labors and the invisible mingling of those labors, which make it hard for us to see our social relationships with one another, remind me strongly of passages in Marx's *Capital*. Marx suggests, on the one hand, that workers are unlikely to see the social relationships among them because, although they are brought together and coordinated by enormous productive systems, their only stake in those systems, the only economic reason they work, is their paychecks. On the other hand, Marx observes, when they look at the products of their collective labor, the price tags divert attention from the productive history of the commodities to their inert presence as consumer items. While workers are social beings connected to one another through shared labor, uninstructed workers are able to greet each other only through the medium of commodities, that is, through things. The infinitely dense expressions of value that their mutual efforts have produced remain as unknown to them as their lasting social intimacy.

Our useful labor as teachers, I thought, is embedded in other people; and so, to use Marx's terms, while we might not be misled by price tags, there are few opportunities for us to see the combined expression of our multiplied efforts. We may meet a former student and sense the influence of other teachers alongside our own; or we may discover in ourselves, by introspection, the many and several voices of former teachers; or we may find ourselves in someone else's classroom (say for

> *Our useful labor as teachers is embedded in other people.*

an open house) and glimpse this mutual effort, as I did, indirectly and by chance.

But why had my dawning recognition that the fifth-grade teacher and I shared a common effort seemed so negative? Why had it been accompanied by such a strong sense of loss? Was the reason only my subjective coloring of the episode? On reflection, this seemed improbable; the negativity was more likely a function of my misunderstanding of repetition. And wasn't the usefulness of what we did as teachers dependent on that very repetition, as Chekhov's Ippolit Ippolitich understood?

Then why would burning in be associated so strongly with loss?

Our usefulness as teachers is undoubtedly similar to the usefulness of other kinds of labor. In Marx's terms, this value is what workers sell to their employers in return for wages, the exchange value or the price of a worker's labor. But while exchange value indicates the quantitative relation between market items, use value is qualitative. Just as the use value of a pound of pasta is consumed by its purchasers, so the use value of labor power is handed over in exchange for wages and thus is consumed by *its* purchaser, the employer. But Marx notes that on a basic human level we also consume ourselves in the process of creating use value. Labor, for Marx, is one of the fundamental creative acts, but the laborer pays a price in its exercise. I wondered if burnout, then, as loss, might be merely the consumption of our human resources, as teachers, in creating useful values in our students. As teachers we labored as a group to embed useful value in our students. A fraction of the value of our effort was returned to us in the form of paychecks; another fraction was returned in learning and in the satisfaction of having enriched the lives and labor power of others.

But value was lost to us as well, twice. First, according to Marx, when our students' now-enriched labor power was traded to their employers for wages, our students' use value was greater than the wages they received. Thus our efforts to enhance our students' lives ended by disproportionately lining the pocketbooks of their employers. So instead of being able to turn around and (through taxes or other means) give back to us more of what we contributed to them, our students increased our loss through their own. Second, we simply used ourselves up on the job. And just as we returned to the job week after week, year after year, working on the same important lessons, so the lesson of this double loss was taught to us again and again.

I believe that we learn that lesson all too well and succeed at last in entering an almost seamless, claustrophobic, frightening, and apparently inescapable world, one that at first can be perceived only accidentally, indirectly, partially, as if it were some distant and exotic place light-years away and not the environment in which we find ourselves working and which is working in us: burning in us. Since in our repeated efforts to teach we harness so much of ourselves, working with such determination and sincerity, drawing so deeply on the memories, ingenuities, and drives we think of as ourselves, is it so surprising that the prospect of self-consumption, or burnout, looms so large in our imaginations or that it is connected so specifically to habits, the habits of work and the habits of submission?

Works Cited

Chekhov, Anton. "The Teacher of Literature." *Anton Chekhov's Short Stories*. Trans. Constance Garnett et al. Ed. Ralph Matlaw. New York: Norton, 1979. 109–28.

Freud, Sigmund. *Beyond the Pleasure Principle*. Ed. and trans. James Strachey. New York: Norton, 1975.

Kozol, Jonathan. *Savage Inequalities*. New York: Harper, 1991.

Marx, Karl. *Capital: A Critique of Political Economy*. Vol. 1. Trans. Ben Fowkes. New York: Vintage-Random, 1977.

English in a Postcolonial Situation: The Example of India

R. K. Gupta

The situation of English in India may be likened to that of a loving yet constantly bickering couple who can live neither with nor without each other. Such ambivalence may well be characteristic not only of India but also of other former British colonies, which seem riven by the conflict between the desire to retain English for its great utility in practical life and the emotional urge to discard it as a symbol and instrument of colonial oppression. An analysis of the way English has developed in India and fared since the end of colonial rule may yield useful insights into the problems and issues of English studies in the postcolonial situation.

I

The institutionalized study of English in India began, as is well known, with the 1835 Macaulay Minute on Education. Thomas Macaulay proclaimed that the only sensible educational policy for India would be to introduce Indians to European ideas and learning through the medium of English. Even before Macaulay's pronouncement, however, there had been a spontaneous and persistent demand from leaders of public opinion in India such as Rammohun Roy and Sir Syed Ahmed Khan for European sciences and knowledge in place of traditional learning. When early in the 1820s the government favored the idea of establishing a Sanskrit college, Rammohun Roy, himself a profound scholar in traditional Indian learning, protested strongly (301).

With the establishment of the three universities of Bombay, Madras, and Calcutta in 1857, English was formally introduced in the Indian educational curriculum. It is widely believed in India that the primary purpose of the British in introducing English was to train clerks for government offices, to produce senior minor functionaries who would fit smoothly and without friction in the intricate administrative machinery of the British government in India. To this day Indians find an easy scapegoat for many of their educational ills in what they regard as a baneful educational policy imposed on them by the British in days long past, a policy that, they argue, was designed to stifle creativity and promote uncritical subservience. However, the facts do not entirely bear this belief out. There is ample evidence to show that the British had, in addition to other possible motives, a genuine desire to disseminate modern knowledge in India and that they believed English to be the necessary instrument. Macaulay himself, with obvious sincerity, told the British Parliament in 1833:

> It may be that the public mind of India may expand under our system till it has outgrown that system; that by good government we may educate our subjects into a capacity for better government; that having become instructed by European knowledge, they may, in some future age, demand European institutions. Whether such a day will ever come, I know not. But never will I attempt to avert or retard it. Whenever it comes it will be the proudest day in English history.   (163)

II

Thus English was introduced in India with the lofty purpose of making accessible to Indians the knowledge and learning of modern Europe. However, three problems beset the teaching of English in India from the beginning, problems that have continued to affect the shape and direction of English studies in the country.

The first problem was the heavily literary bias in the way English was taught, even at the undergraduate level. Course texts for the BA and MA degrees at Bombay

The author is Professor of English at the Indian Institute of Technology in Kanpur.

University in the nineteenth century included Shakespeare's *Troilus and Cressida*, Hobbes's *Leviathan*, Locke's essays on tolerance and human understanding, Wordsworth's *Prelude*, Coleridge's *Aids to Reflection*, and Ruskin's lectures on architecture (Nagarajan 665). Undergraduates often lacked the linguistic competence to understand Shakespeare and Coleridge, to say nothing of being able to respond to them critically. But the teachers somehow assumed that undergraduates' knowledge of English was sufficient for studying the classics of English literature. There was hardly any methodical attempt to develop courses in English language, rhetoric, and composition. Even in courses devoted to the English language—often called general English courses—the texts were usually literary classics that required a high degree of sophistication in the use of English. The disparity between expectation and reality gave rise to heavy reliance on detailed paraphrase as the major classroom strategy. On examinations, students depended on rote memory to grapple with material only dimly understood. As recently as 1983–84, I faced a similar situation at the University of Ibadan, Nigeria, where I found myself teaching the convoluted prose of Jonathan Edwards in an American literature survey course, whose students were ill equipped linguistically to cope with such fare.

The second problem was that the study and teaching of English in India was conducted with little reference to the cultural background of the student. In 1869 Robert Napier, governor of Madras, was amused to hear Indian schoolboys reciting verses that celebrated "the beauty of the snowdrop, the comforts of the fireside, the affecting associations of the country churchyard" (qtd. in Nagarajan 667). In the early stages of English teaching, many of the teachers were Englishmen who taught literature to Indian undergraduates more or less as they would to undergraduates at a British university. Even when Indians took over as teachers of English, things did not change appreciably, and the same approach to teaching English language and literature continued.

The third problem was perhaps the most serious. The study of English in India was to some extent designed to help Indians understand and evaluate their own heritage more critically and interpret both that heritage to the West and the heritage of the West to their compatriots. The future of India, the Sadler Commission of Calcutta University (1917) said, depended on the creation of a new civilization harmoniously blending the best elements of Hindu, Islamic, and European civilizations (Nagarajan 665). Macaulay expressed the hope that English-speaking Indians would in turn refine and enrich the Indian languages to render them fit vehicles for conveying knowledge to the masses. However, the fact remains that English in India developed more or less independently of Indian languages and literatures, and without mutual interaction and enrichment. This led to the anomaly that the students received no introduction to their own cultural heritage, while the English cultural material they were offered was too remote from their experience for them to understand it or profit from it. Moreover, since knowledge of English was confined to a small number of people, the country became divided into an English-speaking elite and the non-English-speaking masses, with hardly a bridge between them. Thus, as Nagarajan remarks, if "the study of English literature brought about an intellectual revolution in the country," it was

> a palace revolution confined to a few intellectuals. The great mass of the people remained wholly unaffected. None of the new ideas of the West such as liberty of thought and expression, responsible and objective criticism, tolerance of different opinions, government by discussion, or the importance of the individual filtered down to the masses. (666)

III

The situation of English in India changed considerably, and predictably, after the end of colonial rule in 1947. The elevated status that English had enjoyed as the language of the rulers and consequently as the language of social and economic opportunity began to diminish. In some minds English became identified with colonial oppression and cultural invasiveness. It came under increasing attack, especially from three quarters—nationalists and cultural revivalists, intellectuals committed to postcolonial ideology, and politicians in search of populist vote-gathering slogans. The revivalists and the postcolonials, otherwise anathema to each other, came together in their attack on English and their support of nativism, which goes to show that it is not politics alone that makes strange bedfellows. Ironically, they often invoked the name of Mahatma Gandhi in support of their nativistic stance, forgetting, or perhaps not even knowing, that Gandhi had consistently advocated liberalism and cosmopolitanism in intellectual matters.

Two major arguments used against English were, first, that it symbolized the most exploitative aspects of colonialism and even now continued to be a means of intellectual and cultural enslavement, and second, that it retarded the growth of Indian languages (Viswanathan; Devy). These arguments were asserted with increasingly oracular self-assurance but usually with no supporting evidence. Neither seems to have much validity. That English has been and continues to be a means of intellectual enslavement seems hard to believe; many leading figures in the Indian freedom struggle had had an English education, and some, like Gandhi and Jawaharlal Nehru, actually studied in England and had thoroughly assimilated the philosophy of Western democratic liberalism, which they then proceeded to use in their arguments against the practice of British colonialism in India. Their knowledge of English enabled them to address an international audience and to gain international support for their cause and thus contributed in no small measure to the end of British rule in India. To that extent, the English language functioned in a self-subversive manner. As for the argument that English retarded the growth of Indian languages, the fact is that India's major languages are highly developed and expressive instruments, with rich and substantial literatures, especially those in Tamil, Hindi, Bengali, and Marathi. A number of leading writers in Indian languages have acknowledged having greatly profited from their extensive contact with English literature, whereas those Indian writers who have remained uncontaminated by English do not seem visibly enriched from that.

A crucial factor that distinguishes India from some other postcolonial countries is its multilingualism. In postindependence India, states were reorganized on a linguistic basis. At present there are more than a dozen major languages in India, each the primary language of at least one state, plus a great many dialects. Hindi, the national language, is spoken by less than half the people in the country. The language issue evokes high emotion, and political opportunism uses that emotion with devastating success. Nehru, India's first prime minister, stipulated that although Hindi would be the national language, English would continue as an "associate" language as long as non-Hindi-speaking states wanted it (which in effect meant indefinitely). People from the southern non-Hindi-speaking states use Nehru's assurance to support their demand that English continue as the medium of official communication. Many people in the north, which is the Hindi-speaking area, imperiously demand that English be replaced by Hindi at all levels of education and for communication between government agencies. The southern states, especially Tamilnadu, resist what they call the imposition of Hindi and demand an indefinite continuance of English. There have been riots in the north against the imposition of English. There have been matching riots in the south against the imposition of Hindi; in Tamilnadu angry young men have immolated themselves in

protest. It is a fact of life that often English is the only way an Indian from one linguistic region can communicate with an Indian from another.

Although in theory colleges and universities in India enjoy considerable autonomy, in practice the government often influences vital academic decisions. The governor of a state is usually also the chancellor of the universities in that state. The vice-chancellor, the highest officer in a university, is appointed by the government. Almost all higher education in India is heavily subsidized by the government through the University Grants Commission, the chairman and members of which are appointed by the government. There are government representatives on university decision-making bodies and on the boards of education that control primary and secondary education.

The importance of English in finding employment with the government has diminished somewhat. The Union Public Service Commission, the major recruiting agency for government jobs in India, has removed the required English essay from the prestigious Indian civil service examination, the candidates now having the option of writing the essay and of answering questions about various subjects in any of the major Indian languages. Most candidates, however, choose English for answering questions.

The language issue evokes high emotion, and political opportunism uses that emotion with devastating success.

Doctrinaire opposition to English gives rise to bizarre situations. Courts have ruled that candidates may submit their PhD dissertations in Hindi or other Indian languages but that such dissertations must be accompanied by an English translation to make possible their evaluation outside their linguistic region. The chief minister of the state of Bihar, finding that the students from his state (where English had been made optional) were faring poorly in competition with students from other states, made English a compulsory subject, only to rescind that order a few days later under political pressure. The theater of the absurd was rendered complete when a former prime minister and a former president of India took part in a sit-in against the use of English in civil service examinations.

There is enormous disparity in the level of English proficiency among the different states. In some states, the teaching of English begins early and is a requirement until graduation. In other states, English is only an elective subject that may be taken fairly late in secondary school. Students who enter a university, coming from schools in different states, may therefore have greatly different levels of competence in English.

The present state of English in India is an often confused and confusing product of the complex interaction of these political, economic, social, and cultural factors. When one surveys the situation, one cannot help being struck by its many paradoxes. There is considerable ambiguity in the policy regarding English, and there is a wide disparity between profession and practice. Malcolm Muggeridge noticed Indian parliamentarians denouncing English—in impeccable English. At a seminar on nativism held at my institute in January 1995 and sponsored by the Sahitya Akademi (the national academy of letters in India), the main thrust was anti-English, but all the speakers except one spoke in English, although almost all knew Hindi well. In politically engineered situations, rioters protest against the use of English while wearing English clothes and openly conversing in English. Knowledge of English is still indispensable to a higher education, English being the medium of instruction in colleges of engineering, medicine, law, and business. People secretly believe, if not openly say, that competence in English makes a considerable difference in their career prospects. Applications for employment are often in English, as are the interviews conducted to screen and select applicants. Parents feel that a degree in English improves the matrimonial prospects of their daughters; and, indeed, many matrimonial advertisements express open preference for girls educated in English-medium schools or having degrees in English. Politicians and bureaucrats denounce the elitism of such schools but surreptitiously send their children to them. The Chandla Committee, set up by the government, discovered in a recent poll conducted in Delhi—as reported in the *Hindustan Times* by Rakshat Puri—that "most people [61%] preferred English as the first language" and wanted it also to be the language of instruction. The committee wryly remarked: "It is ironical that despite so much hue and cry having been raised by the Government about scrapping English [in primary schools], people prefer the language to any other. Because, after all, even a rickshaw puller would like his children to learn English" (Puri). Puri added, "Presumably, the Chandla Committee's findings . . . reflect to some extent opinion all over the country." An editorial in the same newspaper about two weeks later commented:

> The tendency among many State governments to view
> English as a foreign curse which should be got rid of at the

earliest, is unfortunate. Perhaps the only benefit which the country has gained from British rule is the English language which is also the main international language. . . . There is no rationale behind the argument that the way to develop Indian languages is to reduce the importance of English in day-to-day administration, education, business and trade.

> ("Why This Haste?")

A *Times of India* editorial had this to say about the quest for nativism:

> This obsession with roots is an absurdity in a sub-continent that has millennially witnessed an incessant circulation of populations. Along pilgrim trails and trade routes, goaded by invasion or inspired by faith, communities have moved from region to region, taking their customs, folklore and totems with them. In a tradition that has been as open to transformations as ours, it is wings rather than roots that signify a living culture. The sole item on the nativist menu, by contrast, is an unchanging cultural self, believed to lie buried like a tuber beneath the topsoil of foreign influence. While the project of digging for lost tubers may keep the ideological pot boiling, it generates an extremely constricting aesthetic.   ("Recipes")

(A similar paradox: In Nigeria and Kenya, opposition to English by a group of young writers seeking "decolonization" of African literature [Gerard 49–50] has coexisted with a blithe acceptance of English by the educated public.)

Thus mired in uncertainty and controversy, the teaching of English in India lacks a sense of direction. The confusion regarding the role of English is reflected in the way it is taught. Because students with widely varying backgrounds and competence in English enter the universities and are herded together in a single classroom, courses in English are geared to those at the lowest level and so tend to be repetitive and circular rather than sequential and progressive. The labors of English teachers thus often take on a Sisyphean character.

IV

Lest readers should mistakenly assume that the situation of English in India is one of unrelieved gloom, let me now introduce a cheery note and deal with some heartening developments that have taken place in the field of English in postcolonial India.

To begin with, repeated attacks on English by nationalists and others have induced a certain amount of self-criticism and introspection among English teachers. Since teachers can no longer take the importance of English for granted, they are now forced to define their goals with clarity and precision and to show a greater sense of accountability to society at large instead of seeking shelter behind the jargon that professionals sometimes use to escape critical scrutiny of their efforts by independent agencies.

The debate regarding the status of English in post-colonial India has also produced awareness of the different functions English must perform for different categories of people. The teaching of English is thus no longer identified solely with the teaching of English literature; the usefulness of other, less literary approaches is being recognized. A number of newly established English language institutes have identified the needs of English students in India and developed specialized programs consistent with those needs, such as the Teaching of English as a Foreign/Second Language, English for Special Purposes, Business English, Communicative English, and so on. However, some language enthusiasts have perhaps gone too far, seeking to banish from English courses not only unsuitable literary texts but all literary texts, substituting for them expository writing that students often find uninspiring and even insipid. This excess has invited a kind of backlash, so that English teachers in India are frequently divided into two camps, the literary camp and the language camp. Here is how V. V. John, an exponent of the literary approach, reacts to the language camp: "If our language studies are divorced from the joy of learning, . . . the end product of our exertions will be scholars obsessed by the mechanics of language, or inclined to get their thinking bogged down in verbalism" (12). John remarks a little earlier, "May be, all that the new gospel of the 'tool' aims at is to take the joy out of learning the language, and give us the illusion that the residual product is highly technical and businesslike" (10).

V

I have shared with you some facts and reflections about the teaching of English in India in the hope that the problems, issues, and developments described here may have parallels and analogies, or at least some remote applications, in other countries where English is not the native language but is nevertheless used extensively for a variety of purposes, especially in those countries that, like India, have a long history of British colonial rule. What conclusions may be drawn from this study?

The first is the sad and stern truth, which may seem too obvious to need spelling out but which academics often refuse to take into account or a least to act on, that political and economic factors play a decisive role in controlling the language-study situation in a country. These factors include not only consciously designed policies but also such adventitious developments as regional rivalries and public opinion. It would be well if we framed the policies and programs of English studies not, of course, in expedient response to these factors but at least with an awareness of them.

The second conclusion is that it is necessary to distinguish the various needs that English must fulfill in a particular community and to design programs and courses accordingly. This again may seem obvious, but it is not something that English teachers usually keep in mind and act on. In India, for a very long time the teaching of English had a predominantly literary character, and there was little attempt to devise language courses suitable for those whose interests were not literary. Although literature can certainly play a useful role in teaching a language, perhaps the bias, approach, and selection of texts, even of literary texts, should be somewhat different in courses where the primary purpose is to teach language skills, not to cultivate literary and critical acumen.

The teaching of English in complete isolation from native languages is a mistake.

The third conclusion is that the teaching of English in complete isolation from native languages is a mistake. Since mastering a new language is a difficult task not easily accomplished by everyone, the use of that new language as the medium of instruction at the outset encourages emphasis on rote memory and can lead to intellectual sterility. Although the Sadler Commission believed that the use of English in India was indispensable, it still considered the native language to be of primary importance.

The fourth and final conclusion is that the teaching of English literature in isolation from a student's cultural and social context can be unproductive. Although the study of a foreign literature is a possible means of expanding mental and emotional horizons, one's appreciation of that literature depends on the depth and range of one's experience. Teaching literary material that is remote from students' experience without necessary adjustments and modifications is not likely to produce happy results. It is therefore desirable to seek links and relations, either as parallels or as contrasts, between the foreign literature and native contexts. In India not only were teachers of English often ignorant of Indian literature, but many of them actually disfavored the use of Indian examples and illustrations. The situation is changing now, fortunately, and teachers of English literature have begun to realize the desirability of introducing Indian social and cultural material in their courses. However, there is need for closer cooperation between English and the Indian languages. John remarks:

> The fences that separate English from the Indian languages departments in our universities have promoted neither good neighbourliness nor the ends of scholarship. This segregation would partly explain the arid and pretentious pursuits of the English faculty and the resentful narrowness of certain Indian language departments. If the fences of segregation came down, English might be able to render to India's education somewhat of the service it failed to do all these years.   (15)

What sort of future might one envisage for English in India and in other postcolonial countries? It seems to me that despite the many vicissitudes it has undergone, English will continue not only to survive but also to flourish in these countries, for a variety of reasons, although it will inevitably be shorn of some of its former glamour and cultural snobbery. The ambivalence toward English and the anti-English sentiments expressed in muted or strident form are usually confined to a small vocal minority and by no means represent the views of society at large. The war cries against English are often strategic and expedient rather than sincere and consistent. Expressing anti-English sentiments can promote academic cronyism and make a person part of an influential network, a beneficiary of the largesse the network can offer. Even English teachers, in a bizarre act of self-flagellation, can be seen crying themselves hoarse in denouncing English. A seasoned colleague of mine believes that it is much easier to get published if one expresses anti-English views than otherwise.

But the widespread functional utility of English as a means of international communication, of communication between different linguistic regions within a country, and of access to modern knowledge in almost all branches of learning will ensure the continuance of English in India and, I believe, in other postcolonial societies. There is, however, another—and to my mind equally important, if less visible—use of English. It involves employing English as what John calls a precision instrument. "There is," says John, "a larger illiteracy than the inability to read and write. It consists of the inability to tell the important from the trivial, the genuine from the spurious, the noble from the ignoble, or in other words, lack of precision and discrimination" (15). By being an effective instrument in combating this larger illiteracy, English will continue to make an enormously valuable contribution in the postcolonial situation.

Works Cited

Devy, Ganesh. *After Amnesia: Tradition and Change in Indian Literary Criticism.* Bombay: Orient Longman, 1992.

Gerard, Albert S. "Literary Tradition and Literary Change in Black Africa." *Journal of Commonwealth Literature* 19 (1984): 44–51.

John, V. V. "The Uses of English." Presidential address at the Eighteenth Annual Session of the All-India English Teachers' Conference. Chandigarh, Dec. 1967.

Macaulay, T. B. *Speeches, Corrected by Himself.* London, 1854.

Nagarajan, S. "The Decline of English in India: Some Historical Notes." *College English* 43 (1981): 663–70.

Puri, Rakshat. "Indian English and Babu English." *Hindustan Times* 1 Feb. 1995: 13.

"Recipes for Writing." Editorial. *Times of India* 18 Jan. 1995: 11.

Roy, Rammohun. "Letter to His Excellency the Right Hon'ble William Pitt, Lord Amherst, in December 1823." *Selected Works.* Delhi: Publications Div., Govt. of India, 1977. 301.

Viswanathan, Gauri. *Masks of Conquest: Literary Study and British Rule in India.* New York: Columbia UP, 1989.

"Why This Haste?" Editorial. *Hindustan Times* 17 Feb. 1995: 13.

Teaching Old English in the Next Millennium: Why? And How?

M. J. Toswell

The study of early medieval vernacular texts in England is divided with remarkable precision into two camps. One refers to the subject as Old English; the other refers to the subject as Anglo-Saxon. At the University of Oxford, the home of Old English, every first-year undergraduate learns a selection of texts and at the end of the year sits the six examinations known as Honour Moderations, one of which is Old English translation and critical commentary and one of which is Old English literature (with an optional third in Old English for those who so desire). The set texts remain largely those that appear in Henry Sweet's *Anglo-Saxon Reader*, first published in 1876 and revised extensively in 1967 by Dorothy Whitelock. As part of the Finals, exams that are the sole determiners of the quality of degree granted to an Oxford BA candidate, students sit a paper on the history, theory, and use of the language, and they have the option of papers in Old English. Oxford undergraduates also have the option of pursuing Course II, whose papers are primarily medieval and philological—including such titles as Middle English Dialectology, Modern English Philology, Old English Literature and Its Background, Gothic, and so forth. Traditionally, at Oxford the study of Old English has been the purview of the Faculty of English Language and Literature, which has grounded itself in a historical and literary consideration of texts. The principal figurehead in the modern generation of this uneasy housing of both Lang. & Lit. was J. R. R. Tolkien, who as Merton Professor of English Literature was involved in the last major overhaul of the syllabus.[1] At Oxford, then, the subject is carefully entitled Old English in an attempt to provide a sense of linguistic continuity, a modicum of historical grounding, a soupçon of literary linkage, and a dash of genealogical origin to the subject.

That sense of continuity, modicum of history, soupçon of literature, and dash of origin grubbing is, as any student of the subject is well aware, largely spurious.

An Old English elegy like *The Wanderer* or *The Seafarer* bears little resemblance to Milton's "Lycidas" and less to Gray's "Elegy." Over the years *Beowulf* has been described as a national epic, a folk epic, a series of lays, a mirror for princes, a Christian saint's life, a set of monster tales, a heroic-elegiac lament—and it has been shoehorned into several other genres as well. It is, of course, none of the above; we are applying nineteenth- and twentieth-century constructions that are not appropriate to a literature for which no manuals of composition, no evaluative considerations, no literary reviews survive. And, when we teach Old English literature, several texts we include as basic to the canon are just translations. Were the same texts taught in a twentieth-century course, we would demand reasons why the texts were not being read in the original. Bede's Latin writings, as they were translated two and a half centuries after his death, remain the canonical texts by which we introduce our students to the conversion to Christianity of Anglo-Saxon England (the story of King Eadwine, including the famous simile of the sparrow and the hall) and by which we introduce—also using an argument that embraces the notion of origins—our version of the translator's version of Bede's version of vernacular poetry and its first harnessing to the exposition of Christian doctrine: the story of Caedmon. In short, much as we like to pretend otherwise and much as we argue otherwise, our students—and even some of our colleagues—fail to see a deep-seated link between Old English and later periods of English literature, later styles of writing, even later contexts within which literature is produced.

The author is Associate Professor of English at the University of Western Ontario.

The second paradigm acknowledges this difficulty explicitly, by separating the field from the world of English and establishing it in a ghetto of its own. At the University of Cambridge this paradigm is the standard. While Old English, now called Anglo-Saxon, is available as an option to students sitting the tripos in the Department of English, those seriously interested in the subject enroll in the Department of Anglo-Saxon, Norse, and Celtic. Thus Anglo-Saxon is in the title of the department, recognized as one of three languages current in northern Europe in the early medieval period. There is no continuity even between Anglo-Saxon and Middle English, which resides over in the Department of English, where its name, Middle *English*, marks it as the source of modern English poetry and justifies the oft-repeated description of Chaucer as the father of English poetry. Students of early medieval literature must enroll either in the Department of English, where they will be trained in literature from the fourteenth century onward and will have to reach backward on their own, with tutorials in one optional paper on the earlier period; or they must enroll in the Department of Anglo-Saxon, Norse, and Celtic (which until about twenty years ago was simply the Department of Anglo-Saxon), where perforce they will be trained in medieval Latin, history, Anglo-Saxon, Old Norse, medieval Welsh, early Irish, some archaeology, and so forth. Should a student in the Department of Anglo-Saxon, Norse, and Celtic wish to study English literature later than 1500, that is not possible. Further, should a student in this program express a desire to study literature exclusively, that desire can be satisfied only through a study of literature in not one but at least three early medieval languages.

The second paradigm in many ways comes close to the view held of Old English/Anglo-Saxon by scholars of early medieval history, patristic studies, medieval Latin, and paleography. The study of the vernacular literature of early medieval England is seen by them as a very minor offshoot of the immense Latin culture of the early Middle Ages, an offshoot that because of misplaced English and American patriotism has already received far more attention than necessary. It deserves no more consideration than does Old Saxon, Old Gothic, or Old High German. Such a sweeping condemnation, however phrased, attempts to return the study of Old English literature to its very small place in the world of medieval studies as broadly defined. It argues that the place carved out for that study, certainly at Oxford and perhaps even at Cambridge, is an unnecessarily large one. And it follows what I have been suggesting is the second paradigm, which argues that Anglo-Saxon can be studied only in the context of many other medieval disciplines and, more, that it is a minor study. This is a common argument, but it remains a terribly wrong argument and a terribly damaging one. Old Saxon survives only in a few texts and notably a translation of the gospel known as *The Heliand*; Old Gothic in some Bible translations; Old High German in a few fragments, some glosses, and passages of poetry, notably the *Hildebrandslied* and Otfrid's life of Christ. These are the only texts that correspond in date to the large corpus of Old English literature. Surviving from the vernacular material written in England before 1100 are 30,000 lines of poetry; about ten times that much of prose, predominantly homilies and didactic material propounding Christian doctrine; about 300,000 marginal and interlinear glosses to Latin texts; and other miscellaneous texts, including runic epigrams and carvings. This is neither a slight nor an unimportant literature. Further, dismissing it insists on the primacy of medieval studies more generally and does so to the detriment not just of vernacular literatures but also of the wider field. The study of Old English literature in an undergraduate course remains the gateway for many senior students of medieval studies.

Until now, the argument for the importance of Old English/Anglo-Saxon has been relatively easy to make, because the subject has been taught in enough places, and there has been space in the field to permit the Old English/Anglo-Saxon dichotomy without fear that it would work in the direction of the divide-and-conquer principle of destroying an area. Now, however, the field is, or is about to be, under the most sustained attack it has ever faced. The preliminary salvos have already been fired, and the extent to which this subject will be taught in the next millennium is very much in doubt.

According to my construction of the problem, there is a disagreement inside the subject about where this vernacular literature fits in the university curriculum and, by extension, in the world of scholarly studies. Is the subject really Old English, part of a continuum with modern English? If so, scholars of the subject belong in English departments, equipped with the wide-ranging historical and theoretical knowledge of that discipline. However, the study of Old English/Anglo-Saxon has been marginalized by the mainstream world of English studies; it has also, perhaps defensively and perhaps not, acquiesced to that marginalization. When the MLA bibliography project was bruited in the late 1960s and early 1970s, Old English scholars chose not to participate. Partly out of a just sense that the MLA bibliography would not include many of the papers and monographs necessary for Anglo-Saxon studies and partly out of a sense of annoyance that the MLA was turning still farther away from its origins as a philologically based group, the Old English division withdrew—and largely exempted itself from involvement in the MLA as well as in the MLA bibliography.

In 1972, two influential periodicals appeared: the *Old English Newsletter* (loosely associated with the MLA and published mostly in Binghamton, New York) and *Anglo-Saxon England* (Cambridge Univ. Press). The editors of these journals and a collection of other scholars of the subject assembled in Ghent in 1983 for the first bi-annual meeting of the International Society of Anglo-Saxonists. ISAS today has nearly six hundred members around the world, but they include only two members of the Faculty of English at Oxford. The reason for this lack of support for ISAS, in my view, is that ISAS propounds a view of Anglo-Saxon studies that is a holistic one—not one based on the language and literature of early medieval England. It perceives the subject of our study as the whole range of social, historical, and cultural issues that can be examined with respect to Anglo-Saxon England. This commitment to interdisciplinary studies and to knowledge of a wide range of fields in medieval studies has great merit, but the notion of teaching and studying Anglo-Saxon in this way also places the subject in great jeopardy by failing to anchor it firmly in a discipline.

All this, of course, is something of a prolegomenon to my principal argument: why and how we should and will teach Old English in the next millennium in departments of English. First is the argument traditionally made for learning a foreign language or studying comparative literature: to place our own culture in any kind of context, we need a sense that is more than superficial of at least one other culture. Second is the standard justification for the study of history: to understand the issues of today, we must consider the issues—and literature—of yesterday. Third: students of English literature should be more than just aware of the existence of Old English literature, since it provides them with both a detailed study of some specific texts and a sense of the rich historical tradition that is literature. It is frightening that the actual facts of these issues are not even a part of the public record and that when a governance structure or societal condition is particularly rigid or wrong, it is described, almost automatically, as "positively medieval." So it seems to me crucial that we avoid creating students whose knowledge of literature in English is "positively modern": the most effective antidote to that disease remains an intensive study of the earliest English literature.

Fourth: Old English literature is now one of those rare subjects in which students concentrate on a small number of texts and study one, *Beowulf,* for most of a term. In an honors English program there is a great benefit to a course that studies something in detail, providing material in small bites and with frequent tests. Fifth is an argument that turns back on itself like the Worm Ouroboros: students cannot learn Old English literature without learning something about the social, historical, and cultural context of that literature. Allen Frantzen sees Old English courses as only putatively intertextual and argues that the only real future for Old English studies is as a part of the new world of cultural studies. Unable to withstand the agenda of cultural studies, English departments will in his view transmogrify. My view is both more and less sanguine: English departments are resilient entities and will absorb and adapt, but one of the more likely methods of

> *Students of English literature should be more than just aware of the existence of Old English literature.*

adaptation will include a further telescoping of Old English with Middle English with early modern English. Sixth is the argument thought by some to be the most powerful: language. The belief that in an honors program students need at least one course that focuses their attention on details of the language makes a medieval course still a requirement in many universities. Seventh is the somewhat odd argument that the study of Anglo-Saxon already makes use of modern technology, and our students need knowledge of technology.[2] It seems very likely to me that within two or three years computers will be an ordinary and necessary part of the teaching of Old English. Students enrolling in a course in Old English will find that they have instant access to the most recent technologies of textual manipulation and computer-learning techniques.

Eighth and last: there is the sheer satisfaction of comprehending this difficult literature and enjoying its complexity. At the beginning of each undergraduate course, I argue with some passion that if the literature that survives from the Anglo-Saxon period were boring or simple or uninteresting, then the subject would rightly become a curiosity only occasionally taught. Old English literature, however, is extraordinary and sophisticated stuff. It is a part of the ordinary study of English literature precisely because it is literature of the highest order.

To that end, I have four predictions to make about the way in which Old English/Anglo-Saxon will be taught in the next millennium. The subject belongs, I believe, in an English department as much as any other era, genre, or approach does. At the same time, the way it has been taught does not reflect that belonging, nor has the subject sufficiently adapted itself to the late twentieth century. My discussion about the pedagogy of Old English therefore addresses the influence of technology, the question of the canon, the shift in methods of teaching, and the shift in presentation.

> *We habitually teach Old English in a woefully out-of-date way.*

Over the next few years, it seems reasonable to expect that Anglo-Saxon scholars will continue to lead the field in creating home pages on the World Wide Web, in making a wide variety of materials available to scholars, and in adding more and more manuscript material to the file transfer protocol sites already available on the Internet. Anglo-Saxonists have been traveling this highway for well over a decade. The trend in the direction of hypermedia editions is irreversible in this subject, and rightly so, though hypermedia will not replace the teacher or paper materials in the way some anticipate. In the short term, some humanities students will need encouragement to benefit from these new technologies of learning; not long from now, our students will be wondering why we are not more computer-based in our teaching.

On the question of the canon, the issue of Old English as opposed to Anglo-Saxon remains relevant. Textbooks commonly reflect the current state of play in a subject, simplifying it and coordinating it for the sake of students. The current state of play in Anglo-Saxon studies bases itself on the consideration of a very few prose texts, four lyric poems, and *Beowulf.* All the textbooks available subscribe to this notion of Old English as a language to be learned quickly in order to get the student into the great lyric and heroic poems of the period. Worse, they point the student in the direction of the heroic code and force the impression that the world was an ugly and brutal place, filled with hazards and leavened only by the occasional statement of eternal loyalty, the odd oath of allegiance, and the opportunity to die gloriously in battle. This perspective produces scholars interested largely in the supposedly pagan and heroic culture of Anglo-Saxon England, scholars who are then somewhat bemused by the overwhelming evidence for a culture both Christian and sophisticated—sophisticated not just in the production of poetry but in the development of laws, of rules for land tenure, of wills and charters, of penitentials and rules for ordinary behavior. Further, this culture was bilingual, and its well-educated were comfortable writing in either Latin or the vernacular. The evidence suggests that the laity were not entirely ignorant of Latin tags, and that they demanded translations of important liturgical and doctrinal texts for their own use. New textbooks must try more accurately to reflect the cultural and historical world of Anglo-Saxon England in choice of texts and in method of presenting material.

Our teaching of the subject can no longer afford to result in attitudes such as those Wayne Booth must have, to judge from his dismal recollections of his required Old English course (943–44). We habitually teach Old English in a woefully out-of-date way, with a ferocious introduction to the language organized and intended to be memorized in the same fearsome paradigms and conjugations as were used to teach Latin throughout the nineteenth century and the first half of the twentieth. Latin teaching gave up that frightening technique, the bedazzle-'em-with-the-declensions school of teaching, about forty years ago. Old English, however, continues to employ this approach, except in a very few universities that use custom-published texts. Further, a course that provides as its introductory texts short passages translated from the Bible and therefore requires of its students a detailed knowledge of the Christian scriptures seems doomed in the present day. The standard approach to Old English involves giving an extended grammar, some material about sound changes and word formation, some short sentences, a set of representative prose texts, and some longer poetic texts. The most difficult shift is that between the relatively simple, because logical, prose and the far more complex and sophisticated word orders and vocabulary of the poetry. As the material is presented in most courses, the students have to make links themselves and to figure out not only the material but also how to study it. Students at the end of the twentieth century rarely know any Latin, and what knowledge they have of the procedures for studying a foreign language is often sketchy. They need a friendlier and more helpful presentation of texts, and they need shorter texts for the first stages of their study.

The presentation of the texts thus needs substantial revision. At the moment, the standard approach is a rather fearsome one, involving long paragraphs of Old

English with brief headnotes, textual apparatus flourishing at the foot of the page, annotations and explanations hidden by a difficult referencing system near the end of the book, and a comprehensive glossary at the end. The print is generally so small that no ordinary student can fit in interlinear glosses as a translation aid, and the margins are too small to accommodate any significant annotation or commentary. All in all, the layouts are ideal for the prevention of learning the language or enjoying the literature. We need, then, nonthreatening ways to present the texts we choose to include in the canon.

Let me conclude with a couple of caveats and acknowledgments of how I have presented the facts selectively in this discussion. First, the controversy that swirled recently in the Oxford Faculty of English concerning the compulsory teaching of Old English is well known (for summaries and discussion, see Jackson; Simpson). Less well known, perhaps, is that a subcommittee of the faculty duly revised the curriculum, which was voted on in the summer of 1994—but that the proposed changes did not receive enough votes from the faculty members to be put in place. Once all the smoke cleared and the faculty was left alone to decide, there was no will to change. This appears a wonderfully optimistic result, although a resounding no vote might have been more decisive. However, over the past three years the complement of Anglo-Saxonists with fellowships or lectureships at Oxford has fallen to an all-time low. The only permanent posts held by experts in the area are three: two (both within reach of retirement) plus the Rawlinson and Bosworth Professor, whose post requires only lectures and supervision of graduate students, not undergraduate tutorials. One Celticist, one readership in Old Norse, one five-year appointment, and two graduate students or former graduate students round out the teaching complement; but these are people for whom either this subject is not central or the post is temporary. The rest of the teaching of Anglo-Saxon at Oxford is done by Middle English specialists (eighteen) or specialists in the history of the language (about four). There are now more recently retired people in Old English than there are permanent members of the faculty who specialize in that subject. Because the teaching of Old English became a national issue, the situation is critical not just at Oxford, where colleges have often appointed fellows in other areas, with only short-term posts for the teaching of Old English, but elsewhere in England, at universities that preserve the same historical focus. This means that the Cambridge paradigm may prove triumphant, pushing Anglo-Saxon out

of English departments and into interdisciplinary departments like those of classical and medieval studies that already exist at a number of Canadian and American universities.

For the first time in its century-long history, the study of English will in the next few years be compressing another century into its curriculum. There will be some who argue that Old and Middle English should include the sixteenth and seventeenth centuries as well and that lately the eighteenth and nineteenth centuries have been acknowledged as having unexpected common territory—in order to make room in the academic timetable for a wide selection of twentieth-century literatures. My incipient paranoia is not entirely unfounded, because the subject in which I teach and learn remains the least understood subject in an English department. This lack of understanding worries me greatly, especially because my paper is probably exhorting the converted—and those already converted do not deserve such apocalyptic and evangelistic rhetoric. So I close by noting that attacks on Old English/Anglo-Saxon have come before and are always (in the view of some) being made and that the only good response remains the refrain from the Old English poem *Deor*:

Þæs ofereode; þisses swa mæg.[3]

Notes

I am grateful to Mary Blockley, M. S. Griffith, L. C. Mugglestone, and E. G. Stanley for reading and commenting on this paper; the errors remaining are mine.

[1]For a brief discussion, see Carpenter 136–46.

[2]Students of Old English already have the option of buying and studying a grammar published by the *Old English Newsletter* as its Subsidia 21 (Hieatt). But this is only the beginning. Pages of the *Beowulf* manuscript were recently uploaded to an FTP site by the British Library; not only are these a great resource for the study of the manuscript itself but also they show the future of Old English studies—a future in which libraries steadily make more material available online. The Oxford Text Archive has several thousand authors and texts available; its most frequent order, outselling the Shakespeare corpus by a factor of three, is for the corpus of Old English. Patrick Conner, the guru on the online computer discussion group AnSaxNet, has a *Beowulf* workstation almost complete, by means of which undergraduate students at the University of West Virginia will be able to learn the poem at their own pace. Several short lyrics have been edited, some with hypermedia techniques, others not. Peter Baker's edition of "Wulf and Eadwacer" is available by gopher at the AnSaxDat archive, and Allen Frantzen has a more extensive project focusing on *The Seafarer* in Chicago. Most recently, the Oxford Computing Service has published a hypertext version of *The Dream of the Rood*.

[3]Usually translated, somewhat loosely, as "That has passed by; so may this."

Works Cited

Booth, Wayne. "Where Have I Been, and Where Are 'We' Now, in This Profession?" *PMLA* 109 (1994): 941–50.

Carpenter, Humphrey. *J. R. R. Tolkien: A Biography*. London: Allen, 1977.

The Dream of the Rood. Ed. Nicola Timbrell and David Snowling. Oxford: Oxford Univ. Computing Services, Information Tech. Training Initiative, 1994.

Frantzen, Allen J. *Desire for Origins: New Language, Old English, and Teaching the Tradition*. New Brunswick: Rutgers UP, 1990.

Hieatt, C. B., B. Shaw, and O. D. Macrae-Gibson. *Beginning Old English*. *Old English Newsletter*, subsidia 21. Book and diskette. Binghamton: Center for Medieval and Early Renaissance Studies, 1994.

Jackson, Peter. "The Future of Old English: A Personal Essay." *Old English Newsletter* 25 (1992): 24–28.

Simpson, James. "The Enjoyment and Teaching of Old and Middle English: The Current State of Play." *Old English Newsletter* 25 (1992): 29–31. Rpt. of *Cue News: The Newsletter of the Council for University English* 4.2 (1992): 3–5.

Sweet, Henry. *Sweet's Anglo-Saxon Reader in Prose and Verse*. 15th ed. Rev. Dorothy Whitelock. Oxford: Clarendon, 1967.

The Profession and the National Education Scene: A Collaborative Model

Edward J. Ahearn and Arnold Weinstein

Recent issues of *Profession*, sessions at MLA conventions, and a report of the American Comparative Literature Association have resonated with the concerns of the canon debate, the culture wars, and multiculturalism, not to speak of the discrepancy between PhD research training and the actual conditions of college teaching, and—inevitably amid all this—the future of doctoral programs.[1]

While such concerns are certainly justified, the association has not given much thought to the connection between these university issues and the larger picture, a picture that foregrounds the growing public worry about the American K–12 educational system, including the role played in it, or conspicuously not played in it, by higher education. Indeed, judging by the paucity of attention secondary education receives in our scholarly and professional discussions, we appear to regard our most engrossing professional problems as unrelated to the general education scene. That there might be a relation between our disciplinary practice and our high schools is a question too often either begged or ignored, even though there is much talk outside the academy about the school reform movements sweeping the country. Is it important for us in the academy, as we reexamine our disciplinary and professional roles, to start thinking more broadly about the educational communities in which we live? At what point does this thinking move beyond civic-mindedness and social responsibility and actually affect our teaching and writing, the training of graduate students, and our professional agendas?

This essay posits a simple and urgent answer to these questions: our profession needs to be involved in the education reform movement, and the time is now. The positive vision described here has grown out of the experience the Department of Comparative Literature at Brown University has had in working with several regional high schools.

Comparative literature departments seem a natural base for outreach efforts because they are (or should be) at the hub of a university's language and literature programs. They often bring together programs in traditional fields, such as classics, and in more recently developed areas, such as women's studies. They usually include both Western and other languages, foster interdisciplinary pursuits, and facilitate team-teaching. These factors have helped the Department of Comparative Literature at Brown—where we have a small PhD program and a large undergraduate program with many majors and high enrollments—to play a role in the educational community outside the university that elsewhere has been played by English departments.

We have had the advantage of working with Brown University's Institute for Secondary Education and with Theodore Sizer, a leading education reformer and the author of *Horace's Compromise: The Dilemma of the American High School* and *Horace's School: Redesigning the American High School*. Sizer's Coalition of Essential Schools, founded in 1984, assists schools that are willing to accept certain procedures and principles: assign teachers a reasonable number of pupils; utilize team-teaching; provide blocks of teaching time that fit the subjects being taught, in place of the typical succession of short class periods punctuated by bells and drills; design courses to accomplish specific goals; and measure students' success by demonstrations or performances.

The authors are, respectively, University Professor and Edna and Richard Salomon Distinguished Professor of Comparative Literature at Brown University.

When the Department of Comparative Literature proposed a great books initiative to the National Endowment for the Humanities, it did so with an eye toward expanding the canon in the college curriculum and also with an interest in employing comparative approaches to literature in a university–high school collaboration. The department therefore titled its three NEH proposals "The Great Books Then and Now," "Texts and Teachers: Themes in Comparative Literature," and "Texts and Teachers: The Interdisciplinary Challenge." These programs bring college professors into high school classrooms and high school students into college classrooms. By creating joint courses for two institutional audiences, we believe we have fostered a dialogue that can lead to changes in both high school and college classrooms and challenge some of the presuppositions that have shaped those classrooms.

The courses we organized used, for example, Greek, Chinese, and Western medieval and modern texts about the experience of growing up in different cultures, giving attention to issues of gender and class; works by Paul, Pascal, Kierkegaard, and Kafka on questions of representation, truth, and belief in the fields of literature, philosophy, and religion; and works by Ovid, Du Fu, and modern Western writers on the physical, political, and psychological dimensions of displacement and the role of "originary" languages.

These courses and others developed as part of the project were international and interdisciplinary. They were also thematically organized, treating issues of significance to human beings of all ages. Throughout, we tried to show how the study of literature sheds light on social, ethical, and political issues of the present and the past.

The courses were team-taught, usually by groups of four faculty members specializing in comparative literature, classics, English, French studies, Afro-American studies, East Asian studies, religious studies, political science, public policy, and medicine. This range was possible because joint appointments are common in the Department of Comparative Literature, and Brown University encourages interdisciplinary ventures. Another crucial feature of the NEH-funded courses has been the requirement that all faculty members teach all the materials in the courses—so that an Africanist discovers how relevant *Moll Flanders* is to an Africanist's concerns; so that a comparative literature teaching assistant and a medical student teach both Kafka and scientific articles on addiction; so that a professor of public policy and his students can see, to the surprise of both, the close link between Brecht's expressionist *Jungle of Cities* and the problems of the "underclass" treated by

social scientists. Begun as part of a grant program, the courses are all now part of the regular Brown curriculum; thousands of students from a wide variety of fields (including the social and life sciences) have taken them. We are working with humanistic materials, but we are reaching new audiences.

And that is where the major innovation of this ambitious program is located: we elected to redefine, radically, the population that both takes and teaches these new courses, by forming a partnership with a number of regional high schools, so that the courses could be taught concurrently by university and high school faculty members to their respective students, providing maximal opportunities for those groups to interact. The support of the Institute for Secondary Education was essential in this regard: secondary school teachers from Rhode Island and Massachusetts have been involved in planning and in incorporating materials, either in part or in whole, into their teaching. Seven high schools have taken part in the project. High school students have attended numerous classes at Brown, and the Brown teaching teams (faculty members and undergraduate and graduate teaching assistants) have taught in the high schools.

The high school teachers speak eloquently about the benefits of the collaborative program. Their students read different works on a more sophisticated level, and the students' confidence in their ability to succeed in college is enhanced by having college teachers in their classrooms and by attending university classes. These experiences can be dramatic for certain students. For example, Hope High School, an inner-city school whose past relation with the university can best be expressed in terms of neglect and resentment, now has black and Latino immigrant students who have been magnetized by the courses titled "City (B)Lights" and "Desire and the Marketplace"; who have attended Brown classes regularly; who have invited Brown faculty members to their school; who have achieved higher results in reading, discussion, and writing assignments; who have created special projects; and who have developed plans for attending college.

The department's connection with the Coalition of Essential Schools and NEH support have also made possible a national program of intensive summer seminars that has brought teams of college and high school teachers to Providence to disseminate in eight other regions versions of the collaborative courses we developed.

The success of such courses at Brown and elsewhere has depended on an intense commitment by college and university faculties to enriching high school education; a voracious appetite among secondary school teachers for intellectual stimulation; a mutual respect that prevents a top-down, expert-scholar-to-uninformed-teacher situation; and the excitement of students and teachers at all levels when traditional survey courses are redefined thematically and comparatively.

The Coalition of Essential Schools believes in the need to have a wider repertory of assessment techniques, focusing on the teacher-coach, student-learner model. The challenges thus posed for the university are real: Are we open to accepting performances, portfolios, or other final presentations of knowledge at the close of our courses? How egalitarian do we think the classroom should be? In the pedagogy that the Coalition of Essential Schools recommends, is there a place for lecturing? Are we willing to go the full route in conceptualizing what a student should know or be able to do—not to be confused with information—when a course is completed? How many of our instructional efforts are based on our personal research interests versus students' interests?

Such questions are difficult and point to deeper questions: Why teach these books? Why use this approach? Do these decisions matter? How does one show it matters? How does one know it matters? Good teachers meet these challenges whether they are in high schools or universities. Some university teachers assume such matters to be self-evident and beneath consideration, or they are so committed to the disciplinary discourse on their subject that such quasi-existential concerns go unaddressed. High school teachers are less able to avoid these basic but hardly simple matters, and here is where we college and university teachers stand to benefit from the experience of working with gifted secondary school teachers.

We also stand to benefit from offering courses jointly to college and high school students because doing so makes us aware of the posturing and the hermetic language that not infrequently accompany our work. High school students are adamantly nonprofessionals, and their "take" on our materials and themes sometimes leads us to recognize that we are wearing the emperor's new clothes. A student's blank incomprehension obliges us to think harder about the import and reach of our subject, and if high school seniors cannot be persuaded that our interests make sense or deserve consideration, then it behooves us to ponder why Sizer argues that the enabling principles that undergird courses should be apparent. Often the university curriculum, with its lockstep courses, bypasses considerations of enabling principles. In fact, the high school audience is ideal for getting at the genuine stakes of much of the theoretical criticism that occupies the academy. Indeed, our experience is that when we drop jargon and convey passionately and intelligently our stance on some important matter, we can energize high school students.

Ultimately, the rationale for our—that is, higher education's or MLA members'—involvement in the secondary school is remarkably simple: if our issues and our expertise matter, then they must matter in the schools as well. To put it simply, we are talking about a redistribution of resources in our society, and here is one arena where the redistribution of intellectual resources can actually take place.

As the department's collaborative programs have evolved thus far, they have enriched the curriculum at Brown and in a number of local high school classes, emphasized the importance of a college–high school link, and begun to exert an influence elsewhere in the country. And what we have learned is exciting: beyond the specific books and approaches that we taught, we are creating partnerships with people who never thought that they had much in common with one another and with us. What we see emerging is a community of teachers who cross the high school–college boundary and consult about courses, book lists, opportunities for class visits, joint teaching, and the challenge of intellectual exchange. There is no way to know how far this community will go.

> *If our issues and our expertise matter, then they must matter in the schools as well.*

George Levine refers to our "immediate public responsibilities" in our research, teaching, and education of graduate students (45). We believe that our public responsibilities involve more than creating a smoother fit between research training and college teaching; we think that the entire profession has to reconceive itself along the graduate–undergraduate–secondary school continuum. What are some of the implications of this continuum? One implication, certainly, is that if an issue is of compelling intellectual importance, it can be addressed in terms understandable not only to a coterie of adepts but also to intelligent college and high school students. This formulation itself supposes a view of our activities not as arcane but as directed to the public as a whole. A second involves reflection on training graduate students to think and act along similar lines. How about doctoral programs that imagine PhD course work and research in terms of this broader educational community? The best way to build such doctoral programs would be to involve graduate students in the comparative, internationalist, interdisciplinary, team-taught courses discussed here. The narrowly specialized research model is due for rethinking along these lines.

Our goal in describing the Brown University effort is to heighten awareness among MLA members of the pressing need for colleges and universities to contribute to the enrichment of high school curricula and to recognize the problems of high school teachers and learn from them.

Note

[1]In addition to the last two issues of *Profession*, the 1994 MLA convention session "The Future of Doctoral Programs" (San Diego, 30 Dec.), see the ACLA report, earlier reports, and a number of responses, including one by us, in *Comparative Literature in the Age of Multiculturalism* (Bernheimer). Copies of reading lists for courses described here are available on request.

Works Cited

Bernheimer, Charles, ed. *Comparative Literature in the Age of Multiculturalism*. Baltimore: Johns Hopkins UP, 1994.

Levine, George. "The Real Trouble." *Profession 93*. New York: MLA, 1993. 43–45.

Sizer, Theodore. *Horace's Compromise: The Dilemma of the American High School*. Boston: Houghton, 1984.

———. *Horace's School: Redesigning the American High School*. Boston: Houghton, 1992.

Global Thinking, Local Teaching: Departments, Curricula, and Culture

Russell A. Berman

Thinking through the relation between theory and teaching cannot be a matter of prescriptively determining how teaching ought to look in order to be judged adequate by theory. To do so would both underestimate the variability of classroom practices and overestimate the power of the theoretical imagination. Instead of a conceptualizing hierarchy that puts teaching in the back of the bus and leaves the driving to theory, I propose an examination of the more complex and very material effect of the several discourses we call theory on the practices of teaching in language and literature departments. "Theory" here is not at all primarily pedagogical theory but rather the open-ended set of paradigms that have forced a fundamental rethinking of the study of the humanities. This theory, including the incompatibles of poststructuralism, neo-Marxism, feminism, and postcolonialism, to name a few, has most strongly affected departments traditionally devoted to literature, although it pertains just as well to other humanistic disciplines. The question I want to explore is how the larger theoretical revolution, with its epicenter in the language and literature departments, elicits structural consequences for these departments, for the curricula that are taught, and for the understanding of culture as the topic of teaching. The irreversible transformation in the perception of the field may be fundamentally at odds with the conventional structures of the departments.

As I have already suggested, theory is hardly a homogeneous enterprise. Its diverse strands pose diverse challenges to pedagogy. I want to proceed by reviewing four theoretical discourses and consider their implications for the larger enterprise of teaching.

Language-Based Theory

Language-based literary theory—from structuralist poetics to deconstruction—studies literary texts or works as linguistic objects, therefore locating them comfortably, or seemingly so, near the study of language. Our departments might seem to outside observers to be the natural sum of two distinct but related addends: language and literature. Yet the addition is no simple arithmetic and depends on several operative fictions: the philological claim that the study of language is the primary vehicle for the study of literature; the Romantic claim that literature is the ultimate culmination of language; the educational claim that a student might or even should begin with the study of language and proceed, as if in a dog-eared novel of development, to literature, and that this trajectory should be the norm and define the pedagogical project of the department; and, finally, the departmental claim that language teachers and literature teachers work hand in hand, on equal footing, with mutual respect and collegiality in the interest of a shared agenda.

Of course, these fictions have never held empirically; there has always been much more to literature than philology and much more to language study than literary appreciation. Institutionally, the equality implied by the conjunction separating *language* and *literature* was never an adequate designation of the sorts of hierarchy that have tended to prevail: consider all the differences in prestige, power, and salary. Nevertheless, that Romantic constellation based on a presumption of the organic wholeness of language and literature made the

The author is Professor of German Studies and Comparative Literature and Director of the Overseas Studies Program at Stanford University. A version of this article appeared in the Fall 1994 issue of the ADFL *Bulletin.*

pedagogical enterprise of the integrated department seem coherent. The language skills that a student might learn were, according to this view, perhaps inferior to the poetic language of literature but they were not of another existential status. Hence the model of using literary texts in third-year language instruction (for the commonly taught languages) as if the goal of language instruction was primarily literary appreciation.

All these beliefs have ceased to be tenable; a fundamental rethinking of the pedagogical enterprise—and the departments, which are constructed to house it—is in order; and, paradoxically, it is precisely the linguistic turn in literary theory that has severed the tie between language and literature as instructional material. For whether one designates the goal of language pedagogy as proficiency or competence or fluency, it necessarily implies some facility by a speaker or writer in communicating meaning. Yet it is precisely that communicative character of language that is denied by deconstruction. The central claim of deconstruction, strictly understood, is the absolute incompatibility of speech and writing; indeed, speech is taken to represent a degraded mode of language, since it is linked to the notion of a speaker who is a "subject" who "communicates" "meaning"—all terms hopelessly implicated in the Western metaphysics that it is deconstruction's project to attack. Writing, by contrast, is always separate from the author and never reducible to intention or meaning; it therefore represents language as ultimately undecipherable. Paul de Man's figurality of language (take nothing literally) and Jacques Derrida's grammatological bias against speech (writing is more authentic because it appears to be authorless) point to the always already deficient character of language, a site of confusion and mendacity, not communication and certainly not anything like "fluency." Language proficiency is not a possible goal for deconstruction's language theory.

If the language-pedagogical agenda is concerned with meaning, it stands at odds with this strand of recent literary theory. The former is about how language works; the latter, how language cannot work. A house divided against itself? That alliance of "language and literature," with its Romantic provenance and its shaky structure, finally breaks down. The results? Probably, on the one hand, a heightened professionalization of language instruction and, on the other, a separation of literature

> *Cultural studies pries at the Romantic link between language and literature.*

instruction from language specificity—that is, departments of comparative literature or of literature in general, with most work read in translation. In other words, when language specificity ceases to be the rationale for separate disciplines, the arguments for separate departments of national literatures become weak, and amalgamation into a single unit becomes likely.

An alternative possible consequence of the severing of language instruction and (some) literary theory is more subtle and less drastic. If language instruction is seen less as leading necessarily to literary study, it might plausibly be taken to lead elsewhere or even to lead to several possible sites, pointing to a model of "language across the curriculum": use of foreign language skills in a variety of disciplinary settings, not only in the study of literature, although certainly there too. Using French in art history, German in philosophy, or Russian in political science courses could represent an intriguing vehicle to encourage the development of language proficiency outside the language and literature department, once deconstruction has granted the divorce. Indeed, a wider disciplinary use of foreign language could eventually generate a larger population capable of and interested in using original languages to explore literature.

Far be it from me to argue for this departmental reordering. My only point now is to trace some potential institutional and pedagogical consequences of recent theory. There are others, which point in other directions.

Cultural Studies

Cultural studies also pries at the Romantic link between language and literature, but somewhat differently and in a way that would presumably require less institutional restructuring. Departments of national literature have always had another function, although one implicated in the same Romanticism that viewed language as highest and purest when it was most poetic. For Romanticism located that poetic expressivity in the nation and discerned the nation's genius in the language of the people. Therefore literary material became the preferred route for the study of a nation, culture, or society, just as that nation, culture, or society was the preferred frame for the study of literature.

Neither side of that equation remains compelling. All that we have learned about the artificiality of national canons implies that there are probably better ways to think of literature than as the expression of nations. Further, there are certainly many materials other than literature one might use to study and teach other cultures, which is precisely the project of cultural studies. This branch of theory examines the symbolic orders in which intersubjective meanings and social practices are constituted and contested, including literary works, other artistic material, and nonartistic but nevertheless symbolic material such as modes of public representation, the organization of private and public spaces, and codes of gender distinction.

If deconstruction tends to subvert the viability of integrated language and literature units because of the specific character of its language theory, cultural studies does not, since it has no single language theory. Indeed, in general, cultural studies is a considerably more heterogeneous development, perhaps in part because its empirical orientation has much in common with some historiographic concerns about context, institutions, and change. To be sure, cultural studies has little use for the Romantic intoxication with language, but it de facto preserves the prominence of language, given the focus on specific geographical areas. Instead of teaching literature, which can only very dubiously be restricted to a single nation or language, one teaches a culture—Germany's, for example—for which a language becomes an indispensable tool, although the language is no longer the magical place of the origin of the folk.

But even if we save the institutional coherence of "language and literature" departments by appealing to the cultural studies agenda of "teaching Germany" or teaching German culture (although the rationale for disciplinary autonomy and restricting oneself to Germany is no longer language-based), a larger question emerges pertaining to scholarly identity. Cultural studies cannot evade the immediate challenge posed by its own interdisciplinarity, for it is not only we in—or emerging from?—literature departments who teach Germany or any other culture. So do historians, art historians, political scientists, and others, and despite all the conferences, journals, and associations, an effectively and substantively interdisciplinary curriculum has not been achieved; here and there at the margins there may have been some cooperation, but these small efforts—the rare team-taught course or the coauthored article, for example—are hardly enough to transform the institution of scholarship. Despite some recent developments, the study of culture is still marginal in history departments, and culture is barely a factor at all in the quantitative social sciences. So the interdisciplinarity that devolves from the replacement of literature (narrowly defined) by culture (broadly defined) differs greatly depending on whether it is a matter of "Ger-

man studies," which seeks to bring together Germany specialists from various fields, or of "cultural studies in German," which is certain to remain a largely postliterary phenomenon, that is, the intellectual agenda in language and literature departments after the primacy of literature, narrowly understood, is revoked. The former version, bringing together all the Germanists from various departments—we can call it *Grossdeutsch*—will tend to preserve conservative disciplinary distinctions by simply adding the literary scholar to the historian, to the economist, and so on. Cultural studies as *Kleindeutsch* has the advantage of revitalizing the language and literature model by using an innovative pedagogy that examines a culture through a range of objects, including but not restricted to canonic literature.

This important distinction also pertains to the pressures on the other foreign language fields either to network with other disciplines on the basis of a shared regional interest (area studies) or to redefine separate literature departments within the discipline as cultural studies departments in French, German, Spanish, and so on. This precise location of cultural studies entails reorienting scholarly attention from the literary work of art to the construction of collective cultural identity, and these two alternatives still represent the aporia of the Romantic legacy: literature and nationhood. Area studies, literary studies, or cultural studies: all three signify distinct possibilities in all the traditional foreign language fields; in practice, there is no one solution for all fields, since their disciplinary traditions are different from one another, as are the cultures themselves, the objects of study. In German, the shift to a specifically cultural studies agenda can draw on longstanding intellectual traditions, as well as the history of political obsession with national unification; in Spanish, the relation between culture and territory is configured very differently; and in Russian, the authority of a high tradition impedes any consistently postliterary developments. But both Russian and German fields are about cultures identified with specific territories—Russia and Germany—in ways that English departments are rarely about England. It is precisely this difference—between departments oriented toward other cultures and departments oriented primarily toward the autonomous literary work of art—that is the site of cultural studies.

Literature may be taken to be universal; culture is particular, and the cultural studies agenda of teaching Germany or teaching France has the additional problem that its fundamental conceptualization may be nationalistic or even racist. Paul Gilroy has criticized British cultural studies for inheriting from a Stalinist

Marxism an account of nationhood that necessarily disprivileged minorities. Hence the romanticizing search for the real England of real English workers: if not socialism in one country, then at least one culture in one country. This argument is homologous to the critique of apologetic versions of popular culture and everyday history in Germany: preferring to look at "normal" people in "situations" rather than at exceptions in exceptional circumstances, for example, the persecuted minority. In both cases, the scholarly problem is not irreparable, but its solution would require additional theorization of the "culture" in "cultural studies," recognizing its instability and heterogeneity instead of imagining a pure and organic cultural material. All cultures, today and in the past, are internally diverse, so diversity might be a constitutive category of cultural studies.

Postcolonial Theory

The enlightened correction to cultural nativism is postcolonial theory, which has flourished particularly in English departments and has reoriented curricula toward issues of colonialism in earlier texts and toward the anglophone literature of formerly colonized nations. Analogous work in French and Spanish departments has produced varied results. Some interesting work on cultural aspects of German colonialism is under way, but because of the colonial era's limited span, the precise parallel to English material is rather small.

Yet postcolonialism is simultaneously the vehicle whereby English departments have been able to address increasingly diverse student bodies and sometimes escape the criticism of Eurocentrism. What is at stake therefore is less a conversation between postcolonial theory and cultural pedagogy than the viability of the study of individual European cultures in the historical context of postcolonialism, the end of European privilege, and an increasingly global cultural horizon. To put the issue clearly: given the restricted character of university resources, given an American national culture that is much less oriented toward Europe than it was when the European national literature departments were established, and given the increasing emphasis on teaching and enrollments, are there any curricular strategies worth exploring in departments charged with the teaching and study of European material?

An important part of the answer is of course the post-European move in the focus of French literary studies to francophone Africa or, for Spanish depart-

ments, the shift in the balance between Spain and Latin America. But were that the whole answer, it would be poor indeed; it would surrender the European tradition to a misconstrued expediency and miss a dramatic opportunity to redefine the European material itself. Germany offers a particularly interesting example, therefore, because the brevity of its colonial past effectively prohibits a shift to a German material outside Europe as a formula for broad disciplinary change. What could the formula then be?

We are still at the beginning of a discussion on this point, and I have no definitive answers, except that the promise of a German cultural studies is intellectually viable only if inflected by a postcolonial orientation. In addition, it would be fruitless to relive the culture wars of the eighties and position a cultural fortress Europe against a misunderstood challenge of global diversity. The problem is rather to articulate a curriculum that teaches Germany while taking seriously the postcolonial question of diversity in various inflections relevant to the German material: nationhood and race (tragically topical in Germany in the light of the postunification xenophobia), German-Jewish topics, regional diversity and federalism, multilingualism—these might be some points at which to start to rebuild the curriculum. To rebuild it: not to add these issues on as marginal embellishments but to set them at the core and to renounce, finally, the neurotic compulsion to extend the literary canon of the nineteenth century into the twenty-first. Instead of literary studies slipping from national identity through nationalism to racism, one could imagine a cultural studies that would thematize racism alongside difference, plurality, and hybridity.

Posthermeneutic Theory

Posthermeneutic theory challenges the legitimacy of the departmental strategy that orients the curriculum teleologically toward the interpretation of literary works. Can the curriculum and pedagogy be rethought in a way that would challenge this passivity and give the student an opportunity to engage in more than retrospective thinking? Instead of encouraging students to become listeners and readers who interpret—or consume?—we can begin to envision a strategy designed to elicit active producers who engage in a culture rather than merely receive it.

The theoretical issue here has to do with the construction of alterity. We should not only work toward a conceptualization of culture that is complex enough to allow for internal heterogeneity—diversity is constitutive of all culture. We, engaged in a pedagogy that teaches the "other" culture, should also have a nonreactionary account of the student's relation to the other, an account that does not reify the other culture in its exoticism but that, on the contrary, foregrounds the relation between here and there, the positionality of the student in and toward the other culture. Instead of aiming for a "native fluency," with its goal of a feigned identity—the American's dream of passing as French—one could explore an articulation of difference in which the student could speak for him- or herself as an American encountering France.

And not only speak. The point, however, is that a posthermeneutic pedagogy—one that promotes active skills over passive interpretation—can entail enabling the student to engage in the production of texts, spoken or written, rather than privileging the exegesis of canonic texts. Of course we should continue to teach high culture, but versatility in the interpretation of high culture is not the sole or ultimate desideratum. An alternative might be labeled foreign cultural literacy: the ability of the student to operate effectively in a different cultural setting. This goal can be achieved most successfully through study abroad, which would naturally include the study of language and culture but would also better prepare the student for future encounters with the host culture.

In this light, curricular concerns and the redefinition of the language and literature departments are part of wider issues in higher education, and we should be able to identify what specific contribution the study of other cultures can make to the educational enterprise. The question has shifted from the relative importance of particular material to the significance of why one should learn about foreign cultures at all. Spare me the answer "The national interest." This notion is just a pipe dream of underenrolled departments eager to show their patriotism: the foreign policy elite was never made up of language and literature majors. The right answer might have to do with cognitive and operative gains pursuant to the engagement with material from other cultures, that is, considerable self-reflection, and it is there that the study of literature remains of primary importance.

Yet the understanding of literary history is not the only component of foreign cultural literacy, which in fact suggests a greater contemporaneous component in the curriculum. If the point is to empower students to live and work in France—or with French people in the United States—or even merely to reflect more richly on their own situation by gaining a foreign perspective on the United States, the distant French past is surely important but, equally surely, less important than the twentieth century. The era of national literary history may have come to an end; think of the consequences for departmental structures. Instead of faculty positions assigned to neatly separated historical periods (the sixteenth century, the seventeenth century, etc.), national literary history might shrink to the size of history of philosophy in philosophy departments, with more resources allocated to diverse aspects of contemporary culture: politics, popular culture, mass media, gender, and minorities.

The four theoretical tendencies I have touched on hardly converge on a single point or a simple agenda. Everything is due for review: the connections between language and literature, between literature and culture, between Europe and the globe, and between the literature of single nations and comparative literature. The status of the humanities and, especially, of the departmental organizations we know is likely to change profoundly. It makes little sense to dig in our heels to defend the past. Why should we want to? But we should want to reexamine our past, our intellectual obligations, and the challenges of contemporary theory and then build institutions that are adequate to them. This task requires asking why we think language, literature, and culture ought to be taught at all and whether they belong together for other than merely conventional reasons. Cultural studies provides a useful answer, insisting on the importance of studying foreign cultures, although differently than in the past: linguistic identity—the definition of departments as French, German, Spanish, and so on—has to be liberal enough to accommodate the diversity of minority languages, just as the study of literature will likely surrender some of its traditional privilege. Such a reconfiguration, which could help us impart to students a concentrated familiarity with another culture, is less a theoretical insight than a realistic assessment of students' interests in other cultures and societies, interests that are surely much more practical than they are strictly literary-historical or philosophical. Can our theoretical reflections on the challenges to inherited departmental structures become as practical as our students' concerns?

Dealing with Difference: Being an Administrator in the 1990s

Patricia Meyer Spacks

When David Laurence invited me to prepare a talk for department chairs and directors of graduate studies at ADE's 1994 Summer Seminar East, he first asked me to speak about how the job of department chair has changed in the last quarter century. Then he reminded me that graduate education was on the agenda for the weekend. Finally he pointed out that my remarks were supposed to be a keynote address that would help set an agenda. So I'm going to try to reflect both on the chair's job and on the problems of graduate education and to call attention to a particular aspect of being chair that we often neglect, what with dealing with the budget and dealing with complaints and dealing with the administration. It's easy to believe that what chairs do is precisely that: deal with things. But I'd like to initiate some collective thought about the chair's obligation also to lead the department, to facilitate change: "dealing" of another sort than the kind that involves worrying about office assignments and parking spaces. Leading is harder than managing. It's also more important.

First, though, a bit of autobiography. When I look back on myself as chair at Wellesley, beginning in 1968, it's like contemplating a love affair of my youth. I didn't know *anything* then, I think. How could I ever have been so young? It seems to me now, pondering myself then, that I went through my three-year term in a state of semiconsciousness—but that in fact no more was required of me, even though the late 1960s was a period of political unrest even in a setting so bucolic as Wellesley.

Yale, fifteen years later, was a different matter—a much harder job, for historical as well as institutional reasons. At Wellesley, I, like my colleagues, believed that the administration and the faculty pursued common agendas. The two groups might differ in their specifications of appropriate means to achieve desired ends, but there was little difference about ends. By the mid-1980s, when I took over at Yale, a chair's job included

vigorous representation of the faculty's interests—interests perceived as quite different from those of students and even from those of the institution at large.

Only three years separated the completion of my term as Yale chair from the beginning of my tenure as Virginia chair, but they were years of great change in the academy. Although the economic facts of the moment continue to imply divergent concerns for administration and faculty, my main worry now as chair has involved divergences within the department—not because the Virginia English department comprises an especially disharmonious group (indeed, quite the contrary) but because, once more, times have changed.

This sketchy capsule summary slides over many relevant facts. The three institutions of which I speak differ dramatically from one another, and those differences—including differences in the degree of power assigned to a department chair—doubtless partly account for what I have perceived as change. My own personal development, involving interests and feelings and ideas, is obviously implicated in my ways of understanding my task. Yet even when I try to take full account of a wide range of determinants, I remain convinced that the demands of chairing a department, almost any department, have significantly altered. The job is more arduous now—perhaps I should say more nearly impossible—and probably less immediately rewarding. Nevertheless, I'm inclined to think its challenges more provocative, more compelling than they have ever been

---

The author is Edgar F. Shannon Professor of English at the University of Virginia. A version of this article appeared in the Winter 1994 issue of the ADE Bulletin.

before. I should probably confess at this point that I have recently signed on, with only pro forma protest, for a second three-year term—precisely because the work of chairing a department now so richly engages my capacities.

Wellesley didn't provide graduate education. My experience of chairing at Yale and at Virginia, however, has convinced me that at least some of the problems we currently face in graduate education duplicate those that now characterize the chairing of departments. The problems I mean stem from what one might charitably call diversity: diversity become dysfunctional. For half the department *humanism* is a bad word; for the other half the term is a badge of honor. And that's if you're lucky. More likely, only a third prefer to describe themselves as humanists and so feel themselves to be an embattled minority. The two-thirds who like to identify themselves with cultural studies hold the power of numbers but not of seniority. Resentment reigns.

How can one manage such a scenario? Well, by engaging its issues and trying to shift its terms. By convincing department members that they best serve their self-interest by learning how to work with those they tend to identify as opponents. By refusing to hypostatize difference or to permit others to do so. By dealing with ideological conflict concretely and specifically at a local level, without yielding to perceptions that "it's a national problem."

What kind of peace is imaginable in an academic department these days? It might begin in the rejection of polarities as defining aspects of discourse. It's possible for a chair to insist on a department's collective responsibility for its own functioning, to demand that faculty members seek and discover what they hold in common—and what they can learn from one another. It's possible to focus attention on the work we need to do as teachers and how best to do it.

I'm advocating administrative action that involves reimagining intellectual relations within a department. Twenty-five years ago there wasn't much need to worry about departmental peace, for two reasons. In the first place, we didn't feel such stringency of resources as we have recently been forced to endure. There was room, usually, to add a course if someone entered the department with new ideas. New ideas translated into curricular terms could thus coexist serenely with old ones. In the second place, at least generally speaking, professional harmony demanded no effort. Individuals might dislike one another, faculty members might declare divergent intellectual viewpoints, but the people teaching in colleges and universities generally shared assumptions

about why they were there, even after the New Critics of the 1940s challenged the historical critics who preceded them. By the time I got to Wellesley, in 1959, everybody had been more or less affected by New Criticism, and the intellectual differences among faculty members were for the most part differences only in emphasis. The oldest teacher in the department and the youngest had much in common—and knew it. I remember a department meeting in the late sixties or early seventies at which we tried to agree on a list of texts that every graduating English major should know. By the end of the afternoon, we had proved unable to come to agreement about even a single author. Shakespeare survived for a long time, but then someone declared that

if we wouldn't give him James Joyce, he wouldn't give us Shakespeare, and that was the end of that. In retrospect, though, it seems clear that we weren't really trying to put together a collection of common texts, since essentially we all agreed about the undesirability

What kind of peace is imaginable in an academic department these days?

of a reading list. Our meeting dramatized a preexistent consensus.

If I try to imagine an English department, any English department, holding a meeting for the same purpose now, I fancy identical results: no agreement about anything. But the lack of agreement would hold different meanings and leave a different emotional residue. Some people would yearn for canonical reaffirmation, others would wish to canonize the previously neglected, and many would deny the validity of lists. To reconcile the range of intellectual positions would prove impossible. No one would be happy about any conceivable outcome, and it would take a genius to generate anything useful from the situation.

Well, either a genius or someone very persistent. What a chair may need most these days is administrative persistence: the kind of persistence that, in the hypothetical situation I just outlined, would refuse to accept irreconcilability, doggedly investigating the assumptions on which warring factions base their war. In any single imaginable situation, such doggedness, one might think, would simply take too long. But in a department whose leader has at every juncture and in many ways insisted that a dynamic of trust must replace one of power, sooner or later there comes to be a thick foundation on which one readily raises superstructures.

I feel foolish stating what all my colleagues know as well as I do, but let me recapitulate some of the new differences within our profession. There are, for an obvious instance, gender differences. When I was at Wellesley, men and women alike taught there in roughly equal numbers, and it didn't seem to matter much which species one belonged to. I remember a male colleague remarking, as new waves of feminism began to surge, that when he entered a room he never thought about how many men and women the group contained; he thought about how many Jews were present. His response sounded almost as plausible to female faculty members as it did to their male counterparts. Now that we understand gender as a political fact, though, such a comment would ring quite differently in female ears. It matters vividly these days whether one belongs to the male or the female persuasion, and gender is widely assumed to contribute to one's intellectual attitudes.

Equally self-evident in many quarters is the fact that ethnicity and race signify as part of a teacher's intellectual equipment—and as textual components in the object of the teacher's study. Departments compete vigorously for faculty members of diverse racial backgrounds, presumably with the tacit assumption that racial diversity implies intellectual diversity. Differences of social class often accompany ethnic differences and are, at least in some circles, assigned comparable value. The investigation of race, class, and gender in literary works both produces and is partly produced by increasing awareness of the same elements as significant in the composition of a faculty. But English departments are not melting pots. Fault lines frequently develop—to shift metaphors—along divisions of race, class, and gender. One can feel (I'm sure many of you know the feeling) as though there simply isn't room for everything—or everyone.

Then there are the theoretical differences among us, differences that have also assumed a new, and to my mind exaggerated, importance. Deconstruction, new historicism, cultural studies; Derrida, Foucault, Bakhtin . . . Labels of position and the proper names associated with various intellectual movements possess extraordinary defining force, as though they belonged to individuals as permanently and significantly as gender identities do. The local deconstructionist feels utterly different from the bibliographic scholar down the hall. The two of them, in their respective perceptions, have nothing in common, nor does either acknowledge common concerns with the narratologist who just joined the faculty.

I have not provided an exhaustive list of the kinds of difference characterizing and often seriously dividing today's departments of English, but I've reminded you of at least a few locations for dissension. Each division, each distinct classification, supplies a potential and frequently an actual locus of struggle, overt or subterranean. A department chair can find or make it a full-time job merely to moderate such struggle. And moderating by no means suffices.

The conflict of categories partly involves the implicit range of curricular possibility associated with them. Male or female; African American, Hispanic American, Jewish American, or Asian American; Marmxist, Foucauldian, or new historicist—every label implies a whole set of courses, more than any curriculum could plausibly contain even in an expanding economy and certainly more than shrinking departments can absorb. Here is where the chair's problems begin to coincide with those of the director of graduate studies. For graduate education more even than undergraduate, curricular possibilities have become a matter of peculiar urgency. How should we train prospective PhDs for an academic market controlled by an economics of scarcity? We have all noticed—perhaps some of us have even written—those ads in the MLA job list that declare a department's need for someone who can teach both the eighteenth century and modernism, preferably with a subspecialty of Native American studies. It's not that the ads characteristically call for "generalists." On the contrary, they often specify quite narrowly, while demanding diverse forms of narrowness. What do our students need to know in order to compete in a market of this sort? Will the ads look the same by the time they get their degrees? How can we prepare them for unforeseeable contingencies?

At stake in answering such questions are human as well as intellectual issues, issues involving faculty members as well as students. If, in training our students for tomorrow, we discard the insights of yesterday, we not only lose for a new generation the wisdom of the old but also risk effectively discarding a group of thinkers who have themselves been trained in ways that the current pressures of modishness encourage us to think outmoded. We risk discarding these teachers by relegating them to undergraduate instruction and administration, by discouraging—and there are subtle ways of discouraging—graduate students from taking their courses. We cannot afford the losses such a process would entail. To resist modishness while valuing and incorporating the new amounts to a difficult but an essential balancing act. To make faculty members from every intellectual generation feel appropriately valued is the chair's responsibility as part of that trying task.

Commentators from outside and sometimes from within the academy have worried in recent years about the "politicization" of literary study. A more cogent worry, I think, would focus on the internal politics of the academy. The economic pressures of the moment guarantee the increasing urgency of departmental politics—*politics* in the most fundamental meaning of the word: the play of power. Each theoretical allegiance, each ethnic or racial or gender definition, figures in the operations and manipulations of power within the department. Alliances of what in the larger world are called "special interests" often determine curricular developments and departmental policies. Such alliances, however, can be challenged. Basic questions about what the department as a collective body values and wishes to affirm tend to vanish from consciousness as fragmented interest groups merge and splinter and make things happen. But these questions can return, can be made to return, to the collective consciousness.

Of course, it has always been true that the operations of a department, like those of a university or a city or a state, follow political laws and reflect political actualities. But the politics of ethnic, gender, and theoretical allegiances has generated new kinds and intensities of intradepartmental bitterness because its very possibility calls attention to differences so abundant that they feel dangerously like fragmentation. And in the internecine wrangling the stakes seem higher than ever because there's no longer enough to go around—not enough courses, not enough money, not enough power or prestige. All of us in the academy feel more beleaguered than we used to, I think. Surveys tell us that people still respect college professors more than they do, say, members of Congress and that respondents affirm the value of such ideas as "culture" and "the humanities." Nonetheless, these days we pretty consistently get bad press; we are labeled lazy, self-absorbed, unconcerned with "values," and interested only in our own esoteric and essentially meaningless research. Are we really doing something important? Lacking a sense of significant status in the community, criticized by legislatures and by the media, we compete more avidly than ever for what status we can manufacture within the confines of the department. Courses that loudly declare their teachers' intellectual commitments, like the high salaries and perks that have become so hard to get, provide signs of status. I'm speaking of a difference of degree rather than of kind when I refer to the new intensity of intradepartmental political struggle, but that difference of degree is sufficiently marked to be meaningful.

Local politics thus helps to determine the nature of the curriculum, hence of graduate (and undergraduate) education. It's hard to debate in their own terms questions about what and how graduate students should study when personal and group self-interest so vividly participate in any discussion. It's hard even to know what it would mean to debate such questions in their own terms: is it possible to conceive terms not immediately involved in internal politics? Inasmuch as the chair attends to the department's political functioning, then, that attention necessarily implicates problems of graduate curriculum.

I'm tempted to say that the motto of today's department chair should be "Attack autonomy." For most of our careers, surely, most of us have believed in the necessity of defending autonomy—autonomy in the classroom, autonomy in research. Now, though, we—and by "we" I mean academics in general, not departmental administrators in particular—may have become too autonomous for our own good. Many in the professoriat assume their right to teach whatever they feel

> *All of us in the academy feel more beleaguered than we used to, I think.*

like teaching. It is not uncommon for faculty members to refuse to teach specific courses needed by the department—to refuse because of a desire, say, to teach a subject more closely related to that of their book-in-progress, or to keep more time for research, or not to deal with first-year students. We—or should I say *they?*—model for graduate students, tomorrow's professors, a pedagogy of privilege, of narrowness, of self-concern. *Autonomy* has in academic practice often come to seem synonymous with self-interest.

A yet more fundamental problem of graduate education now is whether we should be engaging in it at all. Will our society make employment available to new generations of PhDs in English? How can we possibly tell? The job market looks atrocious right now, but what about five, six, nine years down the road? On the one hand, perhaps an improving economy will imply the expansion of higher education. On the other hand— perhaps not. We've all heard the arguments on both sides of this question. In fact, we have no way of knowing what the future holds. We do, however, know that a sizable backlog of unemployed PhDs already exists in our field. Many of us worry that to guide students toward doctorates now constitutes an act of bad faith— particularly given our awareness that these students supply an increasingly essential source of cheap labor for the university.

The students know that, too. Graduate students have always, no doubt, resented their securely employed elders: such resentment reflects a particular form of the "perpetual conflict between the old and young" that Dr. Johnson long ago described (*Rambler* 196, 1 Feb. 1752). But the currents of resentment have become markedly stronger in recent years, with students fearing that they serve in effect as cannon fodder—teachers of freshman composition doomed to rapid extinction as academics. Moreover, a number of good universities have made a concerted effort to speed up the process of getting a PhD, exerting financial as well as moral pressure to make graduate students finish faster. They finish faster, and too few jobs await them. Of course they resent us: they have struggled harder, they think, than we ever had to struggle and have obtained far less as a result. They see us exercising our "autonomy" while they provide slave labor; they suspect that they're working only for our convenience. And self-doubt gnaws at them. As a student said to me the other day, "It's hard not to think that it's your own fault if you can't find a job." The obvious alternative to believing failure a function of the self is to blame it on the teachers who have not issued sufficient warnings to or created sufficient opportunity for their students.

We can't manufacture jobs where none exist—at least we can't do that on a sufficiently grand scale to make much difference. We should, however, be able to speak clearly about the value of the enterprise that we and our students engage in, to help them think for themselves about what their study means and why it matters and to what extent it is self-justifying even without a job at the other end. And given our current fragmentation, such articulations of value have become dauntingly difficult. Most of us don't and can't venture to attempt them.

The range of human and intellectual problems I have already evoked is fairly overwhelming. There's the social, economic, educational, and political dilemma of how much sense graduate education in English makes, given today's actualities, and the human dilemma of the living people who want such education but also justifiably want the rewards traditionally accruing to it. To resolve the difficulties of a department or those of graduate education, one must directly confront theoretical and practical, structural and isolated issues. How? I wish I knew.

It's not really the chair's job, as I understand it, to resolve the conflicts that divide a department. Conflicts split every department and always will, although various circumstances alleviate or intensify them. No individual man or woman, only an imaginary Superchair, can erase the fault lines I mentioned above, the ones that open up these days along divisions of race, gender, theory. Nevertheless, I think it a chair's crucial responsibility, in 1994, to enable a department to deal with its own antagonisms rather than to live with paranoia and concealed resentment. This is not a matter of putting out brush fires. It's quite different from resolving individual cases of academic burnout or sexual harassment or goofing off—traditional and irksome tasks of every chair. It involves understanding particular symptoms in systemic terms and helping the system cure those symptoms.

Nor is the chair's job in relation to fundamental conflict that of mediation. Paradoxically, the first crucial task may seem like the opposite of mediation: it may involve heightening consciousness of difficulty. One way that academics, or at least collectivities of academics, often meet serious divisions of opinion or outlook is to paper them over. College and university teachers of English, in my experience, are often remarkably nice people. They don't like to fight, they don't like to think of themselves as being at odds with their colleagues. It may seem infinitely preferable to deny all lack of congruence by insisting that no real difference exists.

A chair can function valuably by helping to specify differences, by calling attention to conflicts where they fester or burgeon, by demanding that the department reflect collectively on its differences and their meanings until it discovers its points of congruence, by insisting that a department find ways of taking responsibility for itself, and perhaps by raising and keeping firmly in view the alarming possibility that we may not be doing our jobs well enough. The chair can both locate difference and deny that people are solely defined by it. In academic departments, harmony no longer implies what it once perhaps meant: shared opinions about the books one should teach, about the kind of significance books hold, even about such matters as the nature of an appropriate relation between teacher and student. The kind of "peace" I now have in mind as a state to be sought and worked for partly entails delineation of difference, shared understanding of how to negotiate that difference, and investigation of what specific differences at issue really mean. The spectacle of departments full of ideological and intellectual disagreement seems most frightening when least scrutinized. The chair can insist on scrutiny.

This will be at best a long-range project: that's why persistence has become one of the chair's crucial virtues. I would by no means suggest that the results of an insistence on scrutiny will prove instantly harmonious; quite the contrary. To make people look at what divides them guarantees conflict, perhaps conspicuous acrimony, perhaps shouting matches during the department meeting. To posit the possibility that a department might not be doing a good job of representing its discipline and teaching its students will make people mad. To suggest that communal responsibility should in some instances take precedence over autonomy will make them madder. The chair won't be popular as people clash, and resentments against a demanding leader may linger even after the group has learned how better to incorporate its own diversities. But people who need to be popular shouldn't let themselves in for this kind of job. If—and I know it's a big *if*—the chair can lead or drive or cajole faculty members into involving themselves fully in the actual experience of functioning as a group in the harsh academic climate of 1994, if people become committed to the exhilarating if unsettling task of collective self-investigation—if these things come to pass, it becomes possible to imagine the development of a graduate curriculum of considered rather than adventitious eclecticism. It's even possible to imagine that a group that had reflected fully on its own workings would arrive at an implicit rationale for the complicated and diversified collective enterprise of teaching about literature and culture at the end of the twentieth century. Such a rationale might help individual departments understand and justify why they continue trying to produce new PhDs.

You may remember the sequence in *Rasselas* in which Imlac explains to young Rasselas the mission and the necessary training of the poet. His specifications become ever more extravagant, until finally Rasselas interrupts him. "Enough!" he says. "Thou has convinced me, that no human being can ever be a poet" (46). It is similarly the case that no man—or woman either—can ever be a department chair: not the kind of department chair who really solves the insoluble academic problems of the 1990s. Like Imlac, I have promulgated generalizations rather than how-to-do-it details. That's partly because those details will differ from department to department and partly because I don't really know how to do it in any ultimately successful sense; I only know how to try.

The reason the departments I inhabit look at me and see a prospective chair, I think, is that I'm an incurable optimist in academic matters. Even in these parlous times, I see cause for optimism. I was an enthusiastic participant in the recent MLA-FIPSE English Programs Curriculum Review Project as a consultant to the Louisiana State University English department. Over a period of two and a half years, I saw that department transform itself. At the beginning it seemed hopelessly divided. By the end, not everybody trusted everybody else, but a large proportion of the department had been involved in the process of changing the curriculum and had achieved agreement about a series of far-reaching alterations in long-established ways of doing things. In my mind, the process leading to the new consensus provides a paradigm of possibility. A good chair has always been one who can lead a department to fulfill its possibilities. Possibilities remain for departments, even now—especially for those with the guidance of chairs who grasp the urgency of new kinds of confrontation and new reasons for it.

Works Cited

Johnson, Samuel. *The Rambler*. Ed. W. J. Bate and Albrecht B. Strauss. New Haven: Yale UP, 1969. Vol. 5 of *The Works of Samuel Johnson*.

———. Rasselas *and Other Tales*. Ed. Gwin J. Kolb. New Haven: Yale UP, 1990. Vol. 16 of *The Works of Samuel Johnson*.

Forum

Special Topic on the Job Market

To the Editor:

Profession 94 provided grim reading, to say the least, for PhD students who are set to enter the job market. While several different employment options were examined in this special group of articles, one very viable option was ignored: teaching in the two-year college.

The two-year school offers prospective job seekers a set of advantages—and challenges—different from four-year schools. First, starting pay, particularly on unionized campuses, is competitive with more prestigious posts. Likewise, the benefits package, usually offering full health and retirement coverage, outstrips that given many short-term appointments at four-year schools. Second, the open admission policy of many schools typically gives the two-year faculty member a highly diverse class profile, and the socioeconomic and generational variety of community and junior college students presents a challenging opportunity for consistent and innovative teaching. Third, because the primary focus is classroom teaching, two-year faculty avoid the pressure to "publish or perish" that drives many assistant professors to distraction. In fact, many community colleges view academic activity—conference attendance, presentations, and publications—worthy of a higher evaluation at year's end, and even small community colleges like mine have modest travel budgets for attendance at local, regional, or national professional meetings. Fourth, lest the job seeker believe that a two-year post means the end of academic research, such study has become easier; interlibrary loan gives even modest college libraries a nationwide reach, and the Internet allows two-year faculty easy access to other scholars. Finally, because the primary function of the two-year faculty member is to teach, many colleges support that mission with tuition breaks at local or regional universities. Rather than taking lower-paying graduate teaching assistantships as part of a PhD program, many two-year faculty instead have found full-time tenure-track positions after completing their master's degrees and are pursuing their PhDs while teaching.

Needless to say, teaching full-time and doing graduate work is no easy task, but the traditional career track is equally difficult, and rather than looking for a job at the end of six or more years of PhD work, the two-year faculty member can look forward to promotion and tenure. Certainly, the teaching load at two-year schools is demanding (generally four or five sections per semester). However, universities are also requiring research faculty to teach more beginning level courses, including composition, and even though two-year faculty may not get to teach high-level specialty courses, most junior and community colleges offer the full sophomore level survey sequence (world, British, and American literature) and other humanities and English electives on a regular basis (introductions to literature, film, or popular culture; genre and period courses; and specialized classes in the literature of women and African and Native Americans, for example). The current pressures on faculty workloads (including TQM and other "accountability measures") seem to have moved the missions of two- and four-year schools closer together lately; thus, the two-year faculty member gains a number of advantages in the job search: having worked within an academic department, the two-year faculty member has shaped a professional identity; having pursued a consistent program of research through conferences and presentations, the candidate demonstrates the promise of further academic production; and being a practiced teacher, the two-year professor offers college and university search committees an effective classroom professional. These are all qualifications necessary to a successful university faculty member. Or, as is more and more the case, highly qualified academics can build fine careers as community or junior college faculty members.

Traditionally, the primary responsibility of two-year college faculty has been to teach and of university faculty to extend their teaching with research. This bifurcation for too long has fostered stereotypes damaging to both faculty groups: little more than glorified high school teachers, two-year faculty are unconcerned with research; spending all their time in library carrels, university faculty do not care about teaching. Both clichés, of course, are false, but the lack of consideration given two-year schools in *Profession 94* suggests the deeper and too often unspoken division between English professionals today: Comp. versus Lit., two-year versus four-year, master's degree versus PhD. However, I would still venture that the ideal job candidate is one whose teaching is fueled by research and whose academic inquiry is sharpened in the classroom. Both pursuits are possible for the two-year as well as the four-year faculty member. The prospective PhD candidate's job search need not begin and end with the "big jobs" in the MLA *Job Information List*. Rather than being seen as a less attractive career option, teaching in the two-year school can be a career in itself, or a stepping stone to something else during this time when both job seekers and search committees must adapt to a changing academic marketplace.

DANIEL T. KLINE
Jefferson Community College, Kentucky

To the Editor:

In *Profession 94*, Erik D. Curren echoes Nelson and Bérubé in calling for reduction in the size of graduate programs to help reduce the surplus of candidates for the paucity of jobs (59). As Bettina Huber's article in the same issue indicates, departments did graduate fewer PhDs from 1975 through 1986 (89), only increasing their number of graduates in anticipation of both faculty retirements and increased undergraduate enrollments. The former has occurred and the latter will, but institutions are not hiring to compensate. In academic planning as in economics, it's often difficult to predict the market.

Merely enrolling fewer PhD students for the short term in an attempt to balance the job market, however, ignores several complicating features. Schools are judged, to some extent, on their graduates. Like OPEC nations that defy quotas on oil production for needed capital, many schools, despite quotas, would continue to enroll graduate students in order to fill the graduate seminars of top professors and to maintain their graduate reputations. Others, especially large public universities, would continue to enroll graduate students to teach their freshman composition courses. If they were forced to curtail graduate enrollment, these same universities, lacking the funds to hire full-time faculty, would probably hire more part-time lecturers to teach composition, exchanging one abused group for another. The problem of too many graduates for the current market has to be solved in connection with other problems besetting higher education.

But I do agree with Marta Caminero-Santangelo's urgings that departments "consider the ethical and practical implications of their hiring practices" (63). One of my department's new PhDs had no scheduled interviews and so did not attend the San Diego convention. (She had said in her letters that she would be available for interviews, meaning she would go if she had any.) A friend saw her name on the message board and learned that she had an interview. After a flurry of phone calls, immediate ticket purchases, etc., the job candidate made her interview with a school that had never bothered to write or telephone her in advance of the convention and took several months to respond after the interview. Another candidate did have prior notice of his interview, and so bought a "respectable" suit, purchased airplane tickets, and made his hotel reservations. His interview, he felt, went superbly. Later, at a party, a junior faculty member from the interviewing institution told him that the school had decided to upgrade the position to associate professor, and so the applicant no longer qualified—and he was simply out the expense of the trip. I absolutely cannot understand such conduct, such lack of concern for our potential colleagues. In light of such practices, our claim to represent the humanities grows exceedingly tenuous.

PETER L. HAYS
University of California, Davis

To the Editor:

Marta Caminero-Santangelo, in "The Ethics of Hiring" (*Profession 94*), asks us to consider our ethical responsibility to job seekers in a buyer's market. What strikes me, however, as a department head who has hired twenty-one new faculty in the past four years, is that there are no ethical guidelines, for either candidates or institutions, about behavior on the other side of the hiring effort. Let me present several case histories, composites of various experiences that I have had or learned about from other department chairs.

Case Study A. Candidate A applies for a junior position, saying his salary has been frozen in his three years in a tenure-track position despite some considerable achievements. Chairman X offers to raise his salary by $8,000. After two weeks, Candidate A calls to say that, much to his surprise, his department chair has met the offer. At this point, Chairman X says that there is another candidate who is waiting to hear from him. Would Candidate A accept if he could persuade his dean to increase the offer by another $2,000? He says he would. Chairman X convinces his dean that he is sure the additional money would bring the candidate to campus and makes the new offer. After several days, Candidate A informs Chairman X that his department has met the offer again and so he will not be able to accept it. By that time, Chairman X has lost his second candidate, and he is not sure what response he will get from his dean the next time he gives her assurances.

Case Study B. After several months of negotiating salary and other matters, Chairman X believes he has met all of Professor B's needs to accept a senior position, only to be told that her partner, at another institution, will need a position as well. Chairman X does all that is necessary to get additional funds and involve another college to establish a second position. All seems to go well, even the final negotiations to meet Partner B's salary expectations. However, both home institutions match the offers and the pair decides to stay put. The double negotiations have taken a full seven months to complete, and Chairman X closes the search for the year.

Case Study C. Chairman X has advertised for a junior position. Among the most interesting of the 200 applicants is a young scholar serving as a sabbatical replacement at a comparable institution. Chairman X learns about him from his current chairman, who says he only wished he had the line to offer wonderful Professor C. Other faculty at Professor C's school write similar letters on his behalf, emphasizing what a loss he will be to them. Chairman X and his search committee read Professor C's book manuscript and are convinced that they have been steered well. Chairman X extends an offer. However, several days later Professor C calls to say that his current school was able to find a new line for him after all. He is embarrassed and apologetic—he had no idea that this was a possible outcome when his department encouraged him to apply—but he chooses to stay.

I do not believe these people felt that they did anything inappropriate. I doubt that Professor A, when he said he would come for an additional $2,000, believed he had made an ethical commitment. He was simply "negotiating." Similarly, Professor B probably rationalized that she deserved the raise she achieved by applying, and that she should help her partner do the same. And the chairman at Professor C's school most likely felt both clever and successful for leveraging an offer at a comparable school to gain a new line in order to retain a valuable faculty member.

Yet there were significant costs in time (and capital) to the department and in opportunities to both the department and to candidates not being considered throughout these fruitless negotiations. For the integrity of our enterprise and to be fair to those who honestly seek new positions, we need to establish some ethical assumptions concerning the job search. The first should be that candidates should only apply for positions they might actually take. Of course, considerable blame must be placed on deans and chairs who require faculty to prove their worth through outside offers that they have no intention of accepting, rather than recognizing and rewarding merit on its own terms. It would also be a more honest profession if we did not seek counteroffers that we have no intention of taking. I prefer the senior faculty member who said to me, "If you promise to make me the best offer you can, I promise you not to seek a counteroffer that I would rather not accept." I did, and he did not, and we completed our negotiations within a week.

My second ethical assumption would be that when a candidate says, "I will come if you can do xyz," he has made a commitment to do so, whatever counteroffer may be tendered. And my third ethical assumption would be that at some point all of the cards must be placed on the table. If there are a series of expectations that must be met before a candidate will accept a position, they should not be presented serially. I have no problem with the faculty member we tried to recruit who said at the outset, "I would need a good position for myself, a position for my spouse, and some special considerations for my child." We were only able to satisfy two out of the three, but we knew what we were dealing with early in the game, and all was negotiated (at both ends) in the best of faith. There is indeed a lot to talk about concerning "the ethics of hiring," but there is more than one conversation on the topic that we need to hold.

ROBERT SECOR
Penn State University, University Park

To the Editor:

I would like to propose an "ethical" solution to the two key problems outlined by Marta Caminero-Santangelo in "The Ethics of Hiring" (*Profession 94*). Caminero-Santangelo describes the "serious economic hardship[s]" and psychological hardships faced by job candidates interviewing at the annual MLA convention.

During 1994, I applied to several academic positions in French advertised in the MLA's February *Job Information List*. Because the MLA convention had already taken place, the departments to which I had applied were forced to come up with an alternate method for screening job applicants. This method consisted of formal phone interviews, scheduled ahead of time.

I had three such interviews, one of which consisted of a conference call between myself and the search committee (two professors on campus, and one on leave in another state). Two out of three of these phone interviews resulted in invitations for campus visits. Finally, one of these campus visits resulted in the assistant professorship I now occupy.

Of my three phone interviews, one was conducted wholly in French (with an interviewer who was a native speaker), one was conducted half in French and half in English (with a committee that included a German speaker), and one was conducted wholly in English. While job candidates will always be nervous about switching between languages in a job interview, this is no worse over the phone than in person. A typical PhD candidate in the foreign languages will have had ample previous opportunities to conduct business over the phone (whether at home or abroad) in the target language.

The phone interview is cost-effective for both job candidates and academic departments, as neither must invest in excessive travel funds to attend the annual MLA convention. These phone interviews are also economical in terms of time. They may be strictly defined as business calls, which have limited time frames. The phone interview is quite humane, as it allows both interviewer and interviewee to conduct business in a relaxed and familiar atmosphere, away from the overwhelming pressures imposed on attendees of a national convention. Nonetheless, phone interviews may be just as rigorous as interviews at MLA conventions. I felt that those who were interviewing me over the phone had been quite thorough in reading the documentation I had mailed to them. There is a great advantage in being able to glance as often as necessary at one's documentation during a job interview. The stresses and strains of eye contact and body language are eliminated, as are those associated with small talk. Job candidates are less likely to make as heavy a psychological investment in phone interviews as they are in face-to-face interviews.

I would strongly recommend that departments that are now hiring counter Caminero-Santangelo's charge of a "buyer's market" in academia by adopting initial phone interviews as standard policy in the hiring process.

LYDIA BELATÈCHE
Mississippi State University

To the Editor:

As graduate students, many of us have internalized the notion that graduate study is a quest romance where we prove our worthiness by remaining true to the goals of intellectual individualism despite the obstacles of carrying a heavy teaching load, dealing with difficult professors, living paycheck to paycheck, and facing assaults on graduate funding from administrators, not to mention the difficulty of explaining what we do to outsiders. Once we have proven ourselves worthy, we become part of the mythological academic feudal kingdom complete with our own ivory tower and a fragment of the grail. Now that mythical kingdom is under assault by the assertion that the academy is a business and, like all businesses, is dependent on market pressure. Unfortunately, the language used in the quest romance mythology does not allow for an understanding of the business end of our profession. The graduate student responses to the terrible job market, published in *Profession 94*, demonstrate how the language of graduate study, founded in the romantic mythology of intellectualism and intellectual freedom, breaks down when addressing the realities of the academic marketplace.

Graduate student Erik D. Curren opened the journal's section on the job market with an essay titled "No Openings at This Time: Job Market Collapse and Graduate Education." As the president of the MLA Graduate Student Caucus and a veteran of three years on the market, Curren is qualified to address the problems of both graduate education and the realities of the job market. However, the language he chooses places his argument in the realm of the romance. Curren argues that "today's graduate students must experience modern language study as an essentially moral profession, a place where higher laws than those of supply and demand hold sway." He pleads that the present "graduate students not be abandoned" (60). As one of the graduate students for whom Curren is pleading, I do not feel that framing the argument in Dickensian terms that make an appeal to higher laws and essential morality in order to prevent my abandonment flatters me or empowers me in the face of massive institutional shifts and difficult economic realities.

The investment in a romantic ideal invites language that leads to particularly unhelpful binaries that construct the situation in value-laden moral terms. For example, Curren warns of losing earnest scholars to cynical careerists. This binary construction supports the recurring theme that when a university acts like a business, it loses its moral base. The romantic subtext remains unchallenged by this kind of either-or rhetoric: if you prove your worthiness (whatever that might mean), you'll get the job you deserve. If you don't get the job, it is not your fault because you were the victim of hardened careerists in cahoots with immoral institutions that functioned as if they were a business.

What is even more problematic in the use of this moral language is the issue of agency. Moral language appeals to higher law, some force that is beyond our control. If we base our perception of our current situation on language that relies on supernatural judgment, we might as well have a pray-in for all the practical good our rhetoric will serve. Our training as literary and cultural theorists cautions us against assumptions of essentiality because we learn that institutions as well as groups are culturally constructed. Therefore, institutions cannot have an essential nature to which we can appeal because what they are and what they do are determined by cultural context and situational needs.

As graduate students facing a terrible job market, we would serve ourselves more effectively if we framed the situation in terms of the marketplace without attaching the connotations of immorality and general evil. Nor should we invoke a utopian past that never existed. There is a shift taking place in institutions of higher learning, and there will be places for some of us, although those may not be the jobs that have been valued by the myth of solitary scholarship and intellectual elitism. For others there will be no jobs. That is a sad fact that has nothing to do with our worthiness. It's time to leave the language of morality behind and begin to assess our situations and institutions in practical terms.

HOLLY MCSPADDEN
University of Texas, Austin

To the Editor:

"Say it ain't so, Joe," some anonymous child is supposed to have begged Shoeless Joe Jackson about Jackson's part in the Black Sox Scandal of 1919. American idealism smashed to bits on the rock of dollars. I thought I heard the child again in two of the pieces by graduate students in *Profession 94*. However just their conclusions, Erik D. Curren ("No Openings at This Time: Job Market Collapse and Graduate Education") and Marta Caminero-Santangelo ("The Ethics of Hiring") base them on the same false idealistic premise. Curren believes that our profession must prove itself to be "es-

sentially moral," one in which "higher laws than those of supply and demand hold sway" (60). Caminero-Santangelo ends her essay with the claim that no responsible university can "base its practices on principles of supply and demand" (63). But who among us, having made the career for which those two writers yearn, has not discovered how completely universities are creatures of our economic system?

Like it or no, supply and demand governs every nook of university life. Why do fresh PhDs in computer science start off at $40,000, while their peers in, say, Spanish begin at $30,000? (To those who have not yet fallen off the turnip wagon, by the way, that means that the person in Spanish will never, never catch up so long as raises are a percentage of base pay.) Why do most public universities dance to the tune played by their professional schools? Why are research committees obsessed with indirect cost recovery? Why is it easier to wring construction money out of a legislator when the aim is a new building for the sciences? What is the connection between an aging professoriat and increases in tuition? What else but the economics of publishing makes us avid of every theoretical fad?

And why, to address one of Curren's issues, did graduate schools in the humanities not long ago drastically reduce their PhD programs? Every one of the dozen possible answers comes, in the end, to economics.

These are mere facts of academic life, facts all tenured persons know. If they do not, they are fools, and if they persist in persuading graduate students that the university is some higher place exempt from the pressures that bear upon lesser sorts like ad executives and car mechanics, dangerous fools. I have a sense from much that I read—from letters of recommendation for job applicants to articles in *PMLA*—that dangerous fools abound.

Perhaps the humanities need a cure far more "radical" than Curren suspects. We need to disabuse ourselves of our holiness, the corrupting fiction beneath the competing ideologies that fracture and marginalize us. We need to make ourselves genuinely relevant to American life in the late twentieth century. But if instead we continue to set ourselves apart as somehow better than the rest of the world, the rest of the world will continue to respond with genial contempt. Worse, we will continue fouling our own nest in the ways Curren and Caminero-Santangelo despise.

DWIGHT H. PURDY
University of Minnesota, Morris

Reply:

If we simply accept undesirable conditions within the university, such as disparities in pay scales, overproduction of PhDs in a glutted market, and so on, as "mere facts of academic life," then a descriptive statement becomes prescriptive: "These conditions will always exist; therefore we need strive for nothing better." Certainly no one can argue with the assertion that universities are and always will be "creatures of our economic system." But the pivotal question is precisely whether we "like it or no." Many choose *not* to like it and to work actively against the sort of purely economic determinism for which Purdy provides such incontrovertible evidence—with the result that some universities do have the same pay scales across disciplines, some humanities departments are reducing their PhD programs, and so on. Economic pressures exist simultaneously, and in constant tension, with the pressure brought to bear by "higher" considerations within the university; indeed, our sense of professional responsibility depends on the latter. (It might be worth recalling that my main argument in the article at which Purdy takes offense was to urge professional commitment to an ethical hiring process, rather than simply an exploitative one, within the university—a point that is completely lost in Purdy's comments.)

Further, despite Purdy's admonition that to set ourselves apart from ad executives is "dangerous," there *is* a fundamental difference between the avowed bottom line of the ad executive (i.e., profit) and that of the university, which, the last time I checked, was supposed to be education. While this goal certainly does not make the university exempt from economic pressures, it does provide an ethical base—an "ideal," if you will—from which we can resist those pressures. Perhaps the most dangerous and corrupting fiction of all is that we can afford to resign ourselves to a world without ideals.

Marta Caminero-Santangelo
DePaul University

To the Editor:

I write in response to the article by Robert C. Holub in *Profession 94* ("Professional Responsibility"), as many colleagues here and at other European universities have expressed some dismay at its implications for the future of the American university.

The job market in the seventeenth century was not necessarily easy. Yet when writing the history of the Royal Society, in 1667 (*The History of the Royal-Society of London, for the Improving of Natural Knowledge*), Thomas Sprat takes pains to emphasize that the new academy has not and will not recognize national boundaries in constructing its fields of study or in recruiting its members. The theoretical justification for this openness is clear to Sprat:

> If I could fetch my materials whence I pleas'd, to fashion the *Idea* of a perfect Philosopher: he should not be all of one *clime*, but have the different excellencies of several Countries. (64)

Even the fervently nationalistic Sprat founds the project of the academy on meritocracy and difference, not on national protectionism.

The hiring practices which Holub recommends may lead to a localized idea of the university with purely national borders. But the local university is almost an oxymoron.

One danger of Holub's argument is that a school of *ressentiment* (on the theory of *ressentiment*, see Gilles Deleuze, *Nietzsche et la philosophie* [Paris: PUF, 1962]) may be produced by undue attention to what is deemed "unfair" in the context of hiring (Holub 84; the adjective is repeated). Yes, it is "unfair" that some people are born into German or French environments, for example, while others have to invest considerable labor in learning these languages. But does that justify barring native speakers of foreign languages from applying for teaching positions in America if they happen not to be American nationals? Furthermore, does it justify resisting the "import" of native speakers into the American classroom because they also have an "unfair" advantage (85n5)? (At the University of Geneva, all students of English function in English regardless of whether or not they are native speakers. If this were not the case, many would want to pursue their studies elsewhere.) Are American graduate students really so weak that they need to be protected in the ways that Holub proposes? From my knowledge of the situation, admittedly that of an outsider and a foreigner, this is difficult to believe, and I point this out because I fear for the effects of Holub's strategy on the image of American graduates outside America. Perhaps it is also "unfair" that some foreign candidates will be better qualified for a position than their American competitors because they have benefited from more rigorous or supportive academic systems in Europe or elsewhere (although Holub's statement that conditions are easier for young scholars in Germany suggests that he may have grown out of touch concerning the problems of *Nachwuchs* there). In that case, though, instead of attacking the appointment of foreign scholars in America (84), might it not be more productive to examine those systems critically and to determine how their more positive features could be incorporated? Is it not an American article of faith, indeed, that competition is supposed to produce improvements? The suggestion that foreign scholars have not "committed themselves" to the American system is particularly weak (84): to present oneself for interview, assessments, tenure review, and so forth is surely a sign of commitment in itself, compared to which the fact of having gone through an American graduate school becomes a secondary consideration.

Holub raises the question of "our responsibility" toward graduate students (82). In the present climate, perhaps the most responsible act would be not to engage in academic protectionism—which will probably lead to a decline in rigor in the long term—but to make it clear to all students entering graduate school that they should have no expectations about being able to pursue a career in their field of study. Such a warning has been commonplace in Britain for the past fifteen years, for instance. A graduate student cannot live on *ressentiment* or the sympathy of others.

Holub concludes with two calls to the MLA, which need to be distinguished. The first is to review and curtail the growth of doctoral programs: this is clearly needed. The second is to review hiring practices that disadvantage "our own" graduate students (85). As that possessive adjective resonates across the Atlantic, Holub begins to sound strangely like William J. Bennett (see Peggy Kamuf, "The University Founders: A Complete Revolution," *Logomachia: The Conflict of the Faculties*, ed. Richard Rand [Lincoln: U of Nebraska P, 1992], 80–81). This rhetorical coincidence is disturbing—if, that is, the MLA is to remain an association with an American base but an international scope, and if the university is not to be reduced to an organ of national self-reproduction. At the present time, who can afford to practice exclusion in the university? There are many American academics working in Switzerland and elsewhere in Europe; so far as I know, there are no movements to make them uncomfortable by pointing out the high rates of unemployment in their countries of occupation. A professorial position at the University of Neuchâtel was advertised in the MLA *Job Information List* recently, and strong American candidates with knowledge of French were more than welcome. It is obvious that the American university system is under extreme economic pressure, like so many others, but does an economic problem have to be addressed in moralizing terms that amount to xenophobia? If so, then

future advertisements in the *List* for positions in American universities ought to include a warning, next to the equal opportunity notes, that only American nationals need apply. In that case one might ask on what basis the MLA would continue to encourage foreigners to be members of it.

I write as a habitual border crosser, intellectually and professionally, who has had the good fortune to study or work in three different countries and to live in a fourth. If crossing borders becomes impossible in literary study, then I for one will lose interest in it.

Roy Sellars
University of Geneva

To the Editor:

This is to place on record my shocked reaction to Robert C. Holub's illogical and xenophobic arguments against the hiring of "foreign-born, foreign-trained" scholars in English and foreign language departments in the US (*Profession 94*). Exercising one's imagination is somewhat out of fashion today, else I would suggest that Holub try to imagine how such "foreign-born, foreign-trained" members of the MLA would feel on reading his recommendations. If the MLA were to formulate a policy against the hiring of foreign scholars, it should first exclude all such persons from membership.

The problem Holub outlines of too many second-rate PhD programs and too few faculty positions is by no means unique to the US. It is being debated in academia around the world. Its solution lies, as he realizes, in closing many of these self-serving, self-generating programs that mass-produce mediocrity. The solution does not lie in a hiring policy based on the principle "My student, good or bad," which is a version of "My country, right or wrong," a principle that has had disastrous consequences for humanity at large.

Taken to its logical conclusion, the argument that "we" as faculty members have an "ethical responsibility" to hire "our" students must mean that every state and every university should hire only its own students. Such an argument has been seriously and bitterly made by many candidates in India who are convinced that they can only get jobs by keeping out better candidates from other Indian universities. This contradiction emerges when Holub argues, "first, [that] there are many fine, established scholars at institutions across the country" who should be preferred to fine established scholars from outside the country, and, second, that every hiring of a foreigner entails "one of our students" not receiving employment (84). Either being "our student" (US-born and trained? California-born and trained? Univ. of Berkeley–born and trained?) is the primary consideration or excellence is. One can't have it both ways.

Holub's proposal for indigenousness over excellence as the basis for hiring is right in line with the racist tendencies of some US immigration policy makers who recently considered refusing short-term visas to non-US professionals, until they realized that several high-tech sectors of the economy would virtually shut down, since seventy percent of the experts in these sectors were "foreign-born and foreign-trained."

Holub's example of German versus American scholars makes the latter appear underprivileged. But many scholars from Asian and East European countries are trained in conditions of underprivilege and deprivation that an American scholar would find hard to imagine, and achieve excellence against great odds before applying for jobs in the US. They have a commitment to excellence in the study of a language/literature and expressed this commitment wherever they happened to be born and trained. Does Holub really think his students "invest" their lives and money in a US university from a "commitment to higher education in the United States" rather than merely because they happened to be born in the US?

We live in a world of expanding boundaries, which most governments and policy makers chauvinistically and futilely refuse to recognize. As persons committed to higher education in the humanities, we have an ethical responsibility to approach professional problems with humanity and humility, hoping that common solutions can be found to common problems and knowing that fairness cannot be based on excluding whole categories of people because of their nationality or circumstances. Perhaps we need to think of students in general, not just of "our" students.

RUTH VANITA
University of Delhi

Reply:

The hiring of foreign-trained nonnationals was one of several points in my discussion of the ethical issues of graduate education. It is a complex issue to which I was not able to devote enough space. Of one thing I am convinced, however. It is easier to make clichéd accusations of xenophobia and racism than to confront the actual issues. I take to heart the objections raised in the letters from Roy Sellars and Ruth Vanita and would ask them and other readers to consider the following points:

1. The discussion of hiring practices can be framed, as Sellars and Vanita frame it, in terms of liberalism, using the language of open borders and free trade. From this perspective I appear to be the ally of William Bennett. But the discussion can also be framed in terms of labor markets, job security, and unemployment. Since the inception of employee organizations seeking to regulate the labor market (e.g., trade unions), reactionary elements have complained that they restrict "free trade." In the United States, Europe, and elsewhere throughout the world the banner of "free trade" and "open borders" is regularly brandished to diminish job security and workers' rights. (I am confused by Vanita's comment that governments and policy makers refuse to recognize the expanding boundaries of the world; the economically "advanced" countries have consistently sought to expand the boundaries of the world for the sake of their domestic corporations. In contrast, underdeveloped countries, disadvantaged by the "free trade" forced on them by the overdeveloped world, have sought to protect their markets, unless these countries are controlled, as they so often are, by puppets of the overdeveloped world. In short, "free trade" and "open markets" most often mean advantages for the rich and privileged.) The way in which the language of labor markets applies to academia is complex and open to interpretation. I consider that we are training people for positions as educators, and we are training too many people for the positions that are available. We should stop training so many people, but until we do, we, the people who are training graduate students for a national labor market, should hire the people we train for that market before turning to foreign labor markets. Importing faculty members from foreign labor markets exacerbates job insecurity and attendant abuses of PhDs in this country—although the main source of these problems remains the overproduction of domestic PhDs.

2. The fact that Europe overproduces PhDs, and has perhaps done so since the seventeenth century, is not an argument that justifies anything anywhere. If Switzerland and India are producing too many PhDs, then perhaps Sellars and Vanita should agitate there for a reduction in the number of advanced degrees. I don't consider myself absolved of responsibility merely by informing students "that they should have no expectations about being able to pursue a career in their field of study." That universities in the United States have produced too many PhDs for the jobs available for a

quarter of a century and that we have not developed effective means to curtail this overproduction is an ethical black mark on the academy. It should be a matter of special concern for faculty members because professors profit directly from graduate students, who teach classes professors do not want to teach, populate seminars so that professors can indulge in their specialties, and do research tasks professors do not want to do (or pay for).

3. The distress of "foreign-born, foreign-trained" MLA members who read my essay and who hold tenured appointments at US universities can perhaps be allayed by the regularity of their pay checks and the security of their position. I suggest Vanita—as well as other colleagues—try to imagine instead the feelings of a PhD who has devoted over a decade to higher education and has then had to seek alternative employment after suffering through the humiliation of dozens of letters of rejection (although many universities have become so rude they don't even bother to acknowledge candidates' applications), callous interviews, and an indifferent faculty at his or her home institution.

4. Let me correct a few things I wrote that Sellars and Vanita have distorted. I did not write that I was against hiring native speakers of foreign languages or foreign nationals. I did not recommend firing anyone. I also did not write that I am against hiring foreign-trained non-nationals as an absolute principle. I do not think it unfair that some people are born into a German or French environment, and I do not believe American PhDs are weak. I am not sure what to make of Sellars's remark "At the present time, who can afford to practice exclusion in the university?" Universities in the United States are multicultural; they admit students from other countries of the world in very high numbers. I never spoke of excluding these students from the United States or of excluding the foreign students who study here from seeking employment here. I support the multicultural university, which is also a multilingual university, since many students do not speak English as their only language, and many students attend from foreign countries. I support faculty exchange with foreign universities. I do not favor universities' hiring their own graduate students (and do not believe this is a logical extension of anything I wrote). I support hiring for excellence, although I am wary of how the words *excellence* and *quality* can be abused when one seeks to justify the hiring of one person over another.

I am simply against hiring foreign nationals trained outside the United States into positions for which there are many qualified persons trained at our own institutions.

In an ideal world there would be no borders, no passports, no unemployment; everyone would obtain adequate and rewarding positions. In the real world, under present circumstances, I believe the American professoriat owes its first allegiance to the students it trains. If it does not have this allegiance, then I believe it ought to get out of the business of training people and let other countries do it.

Robert C. Holub
University of California, Berkeley

Boundaries of the Imagination

To the Editor:

It is truly a pleasure to receive an invitation "to think, and to think deeply," from a scholar like Wayne C. Booth who finds inseparable ties within the rhetorical scope of logos, pathos, and ethos. "Killing for speaking" cannot be justified rationally, emotionally, and ethically in a universal context. Had it not been for the Bakhtinian dialogic relations that have emerged as a result of Rushdie's publication I would not deem it necessary to write this letter. Faced with a diversity of cultures in our classrooms, we need courage to understand the complexity of issues before we plunge into ideological wars.

It is respect for Rushdie's consciousness as an artist that prompts me to denounce the death sentence against him. At the same time, it is out of respect for my Muslim friends that I, as a non-Muslim, will not confuse the artistic context of *The Satanic Verses* with the religious context of the product. Clearly we are living in a period when our "boundaries of imagination" have expanded beyond those of the crusading era, and we realize that a passion for war ignores the common ground that nurtures the possibility of respect and understanding for other voices and perspectives.

Inspired by your articles, I dared to address this topic with some of my Muslim friends. The answer was that the controversy represents a Western boundary against equitable communication with the Muslim world. The efforts to negotiate on this issue have not been successful because the West has reified Rushdie's work by transforming a heretic into a hero. This controversy embodies the crusaders' legacy in the English language, which connotes hatred toward "Saracens," so-called pagans and barbarians. Some of my American Muslim friends regard the *fatwa* as the only recourse to focus on the controversy as "a semantic whole" (M. M. Bakhtin, *"Speech Genres" and Other Late Essays*, trans. Vern W. McGee [Austin: U of Texas P, 1986], 124). They are concerned that their children, who have been uprooted from their cultural and linguistic heritage, would blindly accept Rushdie's words as an admirable feat of art in the English language. They talked about a different kind of fear, which stems from the political realization that lack of understanding and ignorance can impede the healthy growth of communities.

I would be remiss if I did not acknowledge my debt to Booth's *Rhetoric of Irony* (Chicago: U of Chicago P, 1961) in understanding the boundaries of prejudice, ignorance, inability to pay attention, and inadequacy of emotion that deprive us of new forms of knowledge that are available through ironic revelation (222). I am afraid that just as "the author has his own inalienable right to the word . . . the listener also has his rights" (Bakhtin 121). Inherent in this controversy are the microcosmic factions of the crusading era. My Muslim friends consider the Western response to a religious *fatwa* a legacy of Western imperialism aimed to deprive an "Imam" of his religious authority. They view Rushdie's masterpiece as a commercial ploy in the Western media. They argue that the outrage of the Muslim world was not a result of the *fatwa,* and to ignore that response implies Western determination to preserve the divisive rift between historical factions of the Crusades. Their view is that Rushdie's vision is rooted in a form of "Orientalism" that is "contorting" the Western view of Islam (Fuad Sha'ban, *Islam and Arabs in Early American Thought* [Durham: Acorn, 1991]).

By ignoring the response of the Muslim world to Rushdie's artistic creation, we are perpetuating the myth of the "heathen East." Yes, "killing for speaking" is wrong, because dialogue would uphold the "universal" ideals of freedom, justice, and peace. Conversely, lack of dialogue confines our imagination within the divisive perspectives of the past.

Because I respect the enriching perspectives of Muslim scholars, perspectives that are historically lacking in the English language, I see the need for a dialogue on Rushdie's controversy.

For dialogic interpretations Rushdie's controversy is an excellent paradigm for examining a variety of contexts—political, ethical, religious, ethnic, social, and economic.

MABEL M. KHAWAJA
Hampton University

Reply:

It puzzles me that a non-Muslim feels obligated to speak out on the Rushdie controversy on behalf of "Muslim friends." Are they not capable of doing so themselves? On what grounds do they find *The Satanic Verses* objectionable? Because a Shiite "Imam" said so? Are these Muslims Shiites, Sunnis (as is Rushdie), or members of other sects? Muslims are as pluralistic in their sects and views as Christians are. Why is it that the writer singles out Western theorists but lumps the "Muslim friends" in one nameless category? Do these Muslims all speak with one voice? Have they even read Rushdie's work?

I agree with the point that there is a "need for dialogue on Rushdie's controversy" but must add that that debate has long been under way in both the East and the West. Many Muslim writers, intellectuals, and jurists have publicly challenged the legality of the *fatwa* and its ramifications beyond Rushdie's case. As a result of this and the efforts of the International Rushdie Defence Committee, European Union leaders have appealed repeatedly to the Iranian government to renounce its support of the death sentence. The response to date, however, has been varyingly positive and negative, depending on other exigencies.

The Rushdie issue needs to be seen not as a replay of an agelong conflict, going back to the Crusades, but as a contemporary political matter, exploited for its own end by the Iranian government and its fundamentalist clerical leadership. As for the writer's Muslim friends, their grievance, it seems, has one other basis: that "their children . . . have been uprooted from their cultural and linguistic heritage." This "uprootedness" is precisely the condition that Rushdie's works address: something, perhaps, that may be frightening for the parents but not necessarily so for their children. The children at least, one hopes, will be able to read *The Satanic Verses* as a piece of literature that reflects and confirms their experience.

DONNÉ RAFFAT
King's College, Cambridge University

Reply:

Like Donné Raffat, I am puzzled by this letter—and for the same reasons.

I strongly agree with Mabel Khawaja that we desperately need dialogue across cultures. I cannot, however, see how a *fatwa* constitutes an invitation to dialogue. What kind of conversation can I engage in while my life is under threat? Are we to conduct a rational debate about whether it is a good idea to order Salman Rushdie killed?

"Your money or your life!" Well, ah, er, perhaps we can just have a good long talk about it, furthering the cause of dialogics?

WAYNE BOOTH
University of Chicago

The Righting of French Studies

Editor's note: The editor apologizes for the delay in informing Professor Pavel of the disposition of the letter to the editor he submitted for publication in *Profession 94*. Unfortunately, after the decision not to carry the letter in *Profession 94* was made, the letter was misfiled. The editor regrets the oversight.

To the Editor:

In the article "The Righting of French Studies: Homosociality and the Killing of 'La pensée 68'" (*Profession 92*, a publication subsidized by MLA membership fees, 28–34), Naomi Schor, an officer of the MLA Executive Council, argued that the French, in reaction to American feminism and multiculturalism, are abandoning the radical ideas of the 1960s and revert to their universalist values. She indignantly denounced this move as a "restoration" congenial to conservative views (28).

Schor claimed that this "restoration" is supported in this country by a "homosocial network" of "male," "foreign-born scholars" who, motivated by "anti-Americanism" and antifeminism, engage in "unfriendly takeover bids" to secure control over the French departments in the United States. She added that "it is important to denounce" these people, among whose names I found my own (30).

Notice that although many professional journals often ask scholars who are the targets of critical articles to express their point of view in the same issue of the journal, none of the MLA members attacked by Schor were invited to reply to her accusations in *Profession*. Yet, thinking that Schor's verbal violence represented an isolated incident, I refrained from polemicizing with her.

I was wrong. A year later, Schor reiterated her accusations against "men," "especially the foreign-born, who remain wedded to nationalist privilege" (*Profession 93*

71). Reading her letter, I realized that Schor's remarks, far from being a mere idiosyncrasy, had serious implications for the professional and ethical standards of the MLA. Indeed, the situation was the following: *Profession*, an MLA publication sent to every single member of the association, had *twice* allowed an officer of the MLA Executive Council to publish libelous, prejudicial, and derogatory remarks about several MLA members, including myself. These remarks were couched in a blatantly sexist and xenophobic language, in direct violation of the MLA Statement of Professional Ethics, which asserts:

> As a community valuing free inquiry, we must be able to rely on the integrity and good judgment of our members. For this reason, we should not
> - exploit or discriminate against others on any grounds, including race, ethnic origin, religious creed, age, gender, and sexual preference . . . [or]
> - use language that is prejudicial or gratuitously derogatory. . . .
>
> (*Profession 92* 75)

Shockingly, Schor's language resuscitated the age-old rhetoric of denunciation against foreign-born and foreign-inspired conspirators supposed to plot malevolently against a wholesome community. A response was necessary.

In February 1994, I submitted a rejoinder to *Profession 94*, which the journal declined to publish. Having been denied the right to answer, I seriously considered resigning from the association. Yet, before taking such a drastic step, I insisted once more on my right to respond. I was then offered the opportunity to express my point of view in *Profession 95*. Although by the time the present letter is published the incident will be more than two years old, the issues of professional ethics and of French studies are important enough to transcend the short-term conjuncture.

Regarding the ethical issue, I strongly believe that personal attacks, name-calling, and derogatory remarks on race, gender, ethnicity, and sexual orientation have no place in the MLA publications. In order to avoid misunderstandings, I must add that I do not object to the publication of Schor's *article*, but only to the offensive passages. In order to help prevent such incidents in the future, I wrote to the MLA Executive Council, suggesting several changes in the journal *Profession*'s policies. I proposed that

> the editorial statement printed on the inside cover of *Profession* should include the sentence "The materials published in this journal observe the MLA Statement of Professional Ethics";

the members of the association who are the object of criticism published in *Profession* should be invited to reply in the *same issue* of the journal; and

the editorial decisions regarding *Profession* should be made by an editorial committee open to a diversity of intellectual points of view.

To comment on Schor's accusations, I plead guilty to the charges that I am male and foreign-born. Mea maxima culpa. I was indeed born in Romania, but I do not see in what way I "remain wedded" to Romanian "nationalist privilege." Some privilege. Am I homosocial or heterosocial? I rather thought I was bisocial. Anti-American I am not. My life's work is rooted in American linguistics and philosophy, their relevance for literary theory being a major theme in all my scholarly books. I am by no means antifeminist. I have occasionally criticized irrationalism, which I indeed consider to be a treacherous companion to progressive movements, feminism included. But since a Marxist feminist like Odile Hullot-Kentor is denounced by Schor as an antifeminist (*Profession 93* 71), it appears that in her use the term "antifeminist" merely means a person who does not fully subscribe to Schor's personal view of feminism. Schor's technique consists of stereotyping her targets as antifeminists, conservatives, reactionaries, etc. I consider myself to be an independent (unthinkable as this may be in Schor's Manichaean world) and believe that ideas should be judged on merit rather than according to superficial stereotypes.

Schor's approach seems to me closer to melodrama than to argumentation. She invests her own opinions with a quasi religious status, assuming that they are the only way to salvation. Those who offer criticism or just remain indifferent are treated as enemies conspiring to deprive the world of its redemption. But antihumanist feminism (this is what Schor appears to promote) is only one among the numerous varieties of feminism that healthily grow and compete with each other in America and abroad. There are better ways of defending one's convictions.

As for Schor's remarks about intellectual life in France, it is true, and I guess quite normal, that French intellectual trends born thirty and forty years ago have over time been subjected to scrutiny and criticism. Schor's nostalgia makes her forget that with the passing of time new problems arise, old stands lose their relevance, younger voices are heard. Although some of the thinkers of the recent past, in particular Michel Foucault, have retained their influence, the new generation of French intellectuals is more realist than its elders, more committed to democracy, and more interested in

reasoned debate. Yet, this description does in no way imply uniformity. The work of the younger French thinkers is as innovative and intellectually diverse as can be. To accuse them as a group of attempting some kind of restoration congenial to conservative views makes no sense.

Nor does it make much sense to claim, reductively, that French culture is universalist, while only America is feminist and multicultural. Feminism, as well as universalism, enjoys a strong tradition and presence both in France and America. French intellectuals, like their American counterparts, actively debate the benefits of cultural difference and the resurgence of nationalism and religious fundamentalism.

I firmly believe it is the responsibility of French departments in America to monitor the French intellectual scene and introduce its achievements to academia at large. Translations of younger leftist and moderate thinkers including Jacques Bouveresse, Blandine Barret-Kriegel, Luc Boltanski, Luc Ferry, Marcel Gauchet, Gilles Lipovetsky, Pierre Manent, Mona Ozouf, and Alain Renaut are now becoming available in America. It is up to the intellectual public itself to decide whether these authors are entitled to praise or criticism. Schor has every right to disagree with the new French writers for intellectual or political reasons, but not to anathematize them as a group, based on nostalgia and conspiracy theories.

Thomas G. Pavel
Princeton University

Reply:

We have in an odd way been engaged in a correspondence ever since the publication of my piece, "The Righting of French Studies: Homosociality and the Killing of 'La pensée 68,'" in *Profession 92*. At first not only did you refrain from polemicizing with me, you actively sought to enter into dialogue, writing me at least two personal letters clarifying and seeking to persuade me of your positions. I thought we had come to some sort of an understanding and done so in a cordial, collegial fashion, but the very different tone, indeed the disturbing multiplication of your recent public letters—I am responding here to both your second and third—shattered that illusion.

It is your claim that because I was and still am a member of the MLA Executive Council I was somehow exempted from adhering to a code of professional ethics routinely followed in *Profession* and allowed, instead, to spout forth what you call (in your second response), without any legal substantiation and with a fine sense of melodrama all your own, hate-speech.

According to your account my particular crime against professional ethics is, as I understand it, linguistic in nature; what you find offensive in my piece is its "verbal violence," its "rhetoric." The passages you object to in my article are further deemed "libelous, prejudicial, and derogatory," indeed "gratuitously derogatory," and finally, "these remarks were couched in a blatantly sexist and xenophobic language." These are accusations that pain me and that I must take seriously. In order for me to respond to them, I want to set out a few facts that are missing from your account of my alleged crimes.

In the fall of 1991 I read Antoine Compagnon's article, "The Diminishing Canon of French Literature in America," at first with astonishment, then with a growing sense of indignation. Bemoaning what he views as the regrettable shrinkage of the French canon by ignorant and ideologically driven American colleagues, Compagnon singles out feminism as the only (American) form of criticism that can legitimately lay claim to having expanded the canon: "The only real broadening to be found is in terms of feminism" (111). It is only one short step, however, from this recognition of feminism's positive effects on the canon to Compagnon's characterization of feminism as all-powerful, the dominant ideology currently presiding over exclusions from and inclusions in the American canon of French literature; feminism has in Compagnon's eyes replaced Marxism. Need I say more?

Why recall this article? Because you bear some responsibility for soliciting and publishing it in a special issue of the *Stanford French Review* (15.1–2) you edited on the topic, *France-Amérique: Dialogue and Misreadings*.

There was then nothing gratuitous about my piece: it was you who initiated a debate based on national entities and who by your choice of contributors shaped your special issue into a vehicle for vaunting the superiority of the French, the inability of Americans to get it right. The charge you gave Antoine Compagnon leaves little doubt as to your project: you invited him to contribute an article on "aspects of French literary research that should be called to the attention of our American colleagues" (Compagnon 103).

Lest you think that this is my opinion and, as we say in French, I share it ("C'est mon avis et je le partage"), I would cite from Denis Hollier's witty review of this special issue. Commenting on the issue's title, he notes that there exists a radical *imbalance* between the French and the American sides, that the apparent symmetry of the subtitle is belied by the choice of articles and their contents: "France, the land of dialogue; the United States, the land of misreadings."

This brings me to your accusation of xenophobia. I do not believe that it was xenophobic of you to raise these questions of nationalism and the failed transmission of ideas between France and the United States, and by the same token I do not believe that continuing the debate as I did is xenophobic. Let me say straightforwardly that I regret my wording: by insisting on place of birth as an explanatory category, I weakened the thrust of my argument. In fact, my argument was not so much based on the notion of some essential incapacity on the part of "foreign-born" male professors—as large and diverse a group as American-born professors of French; "our American colleagues" can no more be lumped together than our "foreign-born" ones—to acclimate themselves to the significant presence of feminism in the humanities in American universities, a presence that is, I believe, unparalleled elsewhere. What I was pointing to was a set of complex cultural differences that would make scholars educated in different systems and under different socio-symbolic regimes rather more skeptical and occasionally hostile to feminism than their American peers. And I say as much: "The fact that this group is both male and foreign indicates perhaps the culture shock that European men recently arrived in this country experience when they become aware of the presence of feminism in the university" ("Righting" 30).

I come now to your second charge: namely that I am a blatant sexist. If calling men men and defending feminism against simplistic attacks by men and women are held to constitute proofs of my alleged (reverse) sexism, then I plead guilty as charged. But: is it really necessary for you to instruct me that feminism is the site of all sorts of debates and struggles? This is not news. As I wrote several years ago: "The apparently irreconcilable debate that currently opposes essentialists and constructionists is a false debate in that neither of the warring forces has an exclusive hold on the truth. *Feminism is the debate itself.*" ("Feminism and George Sand: *Lettres à Marcie,*" *Feminists Theorize the Political,* ed. Judith Butler and Joan W. Scott [New York: Routledge, 1992], 46).

Splicing together remarks drawn from unrelated parts of my text, you create the impression that political philosophy and not feminist criticism was my prime concern. You cast me not as a feminist but rather a multiculturalist, and multiculturalism seems to be your true target. For reasons that baffle me, you repeat the word twice, whereas I use the word once in my piece. Multiculturalism is hardly the issue at hand, unless, of course, you consider women's symbolic productions as constituting a separate culture. I never suggested that French political philosophers were reacting to American feminism (I wish); the restoration I referred to had nothing to do with the political positions of the new political philosophers you champion. I was referring to the wished-for return on the part of some French professors in the United States to a canon untroubled by questions of gender. That I am neither impervious to nor uninterested in recent developments in France should be apparent from the laudatory manner in which I describe your own work about this younger generation of philosophers as "prescient" ("Righting" 31) and further as "intelligent and illuminating" (32).

What astonishes me most about your response is its timing. Two years is a long time to harbor such *ressentiment*. Much has changed since 1991: my essay was written at the height of the culture wars, at a moment when the stakes were very high and the rhetoric heated. Today the problems in American French studies are rather different: plummeting enrollments, graduate students who cannot find work, institutional downsizing, shifting disciplinary boundaries. The forces urging further expansion of the canon are no longer feminist, they are Francophone, they are queer. Poststructuralism has largely been absorbed into the theoretical discourse, and Derrida is as much concerned with democracy as are his parricidal sons and daughters.

I hope we can now both move forward to more constructive pursuits than endlessly reliving the past.

Naomi Schor
Duke University

Recommendations on Extramural Evaluations

Modern Language Association of America

Extramural evaluations may not be appropriate to the mission of every institution. Many institutions do not currently require them. The following recommendations are addressed to potential reviewers and to those institutions using extramural evaluations in their review processes.

1. Extramural evaluations should be requested only for granting of tenure or appointment to full or named professorships. Extramural evaluations are not appropriate and should not be sought for pretenure reviews.
2. A maximum of six outside letters should be required.
3. Candidates should have the opportunity to suggest some reviewers for any extramural evaluation.
4. Reviewers should be given at least three months to prepare an evaluation.
5. Prospective reviewers should respond to requests promptly and in the case of a favorable response should adhere to the agreed-on timetable.
6. Material sent to reviewers should be carefully selected in consultation with the candidate.
7. Materials should be selected to limit the demand on reviewers' time. Reviewers should be given the option of requesting specific materials.
8. Reviewers should be informed about the outcome of the case.
9. The work of reviewers should be compensated by the requesting institution as a form of consultation.
10. The work of reviewers should be recognized by reviewers' home institutions as a scholarly activity that is a service to the profession at large.

These recommendations were adopted as a statement of association policy by the MLA Delegate Assembly at its December 1994 meeting. The MLA Executive Council, at its February 1995 meeting, endorsed the assembly's action.